People are talking about...
One Man's Vision...One County's Reward

One Man's Vision...One County's Reward is an amazingly detailed and fascinating account of both the CCC and POW camps in Lawrence County. From the beginning to the final pages, the book chronicles one man's passion for his community, his aspirations to reach out and help those in need, and the impact felt—not only at home but around the world. There are few accounts of such events that could captivate the reader in this way, but *One Man's Vision* does this quite easily. This book provides a glimpse into an era, location, and subject which few have attempted to cover; and its pages are filled with sentimental, emotional, and factual accounts rich with the histories of those involved. As a fan of World War II nonfiction, this book fascinated me, bringing to light the little-known subject of POW camps in Tennessee. On the whole, whether you are a fan of local, national, or world history, I would highly recommend that you read this book.

—Michael McCalip,
Hohenwald, Tennessee
World War II History Buff

My heartfelt gratitude goes out to Ms. Gandy for the care and effort that has gone into this historical recounting of events that were so important to our nation's history. So much of the information in her book, *One Man's Vision . . . One County's Reward* is virtually unknown to today's readers, and it contains stories that need to be told and preserved. This book highlights the lives of men and women who poured themselves into rebuilding the nation they loved, during a time of such crisis as we can only begin to imagine. I am grateful to have been a part of that era, and, by the grace of God, to have been able to share in a small part of the retelling.

What a wonderful account of the history of Lawrence County and perhaps the greatest of its benefactors, James H. Stribling! In *One Man's Vision . . . One County's Reward*, Kathy Gandy has woven the historical registry into a delightful read for all history buffs—particularly those interested in the history of Middle Tennessee.

As a small boy during World War II, I remember POWs from Camp Forrest in Tullahoma cleaning fence rows, as well as the stories my grandmother told of her father's role in the Civil War. I was raised to love history, and it is one reason I immensely enjoyed this book. The compelling story of James Stribling's life is fascinating. The history of the CCC—a well-known but little-discussed period of our history—and its impact on the people, give an insightful education in and of itself. This book is profusely illustrated with pictures of the period, gathered from private sources (most never before published), local museums, and newspaper archives. They add an intimacy to this thoroughly researched book. Curtis Peters' and Tim Pettus' enormous contribution to this legacy of Lawrence County and its people deserve our highest praise. The people's acceptance of the hardships of the times are put forth for us in a wonderful manner that makes reading this book a joy. The relationship between the POWs of Camp Stribling and the local population depicts a story repeated in hundreds of small towns all across the United States. This alone is what sets us apart from any other country. These are the people who made our America the greatest nation man has ever produced. Many thanks again to Kathy Gandy for bringing it to us in such an enjoyable book.

—John W. Adams,
Mount Juliet, Tennessee
Typographer and Student of History

One Man's Vision ...
One County's Reward

How the Life of
James H. Stribling
Affected His Fellow Man

Kathleen Graham-Gandy *Kathy*
With Contributions by
Curtis Peters *and* Tim Pettus

Shock Inner Prizes, Inc.
Books to Touch the Heart
Shock Inner Prizes Publishers
Mount Pleasant, Tennessee

DISCLAIMER

As compilers of this work relating to the local CCC camps, the POW camp, and its relevant stories of World War II and other topics, we make no attempt to indicate that we are the authors or originators of such facts. History is retold stories of lives lived, and facts—as retold—which are often enhanced to invigorate the listener or reader. Some stories are repeated in their entirety to give the full gist of the events. Where this is so, we attempt to give full credit to the author or writer of such information. Others are quotes or stories given to us by third or fourth parties and may be decreased or increased as to the actual facts of the true events. With this disclaimer, we do hereby state that should we fail to give each individual credit for his or her work, it rests on the complexities of the facts previously stated as to the many directions of these compiled historical facts. Full effort is made through all compilation of these facts to review comments and facts prior to publication, such that no derogatory wording or issues are printed relating to any party mentioned in this publication. Pictures used were often of poor resolution due to the time frame of the original settings, but they were enhanced to the highest grade possible for your viewing enjoyment. Copies of letters and other documents often depict the aged process of the original documents with no attempt to deface its true antiquity.

Published in Mount Pleasant, Tennessee
by Shock Inner Prizes, Inc., Book Publishing Division
8369 Old Highway 43, Mount Pleasant, Tennessee 38474
1-800-771-0442; Web address: www.shockinnerprizes.com
Email: sales@shockinnerprizes.com

Book design and typography
by Jennifer Zimmerman
at John W. Adams Typographer
1500 Beckwith Road, Mount Juliet, Tennessee 37122
615-773-2576; E-mail: ProtoType@tds.net

Cover design by Charles E. Gandy, Shock Inner Prizes, Inc.

Back cover photos courtesy of John Hatcher,
hatcherimages.com, 113 First Avenue,
Mount Pleasant, Tennessee 38474

Library of Congress Control Number: 2012922653

ISBN 10: 0-9800-8111-4
ISBN 13: 978-0-9800-8111-4

Printed in the United States of America

1 2 3 4 5 6 7 8 BP 18 17 16 15 14 13

To:

*Charles, my husband,
my soulmate, my best friend.
As always, your support and
help have meant so much to me.
Thank you for helping me, again,
to fulfill a lifelong dream.
You truly are "the wind beneath my wings."*

AND TO:

*The men and women who served in the
armed forces during "The War" (World War II).
To those who gave their lives and to those
who survived: your commitment to your
country will never be forgotten.*

AND TO:

*My parents, Donnie Will
and Edna Mosley Graham*

TABLE OF CONTENTS

PREFACE

By Kathleen Graham-Gandy

TWO YEARS AGO I had no clue that a German prisoner of war camp had ever existed in America, much less in my own back yard—so to speak—in neighboring Lawrenceburg, Tennessee. Nor did I realize that the POWs were hired out to work in Maury County—my current place of residence—as well as many neighboring counties, assisting with farming and numerous woodcutting projects for local furnaces.

I was aware that a Civilian Conservation Corps (CCC) camp had existed in Lawrence County through my husband's family who had farmed the Laurel Hill bottoms in the late 1940s. But, again, I had no clue that there were a total of three CCC camps located in Lawrence County during the 1930s to early 1940s. Neither did I realize that these CCC camp enrollees sometimes worked in Giles County (the county where I grew up), as well as many other counties adjacent to Lawrence County. I was also unaware that most of our national parks and TVA dams were built by the CCC.

When asked if I would be willing to work on this project for the extended family of Jim Stribling, I was both honored and flattered to be given this opportunity. The privilege that I have been given to correlate this family, and historical, data into a finished publication for their family treasure, and to share their treasure with the participants and heirs of those locals, who "lived" these historical events to which we allude in this book, is an honor beyond words. To be a link between true history and future recipients of such news is a truly humbling experience that no author should abuse as "my book"; for without the price that each paid for these events—so worthy of preserving—"our book" would not exist.

ACKNOWLEDGMENTS

THIS BOOK could not have been completed without the help of many people. First, I want to thank the Good Lord for allowing me the opportunity to write another historical book. I truly believe that His divine intervention once again put me in a position to work with some amazing people that I would not have otherwise known.

I am deeply grateful to my husband, Charles, who once again took my project and treated it as his own. In other words, his eye for detail and perfection, working long hours, his thoroughness with research . . . most of all, his patience with me, were all invaluable toward accomplishing this book. He does so much to help, yet he wants no recognition, staying in the background while pushing me toward the limelight. "MY" books would never come to fruition without his help. That is why "MY" books are "OUR" books.

Thanks to Curtis Peters for all his vast historical research, pictures, and assistance in ensuring the accuracy of our documentation. All the phone calls, visits, and setting up of interviews with people who had connections to the history of the CCC and POW camps were invaluable. Thanks for all your help. Also, a world of thanks goes to Tim Pettus for his insight to see that these local legends are too invaluable not to preserve for future generations. Thanks, too, for allowing us to come into your office to look at "The Painting" more than once, and for keeping us on track. Your connections for financial and promotional assistance with this project were a tremendous help as well. Thank you.

A special thanks to my family and friends who had to listen time and again about why I was unable to do things with them, simply because I was working on another book. I wish to express my gratitude to my sister-in-law, Connie Gandy, for providing us with many "working vacations." Her trips were great getaways that allowed us to work uninterrupted on the book. Thanks for not complaining about time spent on the road with computers and printouts handed out for all to read "on the way" to our destination. And there is nothing better than a "Connie" meal. Thanks for pampering us. We love you!

And as with any major production, this book would not have happened without the expertise of: designers, type-setters, editors, and specialists. A special thanks to Jennifer Zimmerman and John Adams for a job well done. We made it through another book! Thanks also to those who contributed documents, pictures, and information. Many phone calls and visits were made to ensure that all the facts were straight. There are so many people who have helped along the way that it is impossible to list everyone, but you know who you are. Thank you from the bottom of my heart. A big thanks to Brian Jansma of Bang Printing for your guidance and your patience on yet another book as well. I really appreciate your understanding of my "blonde moments."

A heartfelt thanks to Jan Best who arranged and hosted the meeting with Ray Morris and his wife, Margaret. You truly are "the Best." Your friendship and prayers mean a lot to us.

IN MEMORY

THIS BOOK IS DEDICATED to the memory of my Uncle Short (Clarence Cecil Howell) and to all those who served in World War II.

Howell was in several different invasions during World War II including Bougainville and the Philippines. Howell spent most of his tour on the Bougainville Island where he spent thirteen months underground. It was while he was on this island that Howell received his Silver Star Medal for heroic behavior.

Two officers had been shot during a battle. Howell, along with his medical officer, and without regard for their own lives, rushed to the aid of these two officers. The man that Howell reached had both legs shot off. Howell kept applying pressure on the man's wounds, giving him packets of plasma.* This kept him alive until help arrived with whole blood, and he could then be transported safely to an evacuation hospital. From there the officer

Clarence Cecil Howell
March 13, 1920—June 10, 2002
Army Medical, NCO (Noncommissioned Officer)
129th Infantry—37th Division
January 29, 1942—August 1, 1945

---

*This method of giving plasma until whole blood could be obtained was a procedure used throughout World War II.

was sent back to the States. After the officer returned to the States, he sent a letter to Howell thanking him for saving his life.

Uncle Short was a very humble man and did not mention this incident very often. Very few people in the family knew about his bravery until later in life. Thankfully, one of his nieces took the time to record his experiences and shared that video with his family.

My thanks go out to my uncle and all the men and women who served in the military during this war and other wars throughout the years.

Years later Uncle Short experienced another historical event. On November 22, 1963, Uncle Short and Aunt B. D. (Frances Graham Howell) were in Dallas, Texas, visiting relatives. Having known about President Kennedy's scheduled trip to Dallas, my aunt and uncle planned vacation time so they could see the President.

They arrived in downtown Dallas early so that they could get

Route of President Kennedy's motorcade.

a good spot along the motorcade route. Only moments after President and Mrs. Kennedy passed by them, they heard gunshots ring out. They could see the car slowing down and then speeding away. (They had earlier been told not to take pictures of the motorcade.)

Just after hearing the shots, my aunt and uncle looked toward the building from which the gunshots had originated. From an open window in the building, they could see movement as if someone was running or moving quickly, but they did not see any gun. My aunt took pictures* of the open window where the gunman had allegedly been standing. This was, of course, the day President John F. Kennedy was assassinated.

*Upwards view of the building
where Lee Harvey Oswald was alleged
to have been lying in wait.*

---

*Information and photos courtesy of Frances Graham Howell and Kenneth (Pete) Howell.

INTRODUCTION

By Curtis Peters

IT IS NOT OFTEN that a history buff gets to open a lost chapter of local history. The story of our past reads like a fairy tale; each succeeding generation seems to add to the legend. Time has served only to enhance the fascination of the history of our county. Small pieces of history are forgotten as we move forward in time leaving the past behind us.

Being a retired history teacher of thirty-eight years, I became fascinated in one of these forgotten stories. My wife's family had connections to a local World War II (WWII) prisoner of war camp in Lawrenceburg, Tennessee, and actually had photos and letters related to the camp. As I began my research, more and more pieces of forgotten local history began to emerge. Working with all of the new information was like putting together a living puzzle from the past. The more facts I uncovered, the greater was my curiosity as to what I might find in the future.

This journey through time brought together stories of Mr. James Henry Stribling, a local Civilian Conservation Corp (CCC) camp from 1939, the World War II POW camp and local Service Men's Home. On the surface, these events seem to have nothing in common, but all of these have connecting threads that hold our past together. Although my research has uncovered a wealth of information, there is much more to discover.

This delightful task was like a vacation in time, visiting some of the people who helped create our county's past. It has also been a pleasure to see the excited faces of so many people telling me the past stories of their relatives as they related to my research. The only regret that I have is that I did not start this journey sooner. We wish you a happy reading of this book and invite you to join us in this fascinating journey into the past.

The Civilian Conservation Corps (CCC) at Camp Stribling, Lawrenceburg, Tennessee

HISTORY OF NEW DEAL

The CCC Defined

THEY WERE AN ARMY of volunteers, over half a million strong, waging an economic and environmental battle for almost ten years in all forty-eight states (at that time) and United

Men working the sawmill at Company 448
Lawrenceburg, Tennessee
Photo courtesy of Old Jail Museum, Lawrenceburg, Tennessee

States territories. Yet, not a single shot was fired. Their weapons were manpower, shovels, and seedlings. Their motto was, "We Can Take It." The Emergency Conservation Works (ECW), as established, would later be called—and always be remembered as—the Civilian Conservation Corps, or the CCC.

Franklin Delano Roosevelt (FDR) became the thirty-second President of the United States on March 4, 1933. He saw a nation desperate for relief from a 25 percent unemployment rate, an unbelievable 13 million Americans, out of a workforce of just over 50 million. Many Americans were without a home, had very limited food supply, and were unable to properly clothe their families. Most of those who were employed were only employed on a part-time basis.

FDR promised a New Deal for the American people. Those hardest hit with unemployment, homelessness, and hunger were young men between the ages of eighteen and twenty-five and World War I veterans. With the Great Depression in full bloom, the banking systems had ceased to function. Lifelong savings, jobs, businesses, and homes were lost. Causing even greater economic and survival trauma was the fact that poor farming and forestry methods had eradicated the soil to the point that potential crops were found to scantly produce but survivable quantities for a family. This made popular the saying of earlier years, "enough and to spare," an exaggeration of undesired proportion; for there was "little to nothing" to spare or share with neighbors, or even distant family. The Great Plains had experienced an extreme drought which compounded the economic problems, leaving little and yet expensive produce to ship to the nonfarming communities. The term "Dust Bowl" was coined for the extensive ordeal of the Midwest region's drought conditions that started in the summer of 1932.

FDR had a long-standing interest in conservation, and in a 1931 speech he had articulated the conservationist critique that had been animating the American movement for a half century. He commented, "The green slopes of our forested hills lured our first settlers and furnished them the materials of a happy life. They and their descendants were a little careless with that asset."

Roosevelt had envisioned the CCC during his 1932 presidential campaign. At his acceptance speech during the Democratic National Convention, he talked of putting a million men into forestry work; but the Hoover administration was very critical of the idea, so FDR did not aggressively push the idea during his campaign.

But less than a week after being sworn in as President, on the morning of March 9, 1933, Roosevelt ordered some of his senior staff (cabinet heads of Departments of Labor, Interior, Agriculture, and War) to come up with a way to put 500,000 young men to work on conservation projects by the summer. By that evening, they had a plan that became the focus of more discussions over the next few weeks. Roosevelt began to tackle the crisis threatening the nation with this unprecedented experiment in federal work relief. Above and beyond any other New Deal program, the CCC was Roosevelt's "pet."

Initial figures as to the cost of such an endeavor met with some resistance from FDR himself. On April 5, 1933, striving to keep the financial burden of the struggling nation to a minimum, the president commented on the letter from Colonel Duncan Major to CCC Director Fechner that the $1.92 per day per man was "absurdly high—it must be greatly reduced" (see letter on page 4).

WAR DEPARTMENT
WAR DEPARTMENT GENERAL STAFF
OPERATIONS & TRAINING DIVISION G-3
WASHINGTON

April 5, 1933.

MEMORANDUM FOR Mr. Robert Fechner, Director of Emergency Conservation
Work, Room 5139, Interior Department Building, Washington, D. C.

Subject: Transfer of funds to the War Department for
Civilian Conservation Corps.

Pursuant to the direction of the President, the following estimate
of funds needed by the War Department to receive, transport to camps,
enroll, shelter, clothe, ration, equip and transport to their work a
total of 25,000 men on the assumption that they will remain only 14
days under Army control, is here submitted as the basis of the original
requisition of funds to cover the current expenses involved:

Item	Cost per man	Cost per man day	Cost for 25,000 men for 14 days
Transportation, to camp	$10.00		$ 250,000
, to work	25.00		625,000
Clothing, initial outfit	38.00		950,000
Subsistence		$ .33	115,500
Medical Attention			
Induction Charges	5.00	.35	125,000
Supplies and Extra Service		.07	24,500
Equipment and Supplies		.08	28,000
Motor transportation, gas and oil		.02	7,000
Shelter, repairs, utilities	15.00	.07	375,000
Allowance (accrued)		(1.00)	350,000
			$2,850,000

1.92

It is therefore requested that the sum of $2,850,000 be transferred
at once to the Chief of Finance, U. S. Army, to cover the current expenses of the enrollment and conditioning of the first 25,000 men
selected for the Civilian Conservation Corps.

DUNCAN K. MAJOR, JR.,
Colonel, General Staff,
Acting Assistant Chief of Staff.

APPROVED.

ROBERT FECHNER
Director of Emergency Conservation Work.

This letter posted on archives.com from the National Archives states:

*An April 5, 1933, memo from Colonel Duncan Major of the army
to Fechner estimates the costs to enroll and maintain 25,000
camp enrollees for fourteen days. FDR commented at the top
of the letter that the $1.92 per day per man was "absurdly
high—it must be greatly reduced."*
Photo from Roosevelt Library

Roosevelt sent a more modest proposal to Congress, calling for the employment of 250,000 men by early summer. It was quickly approved and signed into law. The final congressional document awarded broad discretionary powers to the President in setting up an "Emergency Conservation Work" program. (ECW was the initial legal name of the program. In 1937 the more popularly used CCC title became official.)

Louis Howe, the President's personal assistant, and Robert Fechner, the first appointed director of the CCC—apart from FDR himself—were the two most important individuals in getting the CCC successfully launched into a workable program. As a reporter in 1912, Howe became acquainted with Roose-

CCC Repair Shop
Located at Pine Bluff
Company 448
Lawrenceburg, Tennessee
Photo courtesy of Old Jail Museum, Lawrenceburg, Tennessee

velt while covering the New York Legislature. They quickly developed a close friendship and a shared ambition to one day make Roosevelt President of the United States. During World War I, Roosevelt served as assistant Secretary of the Navy. He put Howe on the government payroll as an assistant. In later years, however, Howe became the principal organizer of Roosevelt's successful presidential campaign.

Once FDR was in the White House, he made Howe his personal assistant. Even though Howe was operating from a position with no formal authority, he did more than anyone else to put Roosevelt's vague vision of an "army" of conservation workers into a stable and workable format. Howe encouraged Roosevelt to appoint Robert Fechner, a longtime labor leader with the machinists union, as the first director of the CCC. Howe and the President had dealt with Fechner during the war on navy-related matters. Organized labor had initially been critical of the CCC program and was even more critical of Roosevelt's appointment of Frances Perkins, a non-unionist, as Secretary of Labor. After hearing of Howe's strategic plan of peace with the unions, Roosevelt gave the nod to Fechner over several more experienced conservationists. The appointment proved to win the support of the labor leaders for the CCC program, despite its seemingly meager wages. Organized labor's opposition to a proposed wage scale of one dollar a day for the men was partially muted by leaving pay rates up to the President, who then went ahead with the thirty-dollar-a-month pay rate on his own. In signing the measure into law, Roosevelt justified it as a means "to preserve our precious natural resources" and, even more important, as a moral and spiritual boost to needy young Americans. Most of these young Americans preferred to work rather than just survive off the limited charity during these Great Depression times. Bringing the unemployed multitude into "healthful surroundings," Roosevelt argued, would help to eliminate the threats to social stability that had been created by the "forced idleness."

Thousands of public employees in hundreds of federal offices in Washington, and across the nation, worked in unison to successfully launch the CCC program that spring and, surprisingly, met the President's goal by July 1. Even the hardest working participant in the planning could scarcely believe what they had accomplished. As they reviewed their accomplishments, the closest comparable feat anybody could think of was the spring of 1917. That was when 181,000 men were drafted into the armed services after the United States had declared war on Germany during World War I.

The number of enrollees peaked in late July, 1933, at 301,230 men after FDR enacted the setup of Veteran, Native American, and Local Experienced Men camps. The Forest Service ran 82 percent of these camps, the National Park Service (NPS) had charge of 11 percent, and the rest were variously managed by the War Department, the Bureau of Indian Affairs, and other federal agencies (including the Tennessee Valley Authority).

Once Roosevelt announced his own CCC project, the army was able to wrap their earlier planning into the new proposal. By March 24, 1933, a week before Congress authorized the CCC, the army's staff had a working plan. By mid-April the army had essentially put together the rules and regulations that it used during the entire course of the CCC program.

In the early deliberations over the form that the CCC would take, the precise role that the army would play produced considerable dissension. Although the army's expertise was indispensable in transporting, housing, and disciplining the 250,000 young men the President wanted in work camps in three months' time, the army's heavy involvement would always be a sensitive issue.

The nation, as a whole, had become very critical of seemingly huge profits by war contractors during World War I. From these past critical lessons, CCC officials, from Fechner on down, consequently tried to reduce any appearance of a military-styled operation. It was agreed that there would be no military police or guardhouses, no saluting or weapons training, and no drills. However, due to the surplus available, the men wore modified army uniforms, initially lived in army tents, and followed fairly routine army camp procedures such as daily directives by buglers. The army's experience proved invaluable to establishing the CCC camps on such short notice; but in due time many leaders would find the veterans to be an uncooperative, and even unneeded, partner in a conservation program essentially concerned with labor training and financial assistance to young men and their needy families.

Robert Y. Stuart, of the U.S. Forest Service, and Colonel Duncan Major, of the War Department, were often at war with each other as they struggled over day-to-day camp operations. Stuart felt his department should run the entire program by itself, including camp operations. He foresaw the army's role as simple as gathering the men into what he had inadvertently referred to as "concentration camps." The forest service, at its discretion, would then call the workers to its own work camps.

When it became apparent that the army's experienced personnel were the most competent to set up and organize the CCC camps, Stuart reluctantly agreed that the army should run the work camps and have disciplinary authority over the workers. Stuart did, however, win on one exception. When men were released for work projects in the field, they would be under the supervision of the technical personnel over the project.

CCC Workers Splitting Wood
Company 448
Lawrenceburg, Tennessee
Photo courtesy of Old Jail Museum, Lawrenceburg, Tennessee

Roosevelt himself made light of any anxieties arising from the CCC administrative struggles. His nonchalant comment was, "Oh, that doesn't matter. The army and the forestry service will really run the show. The Secretary of Labor will select the men and make the rules, and Fechner will 'go along' and give everybody satisfaction and confidence."

To FDR's wishful thinking, the CCC almost worked that smoothly. The CCC became the first and probably the most successful of FDR's New Deal Programs. According to one CCC writer, "Within twelve months the work of the CCC boys had advanced the conservation movement by ten years, and it is now recognized as the greatest single conservation program in American history."

The Men of the CCC Camp
Company 448
Tenn. TVA-44
Lawrenceburg, Tennessee
Photo courtesy of James (Chunky) Moore, Jr.

The requirements for becoming a CCC enrollee were:

- He was to be a single male between the ages of eighteen and twenty-five years and in good physical condition.
- He would be under duress from the economic conditions with family members that needed his financial support.
- The enrollee would be physically capable of survival under rugged outdoor living and working conditions (8.8 percent failed their physical the first year).

The Labor Department decided that homeless and transient men would not be eligible. Each enrollee signed up for a six-

month tour agreeing to a forty-hour workweek. The CCC workers erected telephone lines, bridges, dams, recreational structures,
and fire towers. They also cleared and constructed roads, skiing
and hiking trails, as well as building stone walls in many state
and national parks across America (including the Great Smoky
Mountain National Park in East Tennessee). Conservation-wise,
the CCC planted over 3 billion trees, and fought forest fires on
a regular basis. They built 3,400 fire towers and made 97,000
miles of fire roads. Their work and the economy had indeed
become the strength of the country that President Roosevelt
had imagined.

All this work was accomplished at a monthly wage rate of

CCC Workers Doing Road Repairs
Company 448
Tenn. TVA-44
Lawrenceburg, Tennessee
Photo courtesy of Old Jail Museum, Lawrenceburg, Tennessee

thirty dollars with the stipulation that twenty-five dollars would be sent home to one or more dependents (parents and/or siblings), and the CCC worker would receive the remaining five dollars for personal use. The housing, meals, medical needs, clothes, and even educational opportunities were included in the package at no cost to the workers. For many of the workers, considering the conditions back home, it was a pleasant surprise to be able to eat three meals a day. The original housing for the workers was tents left over from World War I surplus, but most camps later built military-styled barracks using local labor and locally purchased material. This was a boost for the local economy and morale. (Little did anyone realize that many of these camps and barracks would, in a short while, house World War II German prisoners of war.)

The five-dollar fee that each worker was permitted to keep from each month's paycheck was generally for the fulfillment of the enrollee's own "wants and wishes." The young boys were a rowdy sight on weekends as they entered the town nearest their camp, with five dollars in their dress uniform pockets, strutting about as if they were millionaires.

Several communities had reservations of the upcoming arrival of their "new neighbors"; but these fears soon subsided as the young gentlemen proved their worth with each hurricane, tornado, flood, forest fire, house fire, or other community emergency by being their *neighbor's keeper* in a way that few communities could match as to quality and quantity of help. Another pleasant advantage to the nearby communities came in the form of assisting the local economy as the camps would purchase much of their needed supplies from local farmers and merchants.

Each CCC camp was under the command of a World War I

army reservist, usually a lieutenant or colonel, and contained approximately 200 enrollee workers. There were over 4,500 camps across America and its territories, with an estimated 3 million families assisted through the CCC program. Poor leadership at some camps was the cause of problems and errors of judgment. The CCC had its flaws, just as did the individual Americans who resided and oversaw the day-to-day operations of each camp. Despite the flaws of some portions of the CCC program, however, it was still a lifesaver for the American economy.

ARMY OVERHEAD: (Left to right). FIRST ROW: Edward Schade, Otis Banks, Arvil Lamb, Lee Milan. SECOND ROW: Everett Morris, Arthur Stewart, Charles D. Timberlake, Arthur V. Nash, Richard Green.

Company 448
Tenn. TVA-44
Lawrenceburg, Tennessee
Photo courtesy of Old Jail Museum, Lawrenceburg, Tennessee

An amendment outlawing racial discrimination was virtually the only congressional limitation of the President's authority with the CCC program. Segregation in the 1930s was not deemed by the Supreme Court to constitute racial discrimination, and separate "colored" CCC camps were set up for young African Americans. One such colored camp was housed at Henryville (Laurel Hill) in Lawrence County, Tennessee. Some African American enrollees studied radio code, which enabled them to run the camp radio stations. (This would prove invaluable both to them and to the military, with the up and coming war.)

Three other groups would be included among the first CCC enrollees.

- Roosevelt authorized the enrollment of 12,000 reservation Indians, with no restrictions on age or marital status. Over the life of the CCC, some 88,000 Native Americans would be helped through the program with most of these continuing to live at home rather than at the camps.
- The second group authorized by FDR to be helped was the Local Experienced Men (LEMs). These would typically be men who lived in the vicinity of the camps and had some kind of forestry experience. Unlike the younger enrollees, they could be hired with no restrictions on age or marital status and no required physical conditioning through camp training. That first summer the CCC hired about 35,000 LEMs for its camps. This hiring helped to alleviate the potential for sabotage of the camps from local labor forces.
- Veterans were the final group of unemployed men whose needs were supplemented by the CCC program.

Roosevelt accepted the suggestion of the head of the Veterans Administration, Frank Hines, and, by resolution, authorized the enrollment of 25,000 war veterans. These veterans were selected by the Veterans Administration to work in special camps of their own, with no restrictions on age or marital status. CCC camps employed about 225,000 veterans over the next nine years. Veteran camps tended to be a bit more relaxed than the typical camps. Most of the men were in their mid-forties and tended to remain in the CCC almost twice as long as the young men of other camps. The canteens of veteran camps sold beer, and sometimes this practice adversely affected their reputations in rural areas. Local relief officials also occasionally complained about veterans moving their families to communities near their camps, thereby becoming burdens on the already strained local relief efforts.

• As the CCC reviewed various groups of the unemployed, one group that was always notably missing was, of course, women. First Lady Eleanor Roosevelt suggested that some of the estimated 200,000 homeless women in the country be put to work in forestry nurseries—perhaps an unconsciously sexist idea—deliberate, yet considerably ahead of the times. She sent the idea over to the first woman cabinet member, Frances Perkins of the Labor Department, but the topic was dropped. The CCC would always remain an organization for men only. However, the Federal Emergency Relief Administration and the Works Progress Administration (WPA) would later set up some "She-She-She" work camps for women. So was

Mrs. Roosevelt's bravery actually the initial conception of the modern "women's liberation movement"? Unfortunately, many viewed the "She-She-She" camps as vacation camps for women, so the program was short-lived. American citizens in the 1930s objected to the use of public resources to support individuals, especially women.

How to occupy the men of the CCC camps in the remaining hours of the day became a major challenge to the army

CCC Camp Store
Company 448
Tenn. TVA-44
Lawrenceburg, Tennessee
Photo courtesy of Old Jail Museum, Lawrenceburg, Tennessee

overseers of each camp. Division of Welfare ensured that each camp received the services of a chaplain, either army personnel or recruited local clergy. From past experience the army made arrangements to show two movies a week in each of the camps, as well as to develop a system of 150 to 200 rotating library books.

The army would also run postal exchanges and use the small profits for the purchase of recreational and entertainment equipment. Based on army experience, each camp would be initially supplied with a dozen baseballs, six bats, ten gloves, basketballs, and four sets of eight-ounce boxing

The men of the CCC camp during worship.
Photo courtesy of Ray Morris, CCC camp alumnus

gloves, a list quite familiar to army personnel. Elaborate athletic competitions, both within the camp and with other camps and local groups, became great pastime events for many of the enrollees. Local civic groups would often make sizeable donations of recreational equipment.

This patch was worn by Earl Reed who was in Camp 447, Camp William Spratt of York, Alabama. This patch was found by Reed's grandson, Michael McCalip, of Hohenwald, Tennessee, as they were cleaning out his grandmother's attic.
Photo courtesy of Michael McCalip

Recreation was great, but some of the civilian officials in the CCC began to think about something more ambitious and potentially more valuable to fill up the boys' free time. Secretary of Labor Frances Perkins began to talk up the possibility of a more advanced educational program, including university extension courses. She envisioned appointing "camp counselors" to supervise unstructured lessons in the camp and could foresee nightly campfires where the men would sing, tell stories, and put on theatrical performances. However, through the long days of summer and early fall, outdoor recreation was enough to occupy the time and energies of most enrollees. Most of the "spare time" of CCC leaders was spent focusing on the next work project and designing and readying the construction of facilities more substantial than the army surplus tents that presently were the "barracks" of many enrollees. But many state foresters, as well as educators, around the country steadily kept the issue of camp education alive.

CCC Basketball Team
Company 448, Tenn. TVA-44
Lawrenceburg, Tennessee
Photo courtesy of Old Jail Museum, Lawrenceburg, Tennessee

On October 15, 1933, Howe, FDR's personal assistant, pushed to formulate an educational plan. An idea was submitted and later revised by Army Chief of Staff General Douglas MacArthur, whereby educational advisers were appointed for each of the camps. So began the difficult task of conceptualizing and implementing a suitable educational program for the CCC. While there is no question that many young men (especially the 57,000 illiterates who learned to read and write in camp) benefited from the educational opportunities the CCC was able to offer, the whole program always had the quality of an afterthought about it and lacked any kind of system or even clear-cut purpose. Placed, as it was, under the effective control of army camp commanders, the educational program would be only as good, or as bad, as those individuals chose to make it. While some commanders cooperated with the advisers, many others saw the whole program as an "unwelcomed chore."

Over the years, there evolved an amazing variety of subjects taught after hours in the camps. However, a critical study

The men in the camps enjoyed the sport of boxing.
Ray Morris (white trunks) of Franklin, Tennessee,
appreciated the few extra dollars from his "wins."
Photo courtesy of Ray Morris, CCC alumnus

↥ *Card games and pool were other popular* ↧
recreational pastimes.
Photos courtesy of Ray Morris, CCC alumnus

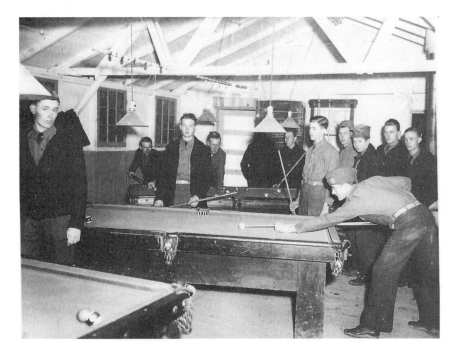

of the educational programs of a small sample of camps found that the cost of camp education was higher on a per capita basis than that of public schools. It also revealed that enrollees dropped out of programs in alarming numbers even after an enthusiastic beginning. Another factor revealed through the study was that the average enrollee received only twenty-seven hours of instruction over a two-year typical enlistment.

"They Shall Have Music" (Company 1458)

Music was a vital part of camp life as it made a fresh connection with families back home through the lyrics that were sung.
Photo courtesy of Ray Morris, CCC camp alumnus

Seeing the popular and productive boost of the CCC program on the American economy, FDR was highly in favor of making the CCC program a permanent program. However, by the time 1942 had arrived, Congress felt that there were more pressing issues than spending money on the CCC program.

CCC Library
Company 448
Tenn. TVA-44
Lawrenceburg, Tennessee
Photo courtesy of Old Jail Museum, Lawrenceburg, Tennessee

The United States was forced into World War II and that war was costing the United States a lot of money. The problems with unemployment that had plagued the country when the CCC program was first initiated was now on an upswing. Congress felt that the money they were spending on President Roosevelt's New Deal program would be better spent on war issues. With most of the CCC workers being at an age for defending their nation, the majority (75 percent) were enlisted for military service and journeyed elsewhere to once again save their nation. In 1942, the CCC camps were emptied of men as quickly as they were filled, and the removal of the program was instituted. Many of the camps have been torn down; however, some still exist on state lands.

Thousands of the 2.5 million former CCC men are still living, which is attested to by the unlimited Web sites of those associated with the National Association of Civilian Conservation Corps Alumni. Area reunions are held annually with hundreds in attendance at the facilities near their old CCC camp sites. They often joke about how they and the trees they planted have grown old together.

The CCC was indeed a New Deal, but it was a deal that had saved many American families during a time of utter hopelessness across the "land of the free and the home of the brave."*

Several notable alumni of the CCC include:

- **Raymond Burr,** actor (*Ironside* and *Perry Mason*)
- **Archie Moore,** Light Heavyweight Boxing Champion of the World
- **Robert Mitchum,** actor (mostly westerns)
- **Chuck Yeager,** test pilot (first to break the sound barrier)
- **Stan (Stan-the-Man) Musial,** baseball player
- **David "Stringbean" Akeman,** country music/Grand Ole Opry singer

TVA's Role in the CCC

Why include the TVA as a part of this CCC chapter? The reasons are quite obvious considering the facts that:

- TVA was a part of FDR's New Deal that continued beyond the years of the CCC.
- TVA oversaw the operation of nearly half of the CCC camps in Tennessee and many in surrounding states, relating to dams of the Tennessee River basin and its tributaries.

*Wikipedia, CCC History, Public Domain.

- TVA was instrumental in soil conservation, flood control, and providing recreational facilities throughout the Tennessee Valley.
- TVA was instrumental in providing electrical power, not only to the majority of the CCC camps, but also to the area residents to enhance the quality of life during this desperate period of time for the nation.

The concept of the Tennessee Valley Authority (TVA) started with Muscle Shoals, a stretch of the Tennessee River where the river dropped one hundred forty feet in thirty miles. That drop in elevation created the rapids or "shoals" for which the area is named and made passage farther upstream impossible. The federal government acquired the land in 1916, with the intent of constructing a dam that would alleviate the navigational problem, generate electricity, and produce nitrates needed to produce explosives for the World War I effort. But the war ended without a dam being built.

The election of Franklin D. Roosevelt altered the balance of power and finally led to action. On April 10, 1933, Roosevelt asked Congress to set up the Tennessee Valley Authority (TVA). On May 18, 1933, President Roosevelt signed the Tennessee Valley Authority Act as part of the flurry of legislation that marked Roosevelt's first 100 days in office. The TVA was one of the most ambitious projects of the New Deal in its overall conception.

The TVA pledged to improve the navigability on the Tennessee River, as well as to provide flood control, to reforest and improve marginal farm land, to assist in industrial and agricultural development, and to assist in the creation of a government nitrate and phosphorus manufacturing facility. The proposed 1916 war-supporting factory became a chemical plant manufacturing fertilizers, and a hydroelectric plant which generated power for parts of seven states at Wilson Dam near Florence, Alabama.

Prior to the Tennessee Valley Authority Act, the region was one of the most disadvantaged in the South. TVA was given an assignment to improve the economic and social circumstances of the people living in the river basin.

The U.S. Department of Agriculture, including the Agricultural Adjustment Administration, U.S. Forest Service, Civilian Conservation Corps (CCC), and state agricultural experiment stations and extension services, were (*and are*) among the agencies that have worked with TVA to carry out a well-rounded program of rehabilitation for both the land and its people.

In October 1933, construction began on Norris Dam, named after Senator Norris, who had campaigned for the creation of the Tennessee Valley Authority. TVA engaged in one of the largest hydroelectric power construction programs ever undertaken in the United States. Sixteen dams and a steam plant were constructed by the TVA between 1933 and 1944. At its peak, a dozen hydroelectric projects and a steam plant were under construction at the same time. Design and construction employment reached a total of 28,000 workers, many of whom were a part of FDR's CCC program.

Rural electrification was based on the belief that affordable electricity would improve the standard of living and the economic competitiveness of the family farm. The Roosevelt Administration believed that if private enterprise could not supply electric power to the people, then it was the duty of the government to do it.

By 1941, TVA had become the largest producer of electrical

power in the United States. That led to even stronger opposition from private power companies, who were angered by the cheaper energy available through TVA, and they saw it as a threat to private development. (*Author's note of interest:* In 1942 the Mount Pleasant Power System was the sixth largest user of TVA power with up to fifteen phosphate plants throughout its system. Mount Pleasant, Tennessee, was the Phosphate Capitol of the World from the early 1900s [when its payroll was greater than that of Nashville] up until the mid-1980s.)

TVA Silt Basin—Roger Hays' farm, fifteen miles northeast of Lawrenceburg. Mr. J. G. Eggleston (left), project superintendent, and Mr. N. B. Dunn, Jr. (right), foreman, Company 448, Tenn. TVA-44, Lawrenceburg, Tennessee.
Photo courtesy of Old Jail Museum, Lawrenceburg, Tennessee

Farming practices in the Tennessee Valley, like those in other farming communities, attempted to pull as much productivity as possible out of fragile lands. Results were often destructive.

Hillsides and valleys were plowed and planted, resulting in the loss of valuable topsoil.

Such crops as corn, tobacco, and cotton left the topsoil exposed during the winter months, which contributed to land erosion. TVA developed programs to teach farmers how to improve crop yields, replant forests, and improve habitats for fish and wildlife. Three Lawrence County CCC camps were a part of these TVA programs.

TVA worked to change old farming practices and taught farmers to substitute nitrates with such plants as alfalfa and clover to naturally add nitrogen to the soil. TVA extension programs introduced contour plowing, crop rotation, the use of phosphate fertilizers, and the planting of cover crops for soil conservation.*

Local CCC Camps

There is much speculation but little history of the facts of the beginning, the ending, and again the beginning of Company 448, Camp Tennessee TVA-44. The following articles appeared in the local papers that leave much speculation of the continuity of the CCC camp at Pine Bluff:

- An article in the April 18, 1935, *The Lawrence News,* spoke of a CCC camp to be located at Pine Bluff, a mile west of Lawrenceburg that would accommodate about 250 men. The proposed occupation date was about June 1, 1935.
- An article in the June 27, 1935, *The Lawrence News,* talked of the improvements to local farms by controlling soil erosion which would be the chief objective of TVA Camp

---

*TVA Web site, TVA and the CCC, Public Domain.

44 that should be in operation within the next few weeks.

- The next article was in August 8, 1935, in *The Lawrence News,* that spoke of 1,521 sandwiches being prepared by the Princess Sandwich Shop of Lawrenceburg for the 260 CCC boys who were being taken to Newport.

- A farewell dinner brochure on display at the Lawrence County Archives for CCC Company 1472 (Henryville/Laurel Hill Camp), TVA-44 (Lawrenceburg Camp), gives a full detail of the menu for the evening including oyster stew, fried chicken, potatoes, yams, peas, salad, pies, cakes, beer, hot chocolate, coffee, cigars, and cigarettes. A full roster of leaders and CCC enrollees were included, as well as a letter, dated September 23, 1935, of commendation from the District C office in Fort Oglethorpe, Georgia, for the officers and all personnel of Company 1472, Tennessee TVA-44. (Note: The mix-up of the two Lawrence County camps came from the Georgia office since very few counties had more than one camp. A quick double glance evidently picked up the wrong company number at one glance and the camp number at the next glance, never realizing that they were two individual campsites.)

- An article in the October 17, 1935, *The Lawrence News,* announced that the CCC campsite at Pine Bluff was to be abandoned. It states that the 188 men of the camp that began four months earlier would be distributed among other camps.

- An article in the October 24, 1935, *The Lawrence News,* spoke of telegrams sent in regard to the local CCC camps. Congressman C. W. Turner stated that the "cooperation

Civilian Conservation Corps
Company 448
Camp Tenn. TVA-44
Lawrenceburg, Tennessee
1939–1941
Photo courtesy of Old Jail Museum, Lawrenceburg, Tennessee

of local land owners in applying for assistance for soil erosion had not been as great as other areas that had much need for the assistance." Several local and state politicians and businessmen made every effort to continue this camp and sixty-one additional camps of the Fort Oglethorpe District that were being abandoned.

- An article in the November 15, 1935, *The Democrat-Union,* mentioned that more than 200 local CCC boys are to be fingerprinted. (This may speak of the Laurel Hill Camp(s) since other news articles reference the Lawrence-burg camp as being abandoned.)

- A historical article by Nancy Miller Brewer of the *Lawrence County Advocate* from an early interview of an enrollee at Laurel Hill, stated that these first enrollees arrived from Unicoi, Tennessee, for the "Henryville" camp (better known as the Laurel Hill Camp) in the autumn of 1934.

- An article in *The Democrat-Union* of June 1939, told of J. H. Stribling purchasing a vacant lot near the Pine Bluff camp on "the west side of town" for a softball diamond for the boys to play softball and baseball. (So, if this camp closed in 1935, it was back in operation as of April 19, 1939 on Pine Bluff—same location—moving here from LaFollette, Tennessee, on this date.)

- An article in *The Democrat-Union* of March 18, 1941, spoke of an open house at all thirty-six Tennessee CCC camps from March 29 through April 5. Local (Lawrence County) Soil Conservationist James Taylor spoke in an accompanying article of the great job being done by the local camp through soil conservation practices. He spoke of over one and a half million trees being planted in sixty-three projects of Lawrence County. (It appears the farmers' cooperation and acceptance of the CCC boys and their work was much greater for the second attempt in 1939 than was seen in the initial startup in 1935.)*

Company 448, Camp Tennessee TVA-44, Lawrenceburg, Tennessee, was organized at Sharps Chapel, Tennessee, on August 15, 1935, consisting of about 206 men from counties of East Tennessee.

While at Sharps Chapel, the camp work projects consisted of work to protect, beautify, and extend the usefulness of the lake to be formed by Norris Dam (then under construction). Planting trees on badly eroded places, clearing of undergrowth, fighting forest fires, constructing a concrete dam to provide a lake to be used as a fish hatchery, and building truck trails are examples of the different work projects of the camp at Sharps Chapel.

On April 20, 1936, this company moved from Sharps Chapel to LaFollette, Tennessee. Immediately after moving to LaFollette, the camp began and—after several months' work—completed one of the largest dams that was built by a CCC company. After remaining at LaFollette for a period of three years, the company moved to Lawrenceburg, Tennessee, on April 19, 1939.

This project work of Company 448, Camp Tennessee TVA-44 of Lawrenceburg, Tennessee, was under the management of the United States Forestry Service and was supervised by the Tennessee Valley Authority (TVA). Terrace outlets, erosion control, and tree planting were the principle work of

---

*Local media excerpts, Lawrenceburg, Tennessee.

COMPANY 448

Tenn. TVA-44

LAWRENCEBURG,
TENNESSEE

LEON J. LIVINGSTON
1st Lieut., QM-Res.
COMPANY COMMANDER

SAM ANDREW ROBERTS
2nd Lieut., CA-Res.
SUBALTERN

LOWELL W. KINKEAD
EDUCATIONAL ADVISER

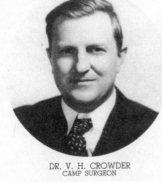

DR. V. H. CROWDER
CAMP SURGEON

Army Commanding Personnel and Camp Physician
Company 448
Tenn. TVA-44
Lawrenceburg, Tennessee
Photo courtesy of Old Jail Museum, Lawrenceburg, Tennessee

PROJECT SUPERINTENDENT-
STAFF and WORK PROJECTS

Tenn. TVA-44

J. G. EGGLESTON
Project Superintendent

JAMES T. VAUGHN
Foreman

W. S. McGANN

TOM S. VARNELL
Foreman

N. B. DUNN
Junior Foreman

Wood Chopper

Wood Detail

Project Superintendent, Staff, and Workers
Company 448
Lawrenceburg, Tennessee
Photo courtesy of Old Jail Museum, Lawrenceburg, Tennessee

MODEL HOME

Constructed by Enrollees

Front View of Model Home—CCC Project

Corner of the Living Room

Another View of Living Room

Model Home Under Construction

An outstanding educational project of the year in District "C", CCC, with Headquarters at Fort Oglethorpe, Georgia, is the construction of a small dwelling house on the campsite of Company 448, Tenn. TVA-44, Lawrenceburg, Tennessee. This four-room structure, strictly modern throughout, *was built, entirely by 14 inexperienced and untrained CCC enrollees* for the purpose of offering practical training to them in construction, and to demonstrate to the remainder of the 8,000 CCC enrollees in camps of this district that the average enrollee is capable of constructing for himself a home in which to live at a very moderate cost.

The total cost of all materials was only $595.91. This figure, of course, accounts only for cost of materials, and nothing for labor. Many materials used in the construction of this building correspond identically with that which the average youth living on a farm sees before him, or has access to in the vicinity of his home, at a very reasonable cost. Foundation for the house, in part, came from the woods. Brick used for chimneys, fireplaces, and porches were salvaged from an old destroyed structure, and at no cost. Sheet rock for the front porch and front walks constituted quarry "throw-outs" which are available to anyone without cost.

This Lawrenceburg Camp 448 Project was used as a model project in all Section C camp directories of Ft. Oglethorpe, Georgia. The house has since been moved but still stands near its original POW site on Pine Bluff in Lawrenceburg, Tennessee.
Photo courtesy of Old Jail Museum, Lawrenceburg, Tennessee

these field projects in Lawrenceburg. Company 448 was in operation until 1941.

An outstanding educational project of the year in District C, CCC, with headquarters at Fort Oglethorpe, Georgia, is the construction of a small dwelling house on the campsite of Company 448, Tennessee TVA-44, Lawrenceburg, Tennessee. This four-room structure, strictly modern throughout, was built entirely by fourteen inexperienced and untrained CCC enrollees for the purpose of offering practical training to them in construction, and to demonstrate to the remainder of the 8,000 CCC enrollees in camps of this district that the average enrollee is capable of constructing for himself a home in which to live at a very moderate cost.

The total cost of all materials was only $595.91. This figure, of course, accounts only for cost of materials, and nothing for labor. Many materials used in the construction of this building correspond identically with that which the average youth living on a farm sees before him, or has access to in the vicinity of his home, at a very reasonable cost. Foundation for the house, in part, came from the woods. Brick used for chimneys, fireplaces, and porches were salvaged from an old destroyed structure, and at no cost. Sheetrock for the front porch and front walks constituted quarry "throw-outs" which were available to anyone without cost.

Note: This house was used as an officer's quarters for the German POW camp established on this site in April 1944.

Two other local CCC camps listed on the roster of Tennessee CCC camps were located seventeen miles northwest of Lawrenceburg, with the nearest post office listed as Henryville, Tennessee. Project S-66, Company 1472, was listed as Camp Henry and was established December 2, 1934. The other camp

Cooks at Company 448
Tenn. TVA-44
Lawrenceburg, Tennessee
Photo courtesy of Old Jail Museum, Lawrenceburg, Tennessee

evidently was not listed as a project number but as Company 3463 and was called Camp William. It was also listed as seventeen miles northwest of Lawrenceburg and was established on the same day. This camp was listed as a "colored" camp, consisting of African Americans. Some local resistance to a "colored" camp was resolved in favor of the local economic gain from business of the camp enrollees. It is speculated that these camps were in the Laurel Hill area since the distance and direction would pinpoint that vicinity.

Nancy Miller Brewer, a reporter for the *Lawrence County Advocate,* also stated in an article relating to the CCC camps in Lawrence County that the Henryville Camps were near Laurel Hill. According to her article and a quote from Robert Taylor, who was an enrollee of the first group to arrive in Henryville in the late autumn of 1934, Taylor stated, "We lived in tents and, with the help of local carpenters, started building a camp to house about 200 men of CCC Company 1472, Camp Cordell Hull, Unicoi, Tennessee," which was the organizing site of the Henryville Company 1472, located at Laurel Hill. Henryville's chief work was the "development of game refuges, roadwork, stream improvement of the Little Buffalo River and its tributaries, replenishing of streams with fish, fire control, planting and development of feeding grounds on game reservations, and marking boundaries."

Through local research, if you asked anyone if they knew of a CCC camp in Lawrence County, most old-timers always mentioned Laurel Hill, probably because of its longer duration as compared to Camp Stribling on Pine Bluff. (It is also speculated that the Laurel Hill site was the "woodcutting site" of the Lawrenceburg POWs in the edge of Lewis County as will be referenced in a later chapter of this book. Jim Stribling also owned the Laurel Hill CCC property.)

A late find on the history of the local David Crockett State Park, across Shoal Creek from Pine Bluff at Lawrenceburg, contains speculation that the POWs—acting as private contractors for eighty cents per day—cleared the land for this park. It has been verified through local media that David Crockett State Park was also laid out and cleared by its owner at his expense and later deeded to the State of Tennessee. James H. Stribling was that owner of said park property and the CCC camp property—which later became the Pine Bluff POW Camp property.

State and national park services utilized the CCC to construct many of the great nature parks we enjoy today, including the Great Smoky Mountains National Park, Gatlinburg, Townsend, Cades Cove, and Lookout Mountain. There were roughly

*Franklin D. Roosevelt dedicated the Great Smoky Mountains
National Park on September 2, 1940, "for the permanent
enjoyment of the people."*
Compliments of National Park Service, Public Domain.

twenty-two CCC camps in the Great Smoky Mountains from
1933–1942, with as many as 4,000 men working in these camps,
reforesting the area and building fire towers and fire roads.

(*Author's note of interest:* On a recent trip to the Great Smoky
Mountains, we paused at the crest of the mountain near the
tap road toward Clingman's Dome to admire the beauty of the
fall leaves—and to catch the only powder room within an hour's
drive of the spot. My brother-in-law commented that he recalled a history book in grade school showing a picture of FDR
delivering a speech from the overlook of the parking area,
declaring the opening of the Great Smoky Mountains National
Park. The seventy-fifth anniversary celebration [mentioned in
the next paragraph] in 2009 and the above photo of the actual
ceremony verify this fact—and from the same spot where we
stood some seventy-seven years after that great historical event.)

In 2009, Smoky Mountain National Park celebrated its
seventy-fifth anniversary in a series of events that highlighted

its landmarks and its people. The rededication of the park some seventy-five years after its inception in 1934, brought a wide spectrum of dignitaries, including Secretary of the Interior, Ken Salazar, governors of Tennessee and North Carolina, Dolly Parton (Official Anniversary Ambassador), and the alumni of the Civilian Conservation Corps.

Approximately 4,000 CCC men served in the Smoky Mountains and ten of them were in attendance to help celebrate the rededication. Each received a commemorative coin with a photo of President Roosevelt during his speech at the original dedication of the park on the crest of the mountain in 1940.*

There are 123 CCC camps listed on the Tennessee roster of CCC camps. Of this list, fifty-seven were for miscellaneous conservation, dam construction, and erosion control under the direction of the Tennessee Valley Authority. Many of the TVA dams were constructed using CCC labor, yielding a "harnessing" of the wild and unmanageable Tennessee River and many of its tributaries, making Tennessee today one of the nation's greatest recreational states.

In 1942 at the start of World War II, the CCC camps were closed and abandoned. The CCC program was not voted out—it was just not approved for refunding and died an unnatural death. The nation was now focused on the fierceness of the war and most of the CCC men (75 percent) volunteered to fight in the military. The CCC camps turned into ghost towns with the exception of the few that were utilized for POW camps for the captured enemy troops.

---

*Great Smoky Mountain National Park Web page, Public Domain.

The Man Behind "The Plan"

JIM'S EARLY LIFE

James Henry Stribling

JAMES HENRY STRIBLING GREW UP in Lawrence County, Tennessee, immediately after the Civil War had ravished everything in the county except the courthouse. His father was Colonel James Lawrence Stribling, a newspaper editor and boardinghouse owner in Lawrenceburg. The young Stribling was an average child who, like many others, longed for bigger and better things to the West.

Thomas (Tom) Sigismund Stribling, a second cousin to James (Jim) Henry Stribling, was a renowned writer who, during the 1920s and 1930s, sold more novels than any other author, including such greats as William Faulkner and Ernest Hemingway. Tom won the Pulitzer Prize for Literature in 1932 for his novel, *The Store.* In 1982, seventeen years after his death, T. S. Stribling's *Laughing Stock* was nominated for the Pulitzer Prize. Stribling's work is still widely read today, mainly in the South, and is a must-read for some secondary schools and colleges.

Tom Stribling wrote articles for many great publications and, with each new offering, had loyal followers who would crowd the newsstand to get his next article. Having been born and reared in the small village of Clifton, Tennessee, in Wayne

County, he always left his readers feeling they were right there beside him as he finished each article or publication.

Tom Stribling related well to his second cousin, Jim Stribling, who lived west of Lawrenceburg on Waynesboro Highway. It was not uncommon to find the two reminiscing on Jim's porch as Tom ventured eastward from time to time when his writings brought him to the area. Tom compiled a collection of stories and historical events from his "sharings" with cousin Jim as the two aged and matured together. Tom shared many of the events with family members; some of these stories were never recorded elsewhere.

Tom's amusing style of portrayal of Jim Stribling revealed him as the country gentleman, yet staunch businessman—the latter of which led to his fame and fortune. The historical information contained therein is essential to the full story of Jim Stribling's life, since so many of his deeds and so much of his personal life in general were kept confidential. To have been so influential in the public domain, his private life remained somewhat of a mystery, even to close family members. Jim revealed very little about his charitable deeds because he was not doing them for the recognition.

Tom's closeness to Jim and his family is revealed through the letters and pictures of later chapters in this publication. Jim's family feels it is their right and obligation to share this declared history of their loving relative, Jim Stribling, who did so much to shape their lives and that of the residents of Lawrenceburg, Tennessee, and its surrounding communities.

Tom Stribling often received letters of request for financial assistance to help a widow, or some poor orphaned child, or the rebuilding of a church destroyed by fire or some other act of nature. Tom always graciously forwarded these "opened-by-mistake letters" to his cousin, Jim Stribling, for whom he was sure they were intended.

Tom, in one of his discussions with Jim Stribling, did a summary of Jim's wealth and the ironic, accidental, and yet providential way that his wealth had been acquired. It was almost as if the virtues of his reward were a "loan" for more heavenly purposes later in Cousin Jim's life.

Jim Stribling in his vest
Photo courtesy of Stribling estate

Jim Stribling, despite his wealth and fame, never wore a tie, was usually found in a vest, and for dressy occasions, sometimes wore a small diamond stud in his dress shirt's top buttonhole. Jim always stuck to his unconventional dress code even when addressing the dignitaries of his business friends of the Louisville & Nashville Railroad, or even Chicago's Swift & Company. His one-fourth-carat diamond stud always made its statement and reflected Jim's prestige, despite his unwillingness to conform to more conventional attire. His unique and personal charisma was key to his wealthy corporate friends, who were the result of his acquired wealth.

As Tom interviewed Jim as to how he acquired his wealth and what inspired his desire for fortune, Jim told him that an orphan boy inspired him to seek his fortune. Tom was moved that Jim's wealth was to help an orphan child. But Jim was quick to clarify that the orphan child inspired him because the young man was being set free after his years at an orphanage and was given a new suit, a new horse, a new saddle and bridle, and a hundred dollars in cash. Jim went on to explain that he had none of these things; and that someday, with the good Lord's help, he would be richer than this orphan boy.

Tom was always surprised that despite the wealth Jim had attained, he always saw himself as poor and lived accordingly. Tom theorized that the great American dream visualized the rich as poor and the poor as rich, thereby establishing the Constitutional right that "all men are created equal."

So the sight of an orphan boy's "wealth" inspired Jim Stribling to become a millionaire. He said farewell to his parents and their farm and set out to seek his fortune. Now Jim had always believed the true Southern fable that fame and fortune always lay within the realm of owning a grocery store. The idea was that all that the grocer had to do was sit back and watch the groceries flow in and out of his store, and the fortune would flow as he counted his newly acquired wealth at the close of each day.

Jim's fortune did not start out in this fashion since he had no money with which to purchase his grocery store. So Jim started by hiring out himself as an apprentice to Mr. C. W. Spotswood as a drug clerk. "Hiring out" is an improper term. Jim was paid no wages but was "hired" for his room and board. An old English custom and Southern tradition was that the druggist would pay the apprentice—upon his departure and as a gift—what his services had been worth to the druggist. During the early days of drugstores, a formal education was not required, so Jim got his "degree" in medicine at a three-day lecture from Mr. Spotswood on the essentials of mixing and dispensing different concoctions of medicine. Through this formal training Jim became a full-fledged pharmacist.

Jim worked for Mr. Spotswood for eight months before being congratulated for his accomplishments by being fired in late winter, with his only parting wages being a heavy overcoat. Of course, with summer approaching, the parting wages were viewed with mixed emotions as to whether gratitude or sarcasm was intended.

But with Jim's "degree" in pharmacy, he now had the essential tools to start a career. However, his race against the orphan boy seemed to be on the decline; but as Fate was with him, he learned of a new drugstore opening in Linden, Tennessee. The new store owner, Mr. S. S. Tripp, needed an experienced druggist for his new business. Jim took the job and ordered and filled the prescriptions of the new operation. Jim was now the experienced druggist who taught Mr. Tripp how to interpret and fill each order. Upon completion of his pharmaceutical training of Mr. Tripp, Jim charged him one hundred dollars for professional services and returned home.

As Jim returned to Lawrenceburg, he found a local druggist, Mr. Jim Henderson, who had his eyes set on bigger and better things to the West. He desired to sell his drugstore business to any interested party. Jim offered Mr. Henderson his one hundred dollars for one-half interest in his store, which Henderson gladly accepted. Jim stayed in the drugstore for one year, and then sold his half-interest for fourteen hundred dollars.

Jim, having envisioned his own venture to the West, purchased a ticket for Denton, Texas, and there decided to pursue his "competition with the orphan boy" by the Southern grocery-man philosophy. Here he rented a nook of a store sandwiched between a barber shop and a saloon. He purchased a thousand dollars of grocery stock and his dream was underway. As a precautionary measure, he set up a shoe repair shop in the back of the store for tough times, just in case the grocery business was slow or became a nightmare instead of a dream. The rule of the day for grocery-store owners was for each customer to collect their groceries as needed and then, on the beginning of each month or other appointed payday, the customer would pay his or her bill in full or in part as means permitted. But Jim's little grocery store was one of a cash-only basis since his stock and cash were so greatly needed for day-to-day survival of the business.

For some time it appeared that Jim's investment was a mistake, since the only customers were the less fortunate who purchased small orders due to their extended credit with the bigger stores. However, it was the neighboring barbershop itself that changed the fate to fortune for Jim Stribling's grocery business. In those days the wealthy customers had pigeon-holes along the wall of the local barbershop with their own private soap mug. Each waited his turn to be shaved. Jim's fortune came as each barbershop customer would meander over to his shop to enjoy cheese, or bologna, and crackers. Now there was no set fortune in selling a small amount of cheese and bologna to a few patiently waiting barber customers, except for the fact that some of those customers were wealthy and influential Texans.

One such wealthy barbershop customer would leave his paper in the chair at the barbershop to reserve his place for his shave each morning and then would step next door and help himself to a slice of cheese, or a hunk of bologna, and a few crackers. He would chat with Jim as he waited his turn with the barber. He never offered to pay for his "takings," and Jim found himself a little shy about bringing this small matter to his attention, seeing that he was a man of stature.

On one particular morning this "faithful" customer made mention to Jim that the Exchange National Bank of Denton was issuing some new capital stock. Jim politely expressed a meager interest in this fact. Then the customer inquired as to whether Jim might be interested in fifteen or twenty shares of the stock. Jim assured the gentleman that he could not afford fifteen or twenty dollars, much less the shares of stock as discussed. The cheese eater assured Jim that the stock was fully subscribed whether or not it was fully paid. The gentleman told Jim that he would try to put him down for some shares. He also said he would try to send some business Jim's way. Jim took all the commenting as a typical Texan's brag and thought nothing more of the matter.

Several days later a local cowhand entered Jim's store and inquired of the cost of fancy candy. Upon telling the price, Jim inquired as to how much of the candy he wanted. The reply came back, "All of it!" The cowhand continued his tour of the store; and with each inquiry of price came the same reply, until Jim's store was completely wiped out. The cowhand, with Jim's help, loaded Jim's entire stock into his wagon. Jim had documented each item, its cost, and the quantity purchased.

As the gentleman began to leave, Jim was fully expecting this to be one of the great Texas jokes; but then the cowpoke turned to Jim and told him to take the bill to Judge Carroll down at the Exchange National Bank. Well, with his stock all properly disposed, he nervously closed his store and made his way to the bank to find out if Judge Carroll really existed. As he walked into the bank and asked for Judge Carroll, he was pointed to the office of his "cheese eater." To Jim's relief this risky sale to an absolute stranger turned out to be the beginning of Jim's great fortune. Judge Carroll assured Jim that he had also acquired twenty shares of stock in Jim's name.

Jim left the bank thanking the good Lord that, first off, the sale of his entire stock was a reality and not a Texas heist, and, secondly, that He had allowed him to find such great business friends. (This cowhand, along with Judge Carroll's many other ranchers, emptied Jim's store every few days.)

Despite the great fortune that had come Jim's way, there were still disasters that fell Jim's lot. On one such occasion Swift & Company of Chicago shipped him a bag of spoiled side meat. Jim, knowing the power—and greed—of the great Northern corporations, realized he would never win if he filed suit with Swift. So he politely wrapped the spoiled meat and returned it to Swift & Company, hoping for the best. In a very short time, he received prime meat for his spoiled meat and several extra sides thrown in for his time and trouble.

Another day of good fortune came when a Mr. Stewart from one of Jim's grocery suppliers, Boring & Stewart, entered the store and looked around at the barren shelves. Jim told the stranger to come back on Tuesday and he would have a new inventory. As the conversation continued, Jim realized he was talking to the one who shipped him his groceries two to three times a week. Mr. Stewart convinced Jim to allow him to ship his groceries by the rail carload with an unlimited line of credit. An agreement was reached and so began Jim's real supply for his source of wealth.

Jim's dealings with the great corporations of his business led him to establish his own theory for wealth:

A corporation is the best possible business friend a man can have. It follows a policy, not a sentiment. It endures

longer than personal friends because it does not get sick, change, or die. It will remember you forever. Its memory is a correspondence file that is imperishable. Its goodwill toward you lasts on and on, unworn by use, untried by time. The best friend a businessman can create is a corporation.

This was a theory that Jim Stribling proved time and again throughout his lifetime.

Jim continued his grocery business in Denton for about three years and made about a quarter of a million dollars. His Southern theory of the grocery business proved correct even though it came through providential assistance.

Jim Stribling and Ardelia Lois (Dena) Cobb Stribling.
(Pictures taken in Texas.)
Photos courtesy of Stribling estate

After the three-year venture in the grocery business, Jim received a letter from home saying that the family missed him and that his father and mother were lonely. (Later evidence verified that Jim's mother was sick.) The letter did not ask Jim to come home, but having left his hometown at the early age of twenty-one, he felt it was time to take his good fortune and head back home to check on his parents. Jim sold his store and returned to Lawrenceburg by train, this time bringing a large sum of money with him. He also brought his new wife, Dena, who had grown up in a Denton orphanage.

Dena and Gladys Stribling, (Mr. and Mrs. Stribling's first daughter).

Little Gladys Stribling as a young child.

Photos courtesy of Stribling Estate

As Jim returned to his hometown of Lawrenceburg, Tennessee, he decided to invest some of his Texas fortune in a farm. He paid $2,000 for the farm and made annual improvements, from four to ten thousand dollars. Jim wanted to set the example of model farming for his fellow Lawrence Countians, so he solicited the help of the local county agents and agricultural extension offices to advise him. Within the first ten years Jim had spent about $90,000 on his farm improvements,

J. H. STRIBLING.   OFFICE OF   J. W. HANNAH.

J. H. STRIBLING & CO.,

DEALERS IN

Staple and Fancy Groceries,

CONFECTIONERIES, TOBACCOS, &c.

Denton, Texas, 7 — 15 188 8

Dear Father,
when mother condition
will admit or approve
of it please hand or
read the enclosed
note to her —
                              your Jim —

Jim sent a letter home to his parents. Inside the envelope was this note asking his father to "hand or read the enclosed note" to his mother "when her condition will admit [permit]." The envelope was stamped July 15, 1888. (Note the letterhead.)
Photo courtesy of Stribling estate

increasing the farm's value to $55,000. He showed the un-educated farmer how to take a $2,000 plot of ground, spend $90,000 for improvements, and convert it into a $55,000 hold-ing. Most farmers—even before the days of calculators—chose not to follow his example. (Author's note: In an article pub-lished in *The Democrat-Union,* March 7, 1963, it appears that Stribling's agricultural tactics were not quite as humorous as laid out by Cousin Tom. Jim was recommended for the UT Agricultural Extension Hall of Fame for his scientific farming practices that were carried out some sixty years prior to the 1963 *The Democrat-Union* article.)

New High School Building.
Lawrenceburg, Tenn.

The new high school building furnished by Mr. Stribling in 1910. There was also a club at the school called the "Stribling Society." This club was focused on noble causes within the school and the community. All members were encouraged to work toward that goal.
Photo courtesy of Old Jail Museum, Lawrenceburg

Jim, feeling as though he had been blessed beyond measure with the money he made in Texas and his investments, decided that it was time to do something more providential. He decided to build a high school for the county.

Lawrence County did not have a high school building to speak of and Jim had become interested in schooling in Texas. Jim, like every man at some point in his life, realized how much better he could have done if he had received just a little more education. So Jim wanted to help the youth of the county in that respect. Jim bought up quite a few lots and built a modern high school, complete with a gymnasium, drinking fountains, indoor toilets, and a kitchen. As it was all finished, he dedicated it to the glory of God and the service of man, and then presented it to the county.

The gift of a school came with one stipulation: That the Bible would be taught in the high school, and Jim would choose the teacher. The county was glad to accept this stipulation in order to get a new high school.

Shortly after Jim's return to Lawrenceburg, he engaged in extensive land purchases and by 1908 he was Lawrence County's largest landowner. Two parcels of his town properties were used to build a hosiery mill in 1913 which manufactured socks, and a potato warehouse that was used for storing and selling potatoes.

Being proud of his adventure with his farm investments, Jim next decided to venture into the dairy business—not for himself but for the whole of Lawrence County. He remembered his corporate friendship with Swift & Company of Chicago. So Jim sent them a letter requesting that a survey be made of the county with hopes of opening a cheese factory.

Swift & Company sent one of their experts who performed the survey and sent back the following summation:

- County doesn't produce enough milk for its own people.
- Cattle are scrubs; there are no milk-producing strains.
- No pasturage for cattle.
- No dairy information among farmers.

Jim was beside himself with the unruly negativity of the agent's report, and he immediately responded with this emphatic message to his friend at Swift & Company:

- YOUR AGENT LACKS VISION.
- GREATEST OPPORTUNITY YOU HAVE EVER BEEN OFFERED.
- FORWARD MORE IDEALISTIC, COOPERATIVE AGENT AT ONCE.

Desiring to retain an old friendship, Swift & Company sent a new representative to review the "misjudged evaluation." Jim was sure the new representative was someone with whom he could work to get the desired results. The new agent arrived and Jim took him over the county, introducing the agent to local farmers. Impressed with Jim's enthusiasm, the new agent sent the following report:

- No milk, cattle, pastures, or dairymen.
- Many admirable sites for cheese factories.

Jim was overjoyed. The agent stated the obvious but showed insight by acknowledging that there were "admirable sites" for a cheese factory. Jim—in his quest to own large tracts of land—had already bought up most of these sites that the agent pinpointed as suitable for the cheese factory. The next step was to have productive milk cattle, productive land, and people who understood the dairy business. Jim, confident that the people of Lawrence County could learn anything, set about getting the best cattle and bringing in farm agents to teach the farmers to become dairy farmers. Jim, who had recently organized a bank, realized he could finance the money for the cattle. He made an agreement with the farmers that they could repay the money after they began to see a profit from their dairy operations.

The grand opening of Swift & Company on October 9, 1929.
As usual, Jim Stribling (right of sign) is wearing a vest.
Notice the large watermelons.
Photo courtesy of Old Jail Museum, Lawrenceburg

The mission was accomplished! Swift & Company agreed to build and run a cheese factory. The cheese factory continued to operate in Lawrence County for many years. Mr. G. M. Stotser was the first manager of Swift & Company in 1929. Lytle Logue, Earl Ropp, Charles Belew, and W. F. Meyers also were some of the first workers there. Belew and Meyers later managed the chicken hatchery next door to the cheese factory.*

Jim Stribling and ladies with a railroad carload of cordwood.
Photo courtesy of Stribling estate

The money that Jim spent on model farms and cheese factories did not come out of farming, and the money he brought home from Texas would never have stretched enough to cover what he was doing. Instead, he had begun a timber operation to bring in the money needed for these projects. He realized that he did not have the monetary means for a modern sawmill—and the labor needed for the operation—so he decided

---

*Submitted by Joann Stotser Abbott, the daughter of G. M. Stotser.

that instead of manufacturing the timber, he would devote himself to selling lumber. After he showed others how to farm and to operate dairy farms to produce milk needed to make cheese, he worked the timber himself. He called this "a division of labor."

He built office space for his lumber operation at a cost of $200 and began a corporate relationship with the Louisville & Nashville Railroad. The L&N decided it needed bridges and depots, so a call was sent out for sealed bids on 22 million board feet of materials needed for construction. Jim, new to the wholesale lumber business, remembered his Texas training in that corporations were "sensitive, responsive creatures to friendship and love." Jim knew that this initial bid was about building a corporate bond more so than making a huge profit from L&N. He worked on his prices until he could not get them any lower. Jim sent in his bid after many long hours of work, but he realized that the sealed bid could not explain everything that he wanted to say. So Jim decided to follow the bid to answer any questions that might arise.

Jim was the only bidder to show up for the opening of the bids. It was a good thing that he went to the bid opening because his bid was about $6,000 higher than the low bid. Knowing the whittling that had gone into his own bid, Jim knew there had to be some explanation to someone having a lower price. Being present for the bid and being allowed to investigate with the bid agent, it was revealed that the "low bidder" had not fulfilled his last two orders to the L&N. Jim, assuring the agent that his lumber was ready for shipment, was awarded the bid. This was the beginning of a long and fruitful relationship.

Two other differences sprang up between Jim and the L&N before they formed a tight relationship. One of these differences had to do with cantaloupes. Jim was in a meeting of the L&N directors where a discussion of rail and bus transportation took place. Jim in his own frank way offered his opinion as to why the buses were overtaking the rail customers. He expounded to the fact that the bus agents were friendlier and more accommodating to the customers. When asked how he arrived at that fact, Jim explained that he made that conclusion through "cantaloupes." The directors asked for further details so Jim went on to explain he had been selling cantaloupes to rail customers. He had found that his business had quickly faded with the coming of the friendlier bus service. He further expounded that the bad attitude of rail agents at ticket counters was a direct pass-through of the same attitudes of top brass at L&N headquarters, thereby passed down the line to the end customer. Ten years would pass with L&N losing most of their rail customers, before they would finally take note of Jim's wisdom.

The second difference Jim had with L&N related to telegraph poles. Jim had concluded that all types of accidents happened to telegraph poles—train wrecks, storms, fires, lightning, old age, and decay. Telegraph poles along the railway were always toppling over for one reason or another. These toppling poles were hazardous to the railway and its passengers. Jim proposed having piles of poles strung out along the whole L&N right-of-way, so telegraph repairs could be made with minimal delay.

Jim politely failed to mention that he had about a half-million telegraph poles on hand that he needed to dispose of quickly or make a sizeable investment in a creosote plant. Jim, to avoid the expense of the creosote plant, developed the plan of saving human lives. The purchasing agent at the L&N could not see the advantage to this idea since they had always bought their poles only when they needed them.

Jim, as usual, took the news hard but did not give up on the idea. Just prior to his surrender to the creosote plant, he read in the newspaper one morning that a hurricane was in the West Indies. According to the proposed path, the storm was headed for all points along the southern tip of the L&N map. Jim called the purchasing agent, explaining the severity of the situation, and a deal was struck. The poles were to be shipped immediately, having priority over all other freight.

The good news is that the poles made it to their destination before the storm hit the South. The bad news is that the storm did not hit the L&N lines as predicted, but the purchasing agent realized that having poles scattered along his tracks was a true asset. So he ordered Jim to service his whole right-of-way. This saved Jim the expense of his proposed creosote plant.

Several years after Jim built the high school, the county decided to purchase the building from Jim for $56,000, and Jim's Bible classes ceased. He prayed a long time about what he should do with the Lord's money that he had received from the school. Jim finally decided to build an orphanage, or Christian Home (as it came to be called). Of course, this was not enough money to build the orphanage; but it did cover the cost of blueprints and cost for setting up the orphanage as a tax-exempt corporation.

The Christian Home building was a colonial-styled home surrounded by orchards of apples, plums, pears, and peaches with grapes, raspberries, blackberries, and watermelon patches. The boys and girls in the home went to the regular county schools, but their instruction was supplemented by Bible lessons at the home. The children received everything

Jim had dreamed of and longed for when he was a boy but was never able to have.

The county began having some financial issues, and because the orphanage was a nonprofit organization, the county could not tax the land where the orphanage was located. The orphanage had a large holding due to all the property that Jim had endowed to it, causing quite a bit of land to be untaxable.

The county tax assessor approached Jim about the lack of income due to the tax-exempt status of the property. Jim told the assessor that when the boys and girls grew up and married, he would be giving each of them a farm as a wedding gift.

Stribling loved to fish with a cane pole. Here he is fishing with some of the children from the Christian Home.
Photo courtesy of Stribling Estate

After the property was deeded over to the young man or woman, it would then be back on the tax books; therefore, the county would receive income from those taxes at that time.*

The housing of children controlled by the Christian Home has long passed. Regulatory standards by state and federal laws made it unworkable after 1980 or so.

Today the two large mansions proudly stand in good repair directly across the road from each other. The girl's side is now used by a local help group for children called, "A Kid's Place." Mr. Stribling established a perpetual trust fund that endows the entity for eternity. There are still 1,200 acres of land adjoining the two mansions. A board of directors, made up of Church of Christ members, oversees the trust and farm. The farm is now mostly planted in pine trees for soil conservation and to provide some income.

Mr. Stribling had a great desire to help children. In September 1939, Adolf Hitler's German Army laid siege to the Jewish section of Warsaw, Poland. The Poles fought back but incurred many casualties, leaving many Jewish children parentless and homeless.

In 1934 Mr. Harold Salant, of Salant & Salant Manufacturing (a Stribling-sponsored plant and the county's leading industry for years), had a direct link to get some of the children out of harm's way. Stribling knew this and contacted Salant about bringing no more than thirty-two of the children to America to live at the Christian Home. Salant countered, "Mr. Stribling, you do know these are Jewish children." Stribling immediately responded with, "Mr. Salant, had you rather have dead Jewish

---

*Information gathered through various letters and collections from the Stribling Estate, including from T. S. Stribling, a Pulitzer Prize winner and a cousin to James H. Stribling.

children or live Christian children?" Salant agreed and put thirty-two children on a ship bound for New York.

Stribling never mentioned this situation to his wife and daughter until one morning at the breakfast table at their home on Pulaski Street. He set his hot coffee cup down on the indented ring in the wooden tabletop. He got everyone's attention by exclaiming, "Oh, my God!" He laid down the morning paper that told the story of a German U-Boat sinking a ship. That ship had the thirty-two children aboard and all were lost. He and Salant did not try to evacuate any more children during the war.

Jim Stribling always did things his way and at his pace. Even though he had a hand in everything that happened in Lawrence County for fifty years, he was a simple man who never drove a car, never wore a tie, and whose favorite pastime was fishing with a cane pole. Many sentences he started began with "My son . . ."

Mr. Stribling practically invented the term entrepreneur; and his hard work, timely investments, and servant's heart brought a brighter hope for Lawrence County when it was needed most.

Mr. Stribling was also an aspiring politician without holding an office. Soon after arriving back in Lawrenceburg from Denton, Texas, Stribling began amassing land. It is estimated that at one time he owned 66,000 acres. His 1909 tax bill reflects such a holding. A good portion of that land would be deeded to the Christian Home, which removed it from the tax records of the county. He also learned of the importance of influencing politicians to gain favor for projects of interest. Two instances that follow reflect his ambitions.

During the legislative sessions, Stribling maintained a suite at the Hermitage Hotel in Nashville. Agricultural promotion and his Christian Home were the passions he expressed to the lawmakers. He was successful in getting an exit off the sacred Natchez Trace Parkway at Napier onto what is now the Squaw Creek Lodge area of Lawrence County. It just so happened that Stribling owned the 6,800 acres into which the road emptied.

Later he befriended local law enforcement icon, Greg O'Rear. O'Rear would later become the Commissioner of Safety in Tennessee during the 1960s. One day Stribling appeared in Governor Gordon Browning's office quite unexpectedly. He very sternly told the governor that he wanted to have O'Rear promoted to captain in the Tennessee Highway Patrol. The governor responded, "I'll get the paperwork started." To which Stribling replied, "I don't think you understand, Governor. He is outside and I want you to *pin* him right now," and the governor did just that.

Locally he often feuded with the county commissioners. They wanted his financial input and influence in Nashville, but they didn't always want his advice or actions that often involved his faith.*

The Democrat-Union in Lawrenceburg reported on June 27, 1941, that Mr. Stribling's house had burned on Sunday afternoon. Sources stated that the house that burned was where Mr. Stribling preferred to live. (He had several homes at that time.) Mr. Stribling had been living in the home for more than forty years. The paper also provided the following article showing the generosity of this man.

𝔗𝔥𝔢 𝔇𝔢𝔪𝔬𝔠𝔯𝔞𝔱-𝔘𝔫𝔦𝔬𝔫
August 24, 1945
J. H. Stribling Offers Park to Local Folks

J. H. Stribling has indicated that he will give the acreage comprising David Crockett Park free to local people and their chil-

---

*Information provided by Tim Pettus, Stribling Estate.

dren, the deed to be made to an organization agreeing to keep same properly maintained.

The park, which Mr. Stribling constructed at his own expense several years ago, is just west of the city limits, adjoining the highway to Memphis and Chattanooga. It has a complete system of roads and paths and other park facilities.*

JIM'S CONVERSION FROM CORPORATE TO ETERNAL INVESTMENTS

J. H. Stribling was a church leader in and around Lawrence-burg, Tennessee. He was an entrepreneur and financier of many

James Henry Stribling
Entrepreneur, bank president, financier, and church leader in Lawrenceburg, Tennessee.
Photo courtesy of Stribling Estate

works among the Churches of Christ. He helped to underwrite the works of men like J. T. Harris, R. H. Boll, and E. O. Coffman as they evangelized in the south central region of Tennessee. The tragic loss of his first daughter, Gladys, at age four, changed Stribling's total outlook on life and wealth. He became a devoted Christian and spent the rest of his life helping his fellow man. This is a beautiful example of how God can take the worst of situations and bring something good as a result. Read further about Gladys and the events that brought her par-

*This article is reprinted by permission, courtesy of Jim and Marie Crawford and family and *The Democrat-Union*.

The headstone of little Gladys Stribling Mimosa Cemetery, Lawrenceburg, Tennessee. *"Suffer little children to come unto Me, and forbid them not, for of such is the Kingdom of God."* Photo courtesy of www.therestorationmovement.com, Public Domain

ents to Christ. The picture on page 50 of a little girl with instinctive childish grace and beauty is inscribed: "Little Gladys Stribling. Born July 22, 1897. Went home December 31, 1901. The only child of James H. Stribling and wife (Dena), of Lawrenceburg, Tennessee, who are heartbroken because of her departure." Her father had this picture, enlarged and beautifully framed, hanging over the vault in his bank.

Of the same beautiful child, a friend writes: "With her little hands, she has linked Heaven and earth closer together for her father and mother. Soon after Gladys' death, God, in his wise Providence, caused Brother T. B. Larimore to be called to our town, to speak the Word of God. He heard of their sorrow, and, with kind, sympathizing words, won their respect and interest. Through his preaching, Brother Stribling was persuaded to obey the gospel and unite himself to the band of Christians worshipping at this place. Brother Larimore's words of consolation and his constant reference to Him who says,

'Come unto me, all ye that labor and are heavy laden, and I will give you rest,' have taught the sorrowing father and mother to bear their loss with Christian fortitude."

Emma Page Larimore, in her book entitled, *Letters and Sermons of T. B. Larimore,* wrote about Brother Larimore's love for children. In their travels the Larimores met so many families and touched so many lives. It always burdened the heart of T. B. Larimore when a family felt the sadness of a lost child.* (A later chapter will give more detail of T. B. Larimore's charismatic persuasion.)

Jim and Dena's second child, another daughter, was named James Lois Stribling (later known as Jim Brock Leonard). "Little Jim," as she was called, devotedly followed her father's teachings and wishes, serving as Chairman of the Board of First National Bank and on the board of the Christian Home until her death in 1988.

Jim Stribling's wealth and influence was felt greatly in his community. He financed the building of the Salem church building just west of Lawrenceburg. He also financed the building of at least two children's homes as well and donated thousands of acres of his land to these orphanages for boys and girls up to age eighteen. The Christian Home (as the orphanage was called) today does not house any children, but it still holds 1,000 acres as an asset along with two mansions on West Point Road.

In the Restoration Movement, names such as *Emily Tubman* and *A. M. Burton* are easily recognized as benefactors of great efforts and works. However, the name J. H. Stribling

---

*Information from www.therestorationmovement.com, Church of Christ history, Public Domain.

should be added to the list as being a man who did great things for the cause of Christ in south central Tennessee.

Shown below are a few of the Stribling contributions given back to the Lawrenceburg community.

Pictured above are the Christian Homes (boys' home on left, girls' home on right) located on West Point Road just beyond Salem Church of Christ and just prior to the Gandy Fire Station. The two buildings are on opposite sides of the road and face each other.

The Salem Church of Christ on West Point Road as seen today.
Photos courtesy of Stribling Estate

The following pages contain articles regarding the Striblings and the obituaries of Jim and Dena Stribling.*

The Democrat-Union
June 26, 1931

Mrs. Jim Stribling dies suddenly

Mrs. J. H. (Dena) Stribling of this city died suddenly at the magnificent home on Pulaski Street following an attack of heart failure. Mrs. Stribling had been in poor health for several years but suffered a heart attack on Tuesday from which she rallied and was feeling very well until another attack came in the night and proved fatal.

Funeral services were conducted at the home on Wednesday before a vast throng of Lawrence Countians who knew and loved her. The funeral was preached by Elder T. C. King who paid a glowing tribute to the many fine qualities of this good woman. Professor Merle Hottle assisted in the conduct of the funeral services. The floral offerings were extensive and very beautiful. While the crowd at the funeral was very large it was not by a tenth what it might have been had the news been received throughout the county in time for the many friends from the different communities to attend.

Pallbearers were J. M. Hottle, Dr. Frank Burns, Marshall Dugger, Robert Durrett, M. B. Watkins, and Walker Barnett. C. L. William was the undertaker. Besides Mr. Stribling she is survived by her daughter, Mrs. Delmar Brock, a brother, Richard Cobb of Denton, TX.

Mrs. Stribling, with her husband, had been one of the most important factors for good ever to be in Lawrence County. Without ostentation, and of times without the fact being even known, she has helped people in strained financial circumstances without asking or expecting any recompense.

When the need arose for a modern high school building it was Mr. and Mrs. J. H. Stribling who came forward and with their own money built and equipped one of the finest institutions of its kind

---

*Reprinted by permission, courtesy of Jim and Marie Crawford and family and *The Democrat-Union*.

in the state. This structure will stand as a fitting memorial to her magnanimous spirit and kindness of heart.

She was also responsible for the education of scores of needy and worthy children whom she aided liberally with funds to allow them an opportunity to attend school.

A great life has come to an end and a great spirit has gone outward and upward to enjoy the release from pain and physical life that were here for many years and to partake of the reward that her noble soul so richly deserves and merits.

While it is not likely that we will soon find another personality such as the one who has gone, the inspiration of her life will be ever before us and lasting good that she had done will always be an influence that will continue to turn the footsteps of many a soul upward toward the right.

Jim and Dena at West Palm Beach, Florida.
(Very few pictures were taken of them together; this picture embodies a very peaceful setting, tying the two together for eternity through their obituaries.)
Photo courtesy of Stribling Estate

JIM'S DEPARTURE

"I have fought a good fight;
I have kept the faith . . ."

𝕿𝖍𝖊 𝕯𝖊𝖒𝖔𝖈𝖗𝖆𝖙-𝖀𝖓𝖎𝖔𝖓

September 21, 1863—December 12, 1951 (Author Unknown)

James Henry Stribling

Several weeks ago, when the subject of observing the First National Bank's Golden Jubilee was discussed J. H. Stribling was adamant on one point. "Let us be sure," he insisted, "that we don't use this occasion to give too much honor to one man. Let us, rather, tell of the work of all of us, of the growth and development of our town and county and be proud that our bank has had a part in their accomplishment. Let these brief words of tribute, therefore, be a simple 'saga of a man who loved his homeland.'"

For if there was one outstanding all-powerful characteristic which took precedence over all else in the life of James H. Stribling it was his love for his town and county and his determination to consecrate his life and efforts toward making them a better place in which to live. Thus it is that we cannot scan the highlights of events which have been great in the annals of Lawrence County development without recognizing the major part played by the First National Bank, and through the bank the man, James Henry Stribling, whose destinies have been so inextricably intertwined with so many of the good things that have come to us in the way of community development.

The writer remembers as a fledgling boy, hearing our father tell of participating in county-wide drives, spearheaded by "Uncle Jim" and other civic-minded persons to remove us from the category of a one-crop county and broaden the field of agriculture until now we rank with the best in the state in every branch of farm production.

The location here of the Swift Cheese Plant, which has furnished a market for thousands of our farmers and has done so much to raise our livestock enumeration from a few hundred head to the impressive thousands that it is today, felt the deft touch of this influence.

Similarly, the huge Salant & Salant factory, which helped greatly to give a proper balance between agriculture and industry in our county would have been impossible at the time but for the assistance of the First National Bank and "Uncle Jim."

In the personal philanthropical field, which is succinctly condensed in accord with his oft-expressed desire, count the local high

Scenes outside of Jim Stribling's First National Bank. He had his office inside where he ran not only the bank's affairs but advised the country people on their personal and business troubles. His door was literally "open" to everyone. Jim said that he lent the money with security to most of the founders of the bank and that it all had been repaid. He was the only living member of the group who subscribed the original stock. (Information taken from back of the picture.)
Photo courtesy of Stribling Estate

school building and the vast Christian Home development which will stand as eternal memorials to his goodness.

Many, many, other accomplishments bear his indelible stamp, but we shall not enumerate in detail. Let us be content to give one example which happened only a few weeks ago and about which doubtless few persons know. When the referendum vote was scheduled on the establishment of a soil conservation district here "Uncle Jim" left his sick bed, yes, what was destined to be his death bed and, brushing aside all protests of doctors and attendants, actually came to town in order to cast his vote in favor of it. When he returned to the hospital, pneumonia developed and he died five days later. Whether the act hastened his death may never be known, but the important thing is the significance of the act itself—his unhesitating response, when the call went out—to do his part and give his best for his beloved county, even to the last ounce of his strength and the last act of his life.

Such, say we, is the stature of true greatness. That a person, great or small, give himself to an ideal—the ideal of service to his fellowman; the ideal of a duty to pattern his life in such manner that when his summons comes it can be said that because of him our world is a better place to live, to rear our families and to worship our God.

He had his critics, 'tis true. Such is the inevitable accompaniment of the accumulation of great wealth, unfortunately fostered by the pettiness and envy of persons who can never hope to match his magnitude.

Let us who are left never forget the impact of his character and the solid bulwark of his principles. Let us here and now re-dedicate ourselves to that nobility of purpose that was his. He has left us a heritage to cherish and given us the incentive and perspective to go on to greater things for our county, state and nation.

Somehow, from the great out yonder the thought seems to wing its way that he would have us pen the final phrase in these words: "My homeland—may she always be right, but right or wrong, my homeland."

The Democrat-Union
December 14, 1951

Jas. H. Stribling Dies Wednesday At Local Hospital

Banker-Philanthropist, Member Of A Pioneer, Lawrence Co. Family

James H. Stribling, member of one of Lawrence's pioneer families, banker, philanthropist, and life-long religious leader, died at the Lawrenceburg sanitarium at 6:10 pm, Wednesday of this week, following an illness of 15 days. Mr. Stribling had not been in good health for several weeks, but was apparently recovering satisfactorily until reverses occurred Wednesday morning. He was 88 years of age.

Funeral services will be held Friday afternoon of this week at one o'clock, at Salem Church of Christ, three miles west of this city, with E. O. Coffman officiating.

Widely known for his philanthropy, Mr. Stribling was one of Lawrence's most prominent and beloved citizens. An ardent advocate of conservation and a devoted friend of the farmer, Mr. Stribling was active throughout his declining years to the betterment of the community and the people he loved. One of the major accomplishments, he brought to fruition was the establishment of The Christian Home, an orphanage near this city, endowing it with $75,000.00 and donating approximately 20,000 acres.

Intensely interested in education, he purchased the present Lawrence Co. High School building and permitted its use without cost to the county for years. In 1902 he established the First National Bank of this city and was president of the institution at the time of his death. He lived on his farm of approximately 200 acres, near Lawrenceburg.

A native of Lawrence county and a son of the late Col. and Mrs. James Stribling, he is survived by a daughter, Mrs. Jim Stribling Brock of this city. His wife, Mrs. Dena Stribling, died more than 20 years ago. A daughter, also, died in infancy.

The Democrat-Union

The following is a "Letter to the Editor" that was sent to *The Democrat-Union* and written by Clarence Junior Clifton. Clifton lived at the Boys' Christian Home for several years. This is his tribute to Jim Stribling.

Thank You, Mr. Jim Stribling

My comment from afar—is concerning the article which appeared in your newspaper on October 18, 2000, in the Letters to the Editor section. This article was written and submitted to you by *a former resident of the Home* (name omitted for privacy). She entitled her article, THE REAL JIM STRIBLING. This article was mailed to me by an avid reader of your newspaper. She and I have much in common for we, too, were residents of the Children's Home in Lawrenceburg. I had one sister and four brothers, along with myself who were accepted and placed in the home there. It's true the boys did rise early and milk and feed the stock. We worked in the fields, and each had their share of responsibilities. Most of us carried these out without even considering it as a form of labor, but rather a means of survival. I was the oldest of my brothers and sister.

I recall when we lived at home with our Mother, we came home from the cotton fields where we had worked diligently from sun up 'til dark, dragging bags of cotton up and down the rows. I was a young boy, but through the trust of the land owner, he would have me drive the horse drawn cotton wagon over the fields gathering the bags of cotton. Night time could not come soon enough. We were tired and hungry. Our meager lunch which Mother had packed in the lard can had not really been enough to sufficiently go around for us all, and to have satisfied our hunger completely. Supper often consisted of hoe cakes and sawmill gravy. We didn't know any better than to think everyone else was eating the same thing and enjoying it as we were. We had our baths, and crowded into clean, make-shift beds which Mom had made up for us. We hovered close to one another to keep warm. The wee morning hours came early when we all arose, dressed, ate our sparse breakfast, and all headed for the fields to work again.

It was sad leaving Mother, waving goodbye as we were taken to the Home. Mother could not provide sufficiently for us. We soon met other boys and girls who had experienced some of the same situations and trials we had gone through, therefore, we all felt we had a common bond with one another. We were assigned bedrooms. I was probably the oldest boy at the home, therefore more responsibility was placed upon me, but I considered this experience as a trust more than a "iron hand" form of treatment. I looked forward to our meals which *the writer* (name omitted for privacy) recalls the girls preparing. I was fortunate to have enough to eat and to have warm clothing.

I recall and refer to my experiences at the Children's Home, as a time in my life when I needed help more than ever before. I retaliated at first, for I did not want to be separated from my Mother and other family members. However, Mother would come to visit with us on the weekends. The saddest part of her visit was when it came time for her to leave and I had to restrain my younger brothers and console them as she walked away with tears streaming down her face, realizing she could not do anything else but leave us, for we were receiving excellent care, and she could not care for us in the same fashion. I also recall playing and developing wonderful and treasured friendships with the other boys and girls at the home. This past July of 2000, I was in Lawrenceburg. I made a trip out to the home. I had my two grandchildren with me and I showed them where their PaPa had once lived. I pointed out various areas I remembered, which now has taken on a little change. I took pictures of the home. We then traveled down some of the roads I recalled driving the bay wagons on and the streams where we had to go and get buckets of water to bring back for use at the school. Memories, both pleasant and humorous came back to me.

On Sunday, while we were there in Lawrenceburg, possibly twelve to fifteen people who had lived at the home and their families all met at the Ponderosa and had lunch together. It was a wonderful time being together again. As I looked around the table into the faces of each of these dear friends, I saw a multitude of strength, character, admiration and support for one another. These were young boys and girls who had now grown into adults, filling their place in society without any feelings of malice or regret.

If I had the opportunity to walk up to Mr. Jim Stribling today, I would extend my hand in appreciation for what I feel he has done for me and my brothers and sister. I feel I am a better person today, by the practices we were taught and duties we were given to do at the home. I place value on what my life has become. I am a happy and fulfilled man. I moved to Florida where I met and married the woman I have been married to for thirty-nine years. I have raised three wonderful children and have two precious grandchildren. Can I give Mr. Stribling credit for that—no I don't think so, however I do feel Mr. Stribling was very instrumental in helping cultivate me into becoming the person I am today. I shudder to think what if there had not been a Children's Home in Lawrenceburg, Tennessee for my brothers and sister to have had the opportunity to go to. I have a very large family, for you see, I consider the boys and girls I was with in the home as my adopted brothers and sisters. I feel I have a grand family. Yes, Mr. Stribling stands very tall in my mind and recollections. He was a giant among men in that time when I needed help and he was there to give it to me.   *Clarence Junior Clifton*

Author's note: The dignity and restraint of Mr. Clifton to not publicly take an opportunity to lash out at the critic of Mr. Stribling shows the true character implanted through Clifton's upbringing. This same strong character was revealed by several other former Christian Home residents whose gratitude for the timely help at the home caused their eyes to overflow with tears of joy as our interview with them was conducted.

CHAPTER 3

The Man Who Was "The Instrument"

LARIMORE'S CHARISMATIC LIFE

Theophilus Brown Larimore

THE CONVERSION THAT TOOK PLACE in the life of James H. Stribling was a transformation that not only changed his life for eternity, but it also made an eternal impact on countless numbers of Lawrence Countians, as well as lives touched worldwide. This was witnessed by the letters of POWs whose lives were humbled through the kind deeds of this great man.

When a man of Stribling's stature is touched in such a way, it bears investigating the logic—or lack thereof—as to what exactly transpired, even though it might be beyond any human comprehension. But to start the encounter of our investigation, let's review a poem by Myra Brooks Welch just prior to reviewing the life of the "instrument" (T. B. Larimore) that was used in this unusual transformation of James H. Stribling.

THE TOUCH OF THE MASTER'S HAND

'Twas battered and scarred, and the auctioneer
thought it scarcely worth his while
To waste much time on the old violin,
but he held it up with a smile;

"What am I bidden, good folks," he cried,
"Who'll start the bidding for me?
"A dollar, a dollar; then two! Only two?
Two dollars, and who'll make it three?

"Three dollars, once; three dollars twice;
going for three . . ." But NO . . . !,
From the room, far back, a gray-haired man
came forward and picked up the bow;

Then, wiping the dust from the old violin,
and tightening the loose strings,
He played a melody pure and sweet,
as a caroling angel sings.

The music ceased, and the auctioneer,
With a voice that was quiet and low,
Said; "What am I bid for the old violin?"
And he held it up with the bow.

"A thousand dollars, and who'll make it two?
Two thousand! And who'll make it three?
"Three thousand, once, three thousand, twice,
and going and gone," said he.

The people cheered, but some of them cried,
"We do not quite understand.
What changed its worth?" Swift came the reply:
"The touch of a master's hand."

And many a man with life out of tune,
and battered and scarred with sin,
Is auctioned cheap to the thoughtless crowd,
much like the old violin.

A "mess of pottage," a glass of wine;
a game—and he travels on.
"He is going once, and going twice,
He's going and almost gone."

But the Master comes, and the foolish crowd
never can quite understand
The worth of a soul, and the change that's wrought
*by the touch of the Master's hand.**

T. B. Larimore was born in East Tennessee, July 10, 1843. His early disadvantages were such of the gloomiest and the most discouraging poverty affords. When he was little more than a child in age and size, he hired himself to a farmer for four dollars a month, or fifteen and one-half cents a day, and

T. B. Larimore

---

*Myra Brooks Welch Web site, Public Domain.

did the work of a man as a plowhand. He was the main financial provider for his mother and sisters, and the cares and responsibilities of the home and family were added to the burdens of his hard work and rough life as a hireling. Every cent of his hard-earned wages had to go for home expenses, and not one penny of the money, for which he worked so hard and endured so much to earn, was he ever able to spend for toys and things that children enjoy and crave. There was sweeter pleasure for him, however, in the consciousness that his labor and hardships helped to support his mother and sisters than he could have found in the selfish gratification of childish whims. The handles of his plow were often marked by blood from his lacerated little hands, and many times he limped from the wounds of rocks and snags in his little bare feet. His eyes were occasionally dimmed almost to blindness with tears from the overburdened heart of suffering childhood, but he never dodged a duty or shirked from his work. He strengthened his spirit and lightened his own burdens by heroic efforts to help others carry their loads, and he never murmured or complained.

From early childhood Larimore was a great lover of books, and he made good use of every opportunity he had to add to his book collection. He was always remarkably exemplary in conduct and religious in disposition. Naturally endowed with a brilliant intellect, vivid imagination, lofty aspirations, and indomitable energy and perseverance, no obstacles could keep him down. By hard work and close attention to business, he made his way against formidable discouragements until an opportunity opened to him, while yet in his teens, to enter Mossy Creek College.

Larimore promptly saw the chance as a gracious dispensation of Providence for which he had long waited and prayed, and he entered college with all the enthusiasm and energy of one with a young and naturally buoyant heart. He was embarrassed by pinching poverty that made stringent economy and close attention to business a necessity. He walked forty miles the first day, starting early in the morning and walking until late in the evening, over rough roads and rugged mountains. He carried provisions to eat along the way to save on traveling expenses. The prospect of an education sustained his spirit as he walked by the way; but there was gloom in his soul and a pain in his heart from the solicitude he felt for his mother and sisters left in loneliness behind him in the little log cabin in the mountains.

When the parting time came, Larimore's courage for a moment failed, and he decided to stay with his family; but they urged him to go because he could do more for them, as well as for himself, by going than he could do by staying. When he left home, such delicacies as they could afford, neatly packed in a little bundle for his lunch by the way, were handed to him with the blessings and prayers of mother and sisters, to whom he had always been a dutiful son and a loving brother. When he stopped at noon under a tree by a spring to eat his lunch, he was hungry, homesick, and foot weary; but the moment he opened his lunch, his appetite entirely disappeared; and he broke down and wept like a lost child in the woods. The lunch was so much better than what he knew the loved ones at home had kept for themselves, that he was overwhelmed with emotion by this token of their love, and not a mouthful of it could he eat.

Soon after leaving Mossy Creek College, he enlisted as a volunteer in the Confederate Army, and served "the lost cause" in some of the most important engagements in the late war.

He was at Fishing Creek, Kentucky, when Zollicoffer was killed, and he went with the special detail under flag of truce to bring away the body of the distinguished Confederate commander from the field where he fell. He was in the battle at Shiloh, and, as the leader of a squad of special scouts, wrote the dispatch that gave notice to Albert Sidney Johnston of the passage of the first federal gunboat above Pittsburg Landing on a flank movement which the Confederate commander anticipated and forestalled.

Near the close of the war, Larimore moved his mother and sisters in a wagon from East Tennessee to avoid molestations and dangers from robbers who infested the countryside. As they went on their way, they camped in a country schoolhouse near Hopkinsville, Kentucky. They were moneyless pilgrims in a strange land, with no means of support but their own labor and the wagon and team that they owned.

His mother was a Christian, and she made herself known to the congregation at Hopkinsville. Larimore earned a living cutting and hauling wood to Hopkinsville at a dollar and a quarter a load until an opportunity opened up in a country school. He taught with credit to himself and to the satisfaction of the patrons and pupils. He attended the meetings of the church with his mother, and he decided to become a Christian and spend the remainder of his life in the service of the Lord.

On his twenty-first birthday, July 10, 1864, at a meeting of the church, he confessed his sins and was baptized. He began preaching in 1866 and attracted attention at once as a persuasive speaker and consecrated Christian. He entered Franklin College, near Nashville, Tennessee, in the fall of the same year. Brother Larimore remained in school at Franklin College about two years. After leaving Franklin College, he went to North

Alabama and preached the gospel with much power and persuasion. While in that section of the state be became acquainted with the Srygley family.

Mars Hill Bible College during its active days.

Brother Larimore next went to Florence, Alabama, and on January 1, 1871, he opened a school and called it "Mars Hill Academy." He continued here for a few years, and as his school grew he changed its name to "Mars Hill College."

Mars Hill College continued for a period of sixteen years— from 1871 to 1887. Hundreds of young men were trained in this college by Brother Larimore. The renowned E. A. Elam taught for a while with him there. This college did more for young people in that section of the country than all other schools there.

Larimore was an accomplished scholar and a popular orator before critical city audiences, but his greatness as a preacher rested mainly upon the hope and joy he carried into the homes and hearts of the poor and unfortunate people who lived in neglected and out-of-the-way places.

In 1868 he married Miss Esther Gresham of Florence, Alabama, who was a true helpmeet in all his labors and trials. She and Larimore had been married thirty-eight years when she died. She is buried in Florence, Alabama, in the old Gresham Cemetery at Mars Hill across from the Larimore home located in west Florence off Cox Creek Parkway. He later married Emma Page, an editor who followed T. B. Larimore and helped him with his scheduling.

Larimore baptizing at his home
in Mars Hill, Alabama.

Brother Larimore's field of labor increased, and the calls for his services multiplied until he had much more work than he could possibly do. He labored to start several colleges in areas where his evangelistic work carried him, including Dixie University in Cookeville, Tennessee (later to become Tennessee Technological University), where he served two years as its president (1909–1911). He traveled and labored in about twenty states and territories and conducted successful protracted meetings in many of the important cities in the South. He also labored extensively in rural regions, and his work was greatly blessed in the conversion of sinners and edification of saints wherever he went. He probably preached more sermons to more audiences and baptized more people than any other man of his day. He baptized more than ten thousand people with his own hands, and he established many congregations of worshippers in all parts of the country where he labored.

Always a poor man, he was always supported entirely by the voluntary contributions of people who appreciated his labors. Perhaps no man of *recent* generations has come from such low depths of poverty and obscurity and has risen to such heights of fame in the brotherhood as T. B. Larimore. His early advantages were very gloomy and his poverty discouraging; yet through

Larimore home in Florence, Alabama, today
a historical treasure.

it all, he arose to heights of great prominence and service among his fellows upon this earth.

He wrote no books, and yet a number of books have been written about him. These books are as follows: *Larimore and His Boys, Letters and Sermons of T. B. Larimore* (three volumes), and *Maine to Mexico and Canada to Cuba*. All of these books breathe the gentle spirit of the great man whose life and work inspired them. They are rich in spiritual blessings to those who may read them.

Last Photo of T. B. and Emma Larimore, November, 1928.

Brother Larimore's preaching has been described by one of his followers like this: "On his face there was a settled expression of goodness and melancholy that touched the hearts of people with a feeling of sympathy and love. There was an indescribable and irresistible pathos in his voice, manner, and general appearance which melted audiences to tears and moved hearts long hardened by sin to repentance at the appeal of the gospel. He preached wherever an opportunity was given him."

Mars Hill Church Building, Florence, Alabama.
Building built in 1904 specifically for the preaching of T. B. Larimore.

Brother Larimore was kind and gentle in his manner and very pleasing in his address. It was not his style or disposition to engage in controversy or to be offensive in his preaching. He chose his subject and presented it in a simple, straightforward way without turning aside to notice any religious error. He preached the truth with earnestness and clarity and said little or nothing about any of the popular religious denominations of the day. He was an eloquent speaker, with music and charm in the well-chosen phraseology with which he clothed the thoughts that he gleaned from the Word of God. All who heard him loved him.*

---

*Excerpts and pictures used in this chapter are taken from the Mars Hill Bible School Web site and reprinted by permission of Dr. Kenny Barfield, past president of Mars Hill Bible School and Web site originator. Additional sources of Web page content are available at the Mars Hill Bible School Web site.

THE TOUCH OF THE MASTER'S HAND

Perhaps this "Touch of the Master's Hand" on the life of T. B. Larimore led James H. Stribling to answer the appeal to "Come unto Me all ye who labor and are heavy laden and I will give you rest."

That "rest" given to Jim Stribling made a profound impact on the entire Lawrenceburg, Tennessee, community, as Stribling spent the remainder of his years serving God and mankind by sharing his wealth with all those he encountered who were less fortunate. Stribling's newfound faith was his continual image—portrayed and shared—with anyone who crossed his path.

Notes from spouse of author: When my wife was asked to help compile the contents of this book, the thought sounded very appealing and I agreed to assist her with this endeavor, yet the content sounded so distant to our own lives. Little did we realize that there was a spiritual lesson to be learned: *History repeats itself! . . . and for a purpose.* Allow me to review with you some of the "repeats" that I found so miraculous in my own life:

- My dad, Hermon Gandy, and my grandmother lived on the property (Mars Hill Bible College) of T. B. Larimore when Dad was just a small child attending Mars Hill public school. They also attended the Mars Hill Church of Christ where Brother Larimore preached. Larimore would pay my dad and grandmother to "pull bitterweeds in his pastures" in order for them to have money to survive during these pre-Depression days (mid-20's). So, yes, my dad was a recipient of "the Touch of the Master's Hand" through the life of T. B. Larimore as well. He, like Jim Stribling, gained the servant's heart by this "touch of kindness" that was never forgotten and that was proven through the life he lived.

One incident in my dad's own childhood relates to an earlier article of "Clarence Junior Clifton" (*Chapter 2*). He, too, thought all kids were just like him when it related to wealth or lack thereof. When he was a small child, Dad's teacher had asked each child to bring some food from home for "the poor kid" at school. So he proudly proclaimed to his mother that he was going to get to help the poor kid at school. His mother scoured the empty cupboards and all that could be found was a handful of dried peas—a "poke o' peas"* if you will—in a small brown bag folded and neatly tied. Daddy proudly displayed his poke of peas on the teacher's desk alongside the canned hams, cans of fruits and vegetables, and the like. He could not wait to see who the lucky person might be who would receive the bounty. His curiosity led the teacher to ask him to help load up the food into his car and help him deliver it to the "poor kid"; then he would drop my dad back off at his home (at Larimore's place). Little did Dad realize until the teacher suddenly turned into his driveway, that he *was* the "poor kid." Again the good graces of his classmates were "paid forward" many times over as he placed himself in the "shoes of others"—time and again—because he had been there.

- I attended Tennessee Technological University (TTU) in Cookeville, Tennessee, graduating in 1970 (BSEE). As stated earlier, TTU was earlier known as Dixie University

*Gospel Publishing House: Sandy Gandy-Curtis, "A Poke o' Peas," Assemblies of God Sunday School Literature, Adult Student Guide, Summer 2007 issue.

(Derryberry Hall only), but it was originally suggested to be named Larimore University by some of T. B. Larimore's followers. He served there as president from 1909 to 1911.

- When I was an infant, my mom used to keep me on a "pallet" in the Laurel Hill cotton fields in Lawrence County, Tennessee, where my dad farmed, raising cotton to pay for his recently purchased 1948 Farmall "C." He spoke often of the old CCC camp that once surrounded the fields. Little did I realize that James H. Stribling owned those same fields that had earlier been the home of the CCC camp at Henryville (as the nearest post office). All locals remember the Laurel Hill CCC Camp. The timber surrounding these Laurel Hill fields was also cut for furnace wood by the POWs from Camp Stribling only a few short years prior. The wood was shipped to surrounding furnaces in the area.
- One of those furnaces listed as receiving wood from the Laurel Hill site was Rockdale Furnace which was located less than a mile from our present home in the Sandy Hook Community near Mount Pleasant, Tennessee.

So, yes, ***history*** has a never-ending cord that forever entwines all of us into the same circles . . . if we research it deeply enough.

CHAPTER 4

The Woman and Her Inherited Plan

JAMES LOIS STRIBLING

JAMES LOIS STRIBLING, daughter of James Henry Stribling and Ardelia Lois Cobb Stribling, was referred to as "Little Jim." There isn't much information on Jim as she was growing up. It appears that Jim was shy and did not like the limelight, as was the preference of her parents. She liked to do things quietly and in her way. Even though the family was wealthy, there were few public records of their lives.

James Lois Stribling (Little Jim) was born May 13, 1903, and was known countywide as her father's daughter. Little Jim grew up in her father's footsteps . . . sustaining his legacy after his death in 1951. She continued working at the bank as president, and later as chairman of the board. She served on the board of the Christian Home

Little Jim with a friend.
Photo courtesy of Stribling Estate

until her death on February 2, 1988. Her husband, Delma Brock (often referenced as Delmar Brock), also worked with the Stribling properties.

Little Jim with household help.
Photo courtesy of Stribling Estate

This picture was taken in 1917.
(Jim would have been about
fourteen years old.)
Photo courtesy of Stribling Estate

Jim as a young woman.
Photo courtesy of Stribling Estate

Jim and Delma Huckabee Brock were married on January 3, 1923. They had thirty-one years together before Delma died on August 18, 1954. Delma worked at the First National Bank with Jim's father, J. H. Stribling, where he (Delma) later became president.

During the 1930s a Civilian Conservation Corp camp (CCC) was built on property belonging to J. H. Stribling. That camp closed after World War II began, and a German prisoner-of-war camp was formed at that location in April of 1944.

Jim and Delma Brock
Photo courtesy of Stribling Estate

Delma Huckabee Brock
Photo courtesy of Stribling Estate

Some of the POWs worked on the Stribling farm doing odd jobs for Mr. Stribling. Other POWs in the camp were "farmed out" to other farmers and businesses in Lawrence, Lewis, Giles, and Maury Counties.

Jim and Delma Brock became close to some of the German POWs and kept in touch with them throughout the years. Jim sent countless care packages to Germany to help the young men to get reestablished in their homes. She wrote an abundance of letters of encouragement to them

Dear Jim:

    Top of the season to you.
I heard great good news tonight. One of my
short stories got put in the Obrien collection
of the best short stories for 1922. You know
not what manner of honor that is but if you'll
ask Marks he'll tell you. Anyway the upshot
of it will be that lots of magazines will write to
me and ask for stories, and I get a good deal of free
advertising out of it.

    And another streak of luck--I finished I think the
beststory I ever wrote Friday and decided to send it
to Cosmopolitan. Well Friday night I received a letter
from the Cosmo asking me to send them a short story.
Now isn't that a coincidence? I am all excited about
it.

    I haven't heard about the English matter yet, won't
for a long time I daresay.

    Wish I could have seen all your Christmas things--
hope a Cadillac Sport is among them but fear not.

    A girl here, Pauline Hassell got the prettiest wrist
watch I ever saw, very tiny and looks just like a small
gold buckle. It's a Gruen. I don't know what I've got
yet but am hoping for the best (of whatever it is).

    Merry Christmas and Happy New Year,

                          Tom

*This letter from T. S. (Tom) Stribling, a cousin, is telling Jim that one of his short stories has been listed in the O'Brien collection of best short stories for 1922. He is also telling her that he had sent one of his short stories to **Cosmopolitan** magazine on the same day that he received a letter from **Cosmopolitan** requesting one of them.*

Photo courtesy of Stribling Estate

Dear Jim,

Being an incurable romanticist myself, let me
wish you all the joy in the world in the romance you
have started with such a gesture.
I was delightfully surprised to hear it. Just to think
of my silent little cousin who has the compound
demureness of ten violets and eight field mice, suddenly
breaking loose and getting married on her own.
Splendid! Splendid! It has all the surprise quality
of an O. Henry story. I certainly hope you'll do something
else as artistic one of these fine days.
I certainly wish you all the joy of your honeymoon.
Being a philosopher, and a psychologist, it would hardly
be sane for me to wish you a continuation of that joy,
and besides it wouldn't be good for you. Joy is like
wine, a drink or two now and then bucks one up in great
shape, but too much of it makes one impossible.
However nature in her economy has never, from the
beginning of the world up to the year 1923, given any
body an overdose of joy as far as my knowledge goes,
so don't hesitate to drink wholeheartedly as long as you
can persuade one shy retiring drop to trickle out of the
flagon.

I hope you will allow me to criticise the technique
of your elopement a little. Now to get on the train,
or motor car and go away when no one knows it, is like
shooting quails on the ground. They never had a chance.
The thing you should have done was to run a notice in the
paper of the proposed flight out of Egypt. Then obtained
two motor cars, one for your folks to pursue you in and
the other for you and Delmar to bat it out in. Then,
on some prearranged signal, you could have started both
cars and had a real thrill. You could have introduced
several elements of uncertainty by having two marriage
licenses, one for Lawrence County the other for Lauderdale,
you could have taken a preacher in your car and have let
him used either or both licenses as the exigencies of the
dash dictated. And think of the dramatic possibilities!

Well, now I know why you were so exceedingly
difficult to entertain when I was down there last, and
you certainly are forgiven. If I had had a marriage in my
head I am sure I wouldn't have been able to talk to anyone
at all, so taking the situation into consideration,
I must say in the words of the psalmist "You done noble"
Next time I come down, I hope to have a much more
consecutive talk with you.

Writing a little more seriously, I really think you were
wise in marrying young. Getting married is like going in
bathing--if you try to walk in gradually and thoughtfully,
you will find you'll get cold feet. The thing to do is
to go in head first and have it over with. And then if
one drowns, they tell me just as one is going under the
third time, one reviews ones whole life in a few seconds,
so after all one has plenty of time to think it over even
if one does jump in head first.
Sunday Jan.7 23.   Lots of love,and good wishes, Tom.

*This letter, dated January 7, 1923, is from T. S. (Tom) Stribling
congratulating Jim on her recent marriage to Delma Brock. Tom
teases her about her elopement. There is more information about
Tom Stribling in Chapter 11.* Photo courtesy of Stribling Estate

and received numerous letters from the POWs as they made their way back home. Some of the men did not make it home until several years later, while many returned home immediately. The night before the men left camp for good, several of the POWs (those who had worked for Mr. Stribling and the Brocks) slipped out of camp to tell the Brocks good-bye. It was a very emotional time as the Brocks and the POWS had become close during their time of encampment in Lawrenceburg.

Chapter 8 goes into more detail about the correspondence between the Brocks and the POWs. (Note: There were no pictures made of the POWs in the camp area by local people. Pictures taken with the Brocks were made outside of the camp.)

Delma Brock (far right), World War I photo.
Photo courtesy of Stribling Estate

Jim and Delma enjoyed walking horse shows and attended and participated in shows in and around Middle Tennessee where they won several awards for their own prized horses.

THE PAINTING

During the time the POWs were imprisoned in Lawrenceburg, many were used to replace the local boys who were away during the war. The Striblings used six of them regularly on their farm west of Lawrenceburg. Among those six was a very bright and talented man named Eugen Hirth. He was a sculptor, painter, and later a dentist in Germany.

For one of Jim Brock's birthdays, Delma Brock traveled to Nashville and purchased quality paints for Hirth to paint a picture for his wife. The paints were slipped under the fence at night.

Painting by Eugen Hirth, former POW in Lawrenceburg.
Photo courtesy of Tim Pettus

However, Delma Brock had forgotten to purchase a canvas upon which the artist could paint. The clever Hirth never hesitated but obtained a white prison bedsheet, heavily starched it, and began painting. His painting depicts his memories of his last night of freedom in the northern end of Tunisia, as he was a member of Rommel's Afrika Korps. The painting now hangs in the office of Tim Pettus, president of First Farmers and Merchants Bank in Columbia, Tennessee.*

Seven years after the death of Delma Brock, Jim married

*A picture of Delma Brock
in his later years.*
Photo courtesy of Stribling Estate

*Pictured from left: Jim Stribling Brock Leonard, Patricia Stribling
Springer, Tom S. Stribling, and Mrs. Tom (Lou Ella) Stribling
(date unknown).*
Photo courtesy of Stribling Estate

*Submitted by Tim Pettus.

Sidney L. Leonard on June 15, 1961 in Lincoln County. Sidney died in February, 1977, in Lawrenceburg. Jim died February 2, 1988, at the age of eighty-four, in West Palm Beach Florida.

*Jim and Delma Brock
with POW guards.*
Photo courtesy of Stribling Estate

*Jim and Delma Brock
with POWs—1944.
Notice the car.*
Photo courtesy of Stribling Estate

The Democrat-Union
February 3, 1988

Jim Stribling Brock Leonard

Mrs. Jim Stribling Brock Leonard Dies at Age 84

Mrs. Jim Stribling Brock Leonard, 84, passed away Tuesday, February 2, 1988 at her home in West Palm Beach, Florida. She was the daughter of the late James Henry and Dena Cobb Stribling and the wife of the late Delma Brock and the late Sidney Leonard. She was a native of Lawrence County, Tennessee, a retired President and Chairman of the Board of the First National Bank, and a member of the Salem Church of Christ. She was the secretary of The Christian Home.

Funeral services will be conducted February 5, 1988 at 11 am at Salem Church of Christ with Brother Andrew Brown officiating. Burial will follow in Mimosa Cemetery. North Funeral Home is in charge of all the arrangements.

She is survived by several nieces, nephews, and cousins.*

Martha Jewell Denson Boston (Niece to Delma Brock)

Martha Jewell Denson grew up, went to school, and worked in Lawrenceburg. After graduating from high school, she worked at Salant & Salant shirt factory. She was eighteen years old at that time. She left Salant & Salant and went to work for an attorney for a short period of time. Later, her uncle, Delma Brock, asked her if she would like to work at First National Bank (this was in 1943). She said yes and continued to work there for forty years.

Martha Jewell married George Edward Boston in 1948 after the war was over. Boston, who was in the service, would visit the Service Men's Home when he was home on furlough (name found in the register of the Service Men's Home). Boston worked as an accountant and adjuster for an insurance office in Lawrenceburg for thirty years.

Delma Brock grew up in the Centerpoint community in southern Middle Tennessee and married Jim Lois Stribling. Brock died in 1954 from an aneurysm, and Jim later married Sidney Leonard from Lewisburg.

---

*This article reprinted by permission, courtesy of Jim and Marie Crawford and family and *The Democrat-Union*.

Martha Jewell Boston worked with Mr. Stribling at the bank. Mr. Stribling never drove a car, so one of the ladies at the bank, Mildred Craft, picked him up every morning for work.

Jim Stribling Brock worked at the bank in the book-keeping department on occasion. Mrs. Jim Stribling Brock became president of First National Bank after her father and husband died.

Jim Stribling Brock's mother, Ardelia Lois (Dena) Stribling, died in 1931; and her father, Jim Stribling, died in 1951.

Martha Jewell shared two of her favorite memories of Mr. Stribling: Lawrenceburg had the Kerr Hotel on the corner of North Military and Depot Street. The hotel served family-style lunches, and Mr. Stribling would take five or six girls from the bank to the hotel every day for lunch (as many as could get crammed into the car). Mildred Craft drove. "It was always fun," Martha Jewell said.

Her second favorite memory is this: When she and George Boston decided to marry, Mr. Stribling told her he had heard that someone was getting married, and she told him "yes." Mr. Stribling told her that she and Boston needed to come by his house after work. She and Boston went to his house and were surprised when Stribling gave her a gift—a Bible. In the Bible was a $50 bill which helped with their honeymoon expenses. That Bible became their family Bible which Martha Jewell still has today. (Note: Mr. Stribling's gift of a Bible to Martha Jewell and George as a wedding gift is in keeping with his religious practices.)

Martha Jewell was close with Uncle Delma and Aunt Jim, and they would visit in each other's homes. When Uncle Delma and Aunt Jim went to the Denson home, they would ask Martha Jewell and her twin brothers, Elwood and Edwin, to play and sing for them. After Brock died, and later Leonard died, Boston helped Aunt Jim with her financial needs. She assisted her in paying her utilities, taxes, and other things that needed to be taken care of, especially when Aunt Jim stayed in Florida during the winter months. They talked every day. Boston became Aunt Jim's "right arm" so to speak.

Martha Jewell Boston has her own history with World War II. She does not remember anything about the CCC camp except that it was in Lawrenceburg, and one of the girls in her class dated one of the boys at the CCC camp. When the POWs were camped in Lawrenceburg, Boston remembers that Uncle Delma and Mr. Stribling took her and several of the girls from the bank out to the farm where the POWs were working. She did not remember anything specific about the POWs. She did know that three of the POW guards married local girls. She remembers one of the girls well, Bernadine Hovelmeier, who married a Lieutenant Luders. There was Dorothy Prokesh who married Robert Noack, and Eva Davis who married Edward Wernet. They all went into Alabama to get married because they did not have to get a blood test to get a license to get married.

She remembers that the POWs had a camp near Napier Ironworks where they cut dyewood and then hauled it to Lawrenceburg for shipping.

Martha Jewell knows that Aunt Jim and Uncle Delma

stayed in touch with some of the POWs and sent them things regularly. Aunt Jim sent one of the wives of a POW crochet thread, and the lady sent Aunt Jim the most beautiful crocheted tablecloth for her large dining table. Martha Jewell does not know what happened to the tablecloth, but it was not seen after Aunt Jim's death. She assumes that Aunt Jim gave the tablecloth to someone before she died.

The following is an account of Martha Jewell's life and her recollection of her participation in the war efforts:

Martha Jewell's family was a musical family where she played the accordion. She was thirteen years old when her father brought home the accordion one day and told her that he wanted her to learn to play. Her accordion is now in the Vaughan Museum in Lawrenceburg. There was a quartet in the family that sang Southern gospel while she and her twin brothers, "The Jewell Denson Family," sang secular and country/western music. (Martha Jewell remembers that in December of 1945, her family went to the POW camp to perform for the men who were still at the camp.)

She and her brothers started singing as a trio when she was about nine or ten years old and sang together until one of the boys went off to war. Her uncle, Dwight Brock, was a pianist for the Vaughan Radio Quartet. In 1942, Mr. Vaughan could not get tires and gasoline to travel anymore, so the quartet disbanded.

Mr. Vaughan knew a Mr. V. O. Stamps of the Stamps Baxter Music Company in Dallas. So, Uncle Dwight called Mr. Vance in Dallas and told him that he had a a quartet comprised of a niece, two nephews, and himself. Mr. Vance told Mr. Brock for all of them to come out to Dallas and let him hear them. They did and they were hired. Boston did not know what the conditions of the contract were; she just knew they were working. They went to Chattanooga where Uncle Dwight became manager of the Chattanooga office of the Stamps Baxter Music Company, and so they moved there and traveled as a quartet called "The Baxter Melody Makers." Her brothers were still in school at that time. One went on to war, and the other became a Methodist preacher who continued to write music.

Her favorite memory during the time of World War II was of the Tennessee Extension Agency. The agency had a program where they would go to the schools every week and show slides on how to can and preserve fruits and vegetables. The agency decided that they wanted some musical entertainment before these presentations so they asked Ottis J. Knippers, who was a representative in the legislature, a judge in the county, and was big in gospel music. He sang solos and asked Martha Jewell to play her accordion for him. There was a young man in town who would go along with them to show the slides.

Knippers, Martha Jewell, and three young men from the national guard went on a war bond tour in Wayne County where they toured Collinwood, Clifton, and Waynesboro. They showed slides encouraging people to buy war bonds. Knippers would sing,

Martha Jewell would play her accordion, and the young men would show slides.

The Nashville Chamber of Commerce took two buses of businessmen on a war bond tour to the eastern and central parts of the state. On their second night of the tour they held a big rally on the square in Lawrenceburg. Knippers sang and Martha Jewell played her accordion. They performed *God Bless America* and other patriotic songs. After the rally the men on the tour asked Knippers and Martha Jewell to join them and perform at their other stops on the rest of the tour.

They left Lawrenceburg and went to Mount Pleasant, Columbia, Nashville, and Murfreesboro where the tour ended. The last stop of the tour was in Murfreesboro because General MacArthur's wife had lived there. The purpose of the tour was to sell war bonds. There were several big-name performers who also performed at some of the rallies, including Minnie Pearl, Roy Acuff, and others.

Martha Jewell remembers that they marched in the parade; and she had to carry her accordion, which was very heavy. She says that because she was the only female on the bus tour that day, the men would auction off the seat next to her to see who could sit by her. She said it was a lot of fun. She was nineteen years old and working at the shirt factory at that time. (The shirt factory was producing the air force shirts and a person could not just "take off." She had to check with her supervisor to see if she could get off for the day to do the tour and was given permission. As a side note, it is interesting that Martha Jewell went on the war bond tour and then sold and issued bonds when she worked at First National Bank.)

Martha Jewell also remembers that while she was at the bank during wartime, the stores had deposits that included ration stamps for food, tires, gas, shoes, and other accounts that had to be posted. She said the day the war was over, they never had to post those ration stamps again!

Martha Jewell Boston continues to make her home in Lawrenceburg. She is the mother to Lynn Boston Pettus and Cindy Boston Peters, the wives of Tim Pettus and Curtis Peters, respectively.*

(Author's note: It was amazing to listen to Mrs. Boston during my interview with her and realize how vivid her memories were. She never hesitated in her recollections as she recounted her life's experiences. It seemed that the memory of each experience was as fresh today as the day it happened.)

Following are a couple of newspaper articles that appeared in the Lawrenceburg paper, *The Democrat-Union,* regarding Martha Jewell Denson Boston.**

The Democrat-Union
By M. M. Niedergeses, May 23, 1942
Lawrenceburg 'Goes' For Big Cavalcade
"Swell Reception" Say Visitors, as They Depart

Lawrenceburg was out en masse on Wednesday night of last week to welcome to this city "Mrs. Douglas MacArthur Bond Selling

---

*Author's personal interview with Martha Jewell Denson Boston.
**These article are reprinted by permission of Jim and Marie Crawford and family, and *The Democrat-Union.*

Cavalcade" of Murfreesboro, when five big busses and a caravan of privately owned cars wheeled into town at approximately 9 o'clock.

The cavalcade was met by the Lawrence County High School band and Co. "G," local unit of the State Guard, followed by the boys' "Victory" company. The parade terminated at the speakers' stand on the north side of the courthouse, where several thousand people waited to hear the program, despite the late hour.

A welcome address was made by Dr. A. G. Buckner, local chairman of the sale of War Bonds, and by Mayor O. R. Downey.

Other speakers included "Dock" Earthman of Murfreesboro, Lipe Henslee of Nashville, collector of internal revenue; W. F. Norris, vice-president of the Commerce-Union Bank of Nashville, Paul A. Mertz, of the War Production Board in Washington, and Dr. Nat Copenhaver, state commander of the American Legion, of Bristol.

Corporal Jim Crawford's new war song, "The Lion and The Eagle," was stirringly sung by representative Ottis J. Knippers, who is also a corporal in the State Guard. Miss Martha Jewell Denson played the accordion accompaniment.

Other talent on the program included Private Todd Hall, N.B.C. impersonator, of the U.S. Army, and singer E. D. Baldwin of Murfreesboro.

The cavalcade left early Thursday morning.

To date, more than $150,000.00 in United States War Bonds have been sold in Lawrence County and sales in the country have already exceeded the quota set for this month, as has been the case each month since the establishment of quotas.

The Democrat-Union
(No Date)

Song Makes Hit as
Denson Is Made Queen

A Lawrenceburg girl who was made "queen," and a home-grown war song that clicked were the distinctions that came to this city last week, when Miss Martha Jewell Denson was named "Queen of the Mrs. Douglas MacArthur Cavalcade," and Corporal Jim Crawford's new tune, "Lion and Eagle," went over with a bang.

Sung by Representative Ottis J. Knippers here Wednesday night, and accompanied by Miss Denson, the Cavalcade promptly drafted the two to complete the bond-selling tour, and they made a hit at every stop.

Miss Denson was presented with a $25.00 War Bond, and the ringing applause for Mr. Knippers was adequate compensation for his stirring renditions.

War Comes Home

TAXES AND CONTROLS

FEDERAL TAX POLICY was highly contentious during the war, with President Franklin D. Roosevelt battling a Conservative Congress. Everyone agreed on the need for high taxes to pay for the war. Roosevelt tried unsuccessfully to impose a 100 percent tax on incomes over $25,000 (equal to $317,471 today), while Congress enlarged the base downward. By 1944 nearly every employed person was paying federal income taxes (compared to 10 percent in 1940).

Many controls were put on the economy. The most important was price controls imposed on most products and monitored by the Office of Price Administration. Wages were also controlled. Corporations dealt with numerous agencies, especially the War Production Board (WPB), and the Departments of War and Navy, which had the purchasing power and priorities that largely reshaped and expanded industrial production.

RATIONING

In 1942, a rationing system was begun to guarantee minimum amounts of necessities to everyone (especially poor people) and to prevent inflation. Tires were the first item to be rationed in January, 1942, because supplies of natural rubber were interrupted. Gasoline rationing proved an even better

UNITED STATES
OF AMERICA

War Ration Book One

WARNING

1 Punishments ranging as high as *Ten Years' Imprisonment or $10,000 Fine, or Both*, may be imposed under United States Statutes for violations thereof arising out of infractions of Rationing Orders and Regulations.

2 This book must not be transferred. It must be held and used only by or on behalf of the person to whom it has been issued, and anyone presenting it thereby represents to the Office of Price Administration, an agency of the United States Government, that it is being so held and so used. For any misuse of this book it may be taken from the holder by the Office of Price Administration.

3 In the event either of the departure from the United States of the person to whom this book is issued, or his or her death, the book must be surrendered in accordance with the Regulations.

4 Any person finding a lost book must deliver it promptly to the nearest Ration Board.

N⁰ 106304 -214

OFFICE OF PRICE ADMINISTRATION

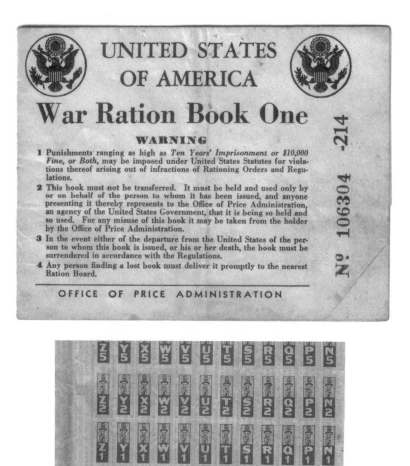

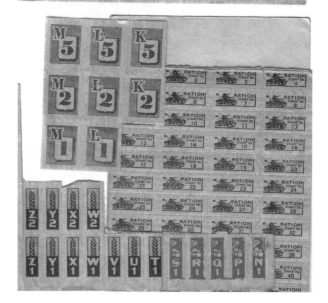

| O. P. A. Form No. R-306 | UNITED STATES OF AMERICA | Not Valid Before 5-20-43 |
| | OFFICE OF PRICE ADMINISTRATION | Date |

Serial No. c63651597 **SUGAR PURCHASE CERTIFICATE** TRIPLICATE

THIS IS TO CERTIFY THAT:

Name: Mrs. Ramon McCrory   Address: 406 E. Gaines St.

City: Lawrenceburg   County: Lawrence   State: Tenn.

is authorized to accept delivery of

Ten   (10) pounds of sugar

pursuant to Rationing Order No. 3 (Sugar Rationing Regulations) of, and at a price not to exceed the maximum price established by, the Office of Price Administration.

Local Rationing Board No. 47-36   Date 5-20-43

Lawrence   Tenn.   By _____ clerk   Signature of issuing officer

County   State   Title

To Be Retained by Original Holder

This sugar ration and the coupons on the previous page are
a few of the many types of rationing methods used
during World War II.

Photos courtesy of Curtis Peters

way to allocate scarce rubber. By 1943, one needed government-issued ration coupons to purchase typewriters, sugar, gasoline, bicycles, clothing, fuel oil, silk, nylon, coffee, stoves, shoes, meat, cheese, butter, lard, margarine, canned foods, dried fruits, jam, and many other items. However, items such as sweets and fruits were not rationed, as they would spoil. Families also grew victory gardens and small home vegetable gardens to supply themselves with food. Some items—like new automobiles and appliances—were no longer made. The rationing system did not apply to used goods (like clothes or cars).

To get a classification and a book of rationing stamps, one had to appear before a local rationing board. Each person in a household received a ration book, including children and babies. When purchasing gasoline, a driver had to present a gas card along with a ration book and cash. Ration stamps were valid only for a set period to forestall hoarding. All forms of automobile racing were banned, including Indianapolis. Sightseeing driving was banned, too.

Gasoline purchase permit.
Photo courtesy of Curtis Peters

The rationing system, which had been originally based on a specific basket of goods for each consumer, was much improved by switching to a point system that allowed the housewives to make choices based on their own priorities. Food rationing also permitted the upgrading of the quality of the foods available, and housewives approved—except for the absence of white bread and the government's imposition of a distasteful wheat meal "national loaf." People were especially pleased that rationing brought equality and a guarantee of a decent meal at an affordable cost.

PERSONAL SAVINGS

Personal income was at an all-time high, but the extra dollars were challenged by fewer goods to purchase. This was a recipe for economic disaster that was largely avoided because Americans—encouraged daily by their government to do so—were also saving money at an all-time high rate, mostly in war bonds but also in private savings accounts and insurance policies. Consumer saving was strongly encouraged through investment in war bonds that would mature after the war. Most workers had an automatic payroll deduction; children collected savings stamps until they had enough to buy a bond. The public paid three-fourths of the face value of a war bond and received the full face value back after a set number of years. This shifted their consumption from the war to postwar, and it allowed over 40 percent of the gross domestic product (GDP) to go to military spending with moderate inflation. Americans were challenged to put "at least 10 percent of every paycheck into bonds," and compliance was very high.

LABOR

The unemployment problem ended in the United States with the beginning of World War II when stepped-up wartime production created millions of new jobs, and the draft pulled young men out of industry and into the war. So great was the demand for labor that millions of retired people, housewives, and students entered the labor force, lured by patriotism and high wages.

Women

Women also joined the workforce to replace men who had joined the military, though in fewer numbers. Roosevelt stated that the efforts of civilians at home to support the war through personal sacrifice were as critical to winning the war as the efforts of the soldiers themselves. "Rosie the Riveter" became the symbol of women laboring in manufacturing. The war effort brought about significant changes in the role of women in society as a whole. At the end of the war, many of the war-related factories closed. Other women were replaced by returning veterans; however, most women who wanted to continue to work did so.

"Rosie the Riveter," working on an A-31 "Vengeance" dive bomber (Nashville, Tennessee, 1943).
Photo courtesy of U.S. Government, Public Domain

Young daughters of these working women learned that to be a working woman was a normal part of life, and later many of these daughters also became working women.

In the prewar era, the 56.1 million workforce found 25.2 percent to be female. The workforce grew to a peak of 66.23 million in 1944 with 29.2 percent of that number being female. By the end of the war, 1946 found a total workforce of 60.52 million with the female portion dropping back to 27.85 percent of the total workforce. Many farmers also returned to full-time farming rather than assisting with factory production.

Farming

Labor shortages were felt in agriculture, even though most farmers were given an occupational exemption and few were drafted. Large numbers volunteered or moved to cities for factory jobs. At the same time, many agricultural commodities were in greater demand by the military and for the civilian populations of the Allies. Production was encouraged, and prices and markets were under tight federal control.

Between 1942 and 1946, some 425,000 Italian and German prisoners of war were used as farm laborers, loggers, and cannery workers. In Michigan, for example, the POWs accounted for more than one-third of the state's agricultural production and food processing in 1944.

Welder making boilers for a ship at Combustion Engineering Company (Chattanooga, Tennessee, June 1942).
Photo courtesy of U.S. Government, Public Domain

Teenagers

With the war's ever-increasing need for able-bodied men consuming America's labor force in the early 1940s, industry turned to teenaged boys and girls to fill in as replacements. Consequently, many states had to change their child-labor laws to allow these teenagers to work. The lures of patriotism, adulthood, and money led many youth to drop out of school and take a defense job. Between 1940 and 1944, the number of teenage workers increased by 1.9 million; and the number of students in public high schools dropped from 6.6 million in 1940 to 5.6 million in 1944, as a million students—and many teachers—took jobs.

CIVILIAN SUPPORT FOR WAR EFFORT

Early in the war, it became apparent that German U-boats were using the backlighting of coastal cities in the eastern and southern United States to destroy ships exiting harbors. It became the first duties of civilians recruited for local civilian defense to ensure that lights were either off or thick curtains drawn over all windows at night.

The Civil Air Patrol was established, which enrolled civilian spotters in air reconnaissance, search-and-rescue, and transport. Its Coast Guard counterpart, the Coast Guard Auxiliary, used civilian boats and crews in similar roles. Towers were built in coastal and border towns, and spotters were trained to recognize enemy aircraft. Blackouts were practiced in every city, even those far from the coast. All exterior lighting had to be extinguished and blackout curtains placed over windows, to avoid helping the enemy in targeting at night. The main purpose of the "lights-out" issue was to remind people that there was a war going on, and to provide activities that would engage the civil spirit of millions of people who were not otherwise involved in the war effort. In large part, this effort was successful, sometimes almost to the extreme, such as in the plains states where many dedicated aircraft spotters took up their posts night after night, watching the skies in an area of the country that no enemy aircraft of that time could possibly hope to reach.

The United Service Organization (USO) was founded in 1941 in response to a request from President Franklin D. Roosevelt to provide morale and recreation services to uniformed military personnel. This request led six civilian agencies—the Salvation Army, Young Men's Christian Association, Young Women's Christian Association, National Catholic Community Service, National Travelers Aid Association, and the National Jewish Welfare Board—to unite in support of the troops. The USO was incorporated in New York on February 4,

1941. (Details of the Lawrenceburg, Tennessee USO are given in Chapter 6.)

As stated before, legions of women previously employed only in the home, or in traditionally female work, took jobs in factories that directly supported the war effort, or filled jobs vacated by men who had entered military service.

A synagogue on West Twenty-Third Street in New York City remained open twenty-four hours on D-Day for special services and prayer.
Photo courtesy of U.S. Government,
Public Domain

Various disposable items, previously discarded, were saved after use for what would be known in later years as "recycling." Families were requested to save fat drippings from cooking for war-related uses. Neighborhood "scrap drives" collected scrap copper and brass for use in artillery shells. Milkweed was harvested by children to be used for life jackets.

DRAFT

In 1940 Congress passed the first peacetime draft legislation. It was renewed (by one vote) in the summer of 1941. Questions arose as to who should control the draft, the size of the army, and the need for deferments. The system worked through local draft boards comprising community leaders who were given quotas, with the authority to decide how to fill them. There was very little draft resistance.

The nation went from a surplus manpower pool with high

unemployment and relief in 1940, to a severe manpower short-age by 1943. Industries realized that the army urgently desired production of essential war materials and foodstuffs more than soldiers. A significant number of U.S. soldiers were not used until the invasion of Europe in the summer of 1944.

Turret lathe operator machining parts for transport planes at the Consolidated Aircraft Corporation Plant, Fort Worth, Texas. Women entered the workforce as men were drafted into the armed forces.
Photo courtesy of U.S. Government, Public Domain

From 1940 through 1943 the army often transferred sol-diers to civilian status in the Enlisted Reserve Corps (ERC) in order to increase production. Those transferred would return to work in essential industry, although they could be called back to active duty if the army needed them. Others were dis-charged if their civilian work was deemed essential. There were instances of mass releases of men to increase production in var-ious industries. Working men, who had been classified "4-F," or otherwise ineligible for the draft, took second jobs.

The prewar years found 540,000 military employees of the 56 million workforce, with a national unemployment rate of 17.2 percent. By 1944, the military comprised 11.4 million of the 66 million workforce, and unemployment had dropped to an all-time low of 1.2 percent. By war's end the 61 million work-force found a decrease of military workers to 3.5 million—with an overall unemployment rate of 3.9 percent—with returning military personnel infiltrating the home-front workforce.

One contentious issue involved the drafting of fathers, which was avoided as much as possible. The drafting of eighteen-year-olds was desired by the military but vetoed by public opinion. Racial minorities were drafted at the same rate as whites and were paid the same, but blacks were kept in all-black units. The experience of World War I regarding men needed by industry was particularly unsatisfactory—too many skilled mechanics and engineers became privates. Farmers demanded and were generally given occupational deferments. (Many volunteered anyway, but those who stayed at home lost postwar veteran's benefits.)

Later in the war, in light of the tremendous amount of man-power that would be necessary for the invasion of France in 1944, many earlier deferment categories became draft eligible.

EMPLOYMENT

Women took on an active role in World War II and took on many paid jobs in temporary new war-related factories, and in old factories that had been converted from luxury products like automobiles. This was the "Rosie-the-Riveter" phenomenon.

Women filled many traditionally female jobs that were created by the war boom, but they also worked at jobs that had previously been held by men. Nearly one million women worked as so-called "government girls," taking jobs in the federal government, mainly in Washington, D.C., that had previously been held by men or were newly created to deal with the war effort.

During World War II, women began to gain more respect, and men realized that women actually could work outside of the home. Women fought for equal pay and made a huge impact on the United States workforce. They began to take over "male" jobs and gained confidence in themselves.

In general, when women replaced men, they came with fewer skills. Industry retooled its machine jobs so that un-skilled workers could handle them. (This opened up many jobs for men who had been unemployed in the 1930s.) Some unions tried to maintain the same male pay scale for women because they expected men to resume their jobs after the war.

Volunteer Activities

Women staffed millions of jobs in community service roles, such as nursing, USO, and Red Cross while the men were at war. In addition, families were encouraged to collect and turn in

Riveting team working on the cockpit shell of a C-47
transport at the plant of North American Aviation.
Photo by Alfred T. Palmer, 1942; Office of War Information.
Photo courtesy of U.S. Government, Public Domain

materials that were needed by the war effort. Women collected fats rendered during cooking, children formed balls of aluminum foil they peeled from chewing gum wrappers. They also created rubber-band balls, which they contributed to the war effort.

Women Air Force Service Pilots

The Women Air Force Service Pilots, known as WASP, and the predecessor groups, the Women's Flying Training Detachment (WFTD), and the Women's Auxiliary Ferrying Squadron WAFS, official from September 10, 1942, were each a pioneering organization of female pilots employed to fly military aircraft under the direction of the Air Force. They primarily flew new planes from the factories to airfields located on the east coast. The women were civilians and not under military discipline.

About 1,000 women were active in WASP. They freed up male pilots for combat service and duties. The WFTD and WAFS were combined on August 5, 1943, to create the paramilitary WASP organization. It was disbanded in 1944 when thousands of male pilots had completed their combat tours and were available for ferrying new planes. These organizations are important in gender history because flying a warplane had always been a male role. Unlike Russia, no American women flew warplanes in combat.

Baby Boom

Marriage and motherhood came back as prosperity empowered couples who had postponed marriage. The birthrate started shooting up in 1941, paused in 1944–45 as 12 million men were in uniform, then continued to soar until reaching a peak in the late 1950s. This was the "Baby Boom."

Woman standing next to a wide range of tire sizes required by the military as needed for aircraft.
Photo courtesy of U.S. Government, Public Domain

In a New Deal-like move, the federal government set up the "EMIC" program that provided free prenatal and natal care for the wives of servicemen below the rank of sergeant.

Housing shortages, especially in the war-related centers, forced millions of couples to live with parents or in makeshift facilities. Little housing had been built in the Depression years, so the shortages grew steadily worse until about 1948, when a massive housing boom finally caught up with demand. (After 1944 much of the new housing was supported by the G.I. Bill.)

Federal law made it difficult to divorce absent servicemen, so the number of divorces peaked when they returned in 1946. In long-range terms, divorce rates changed little.

INTERNMENT OF JAPANESE AMERICANS

Japanese American internment was the relocation and internment by the United States government of about 110,000 Japanese Americans who lived along the Pacific coast of the United States. They were moved to camps called "war relocation camps," in the wake of Japan's attack on Pearl Harbor on December 7, 1941. The internment was applied only on the west coast of the United States. In Hawaii, where the 150,000-plus Japanese Americans composed over one-third of the population, an estimated 1,200 to 1,800 were interned. Of those interned, 62 percent were American citizens.

In 1942 the War Department demanded that all enemy nationals be removed from war zones on the west coast. The question became how to evacuate the estimated 120,000 people of Japanese citizenship living in California. Roosevelt looked at the secret evidence available to him: The Japanese in the Philippines had collaborated with the Japanese invasion troops; most of the adult Japanese in California had been strong supporters of Japan in the war against China. There was evidence of espionage compiled by code-breakers who decrypted messages to Japan from agents in North America and Hawaii before and after the attack on Pearl Harbor. These MAGIC cables were kept secret from all but those with the highest clearance, such as Roosevelt.

On February 19, 1942, Roosevelt signed Executive Order 9066 which set up designated military areas "from which any or all persons may be excluded." The most controversial part of the order included American-born children and youth who had dual U.S. and Japanese citizenship. Germans and Italians were not confirmed.

In February 1943, when activating the 442nd Regimental Combat Team—a unit composed mostly of American-born citizens of Japanese descent living in Hawaii—Roosevelt said, "No loyal citizen of the United States should be denied the democratic right to exercise the responsibilities of his citizenship, regardless of his ancestry. The principle on which this country was founded and by which it has always been governed is that Americanism is a matter of the mind and heart; Americanism is not, and never was, a matter of race or ancestry." In 1944, the U.S. Supreme Court upheld the legality of the executive order. The executive order remained in force until December when Roosevelt released the Japanese detainees, except for those who announced their intention to return to Japan.

Italy was an official enemy, and citizens of Italy were also forced away from "strategic" coastal areas in California. Altogether, 58,000 Italians were forced to relocate. They relocated on their own and were not put into camps. Known spokesmen for Benito Mussolini were arrested and held in prison. The restrictions were dropped in October 1942, and Italy switched sides in 1943 and became an American ally. In the east, however, the large Italian populations of the northeast, especially in war-producing centers such as Bridgeport and New Haven (Connecticut) faced no restrictions and contributed just as much to the war effort as other Americans.

WARTIME POLITICS

Roosevelt easily won the bitterly contested 1940 election, but the Conservative coalition maintained a tight grip on Congress. Wendell Willkie, the defeated GOP candidate in 1940, became a roving ambassador for Roosevelt. After a series of squabbles with Vice President Henry A. Wallace, Roosevelt stripped him of his administrative responsibilities and dropped him from the 1944 ticket, choosing instead Senator Harry S. Truman. Truman was best known for investigating waste, fraud, and inefficiency in civilian programs. In a very light turnout in 1942, the Republicans made major gains. In the 1944 election, Roosevelt defeated Tom Dewey in a relatively close race that attracted little attention.

Author's note: FDR was the only U.S. President to serve three terms and to be elected for four terms. He served for twelve years and forty-two days. He served three full terms and died after serving less than three months of his fourth term. However, his second term was less than four years, since the inauguration date was moved from March 4 to January 20. He served from March 4, 1933, until he died on April 12, 1945. Term limits were placed in reaction to FDR's winning the office four times. And, it wasn't just Republicans who were concerned, but political leaders of all parties. The twenty-second Amendment to the Constitution was passed by Congress two years after the conclusion of World War II, March 21, 1947, and ratified four years later by the states. It was only when FDR was elected to his third and fourth terms that political leaders took the threat of a lifelong presidency seriously.

Propaganda and Culture

The media cooperated with the federal government in presenting the official view of the war. All movie scripts had to be preapproved. World War II posters helped to mobilize the nation. Inexpensive, accessible, and ever present, the poster was an ideal agent for making war aims the personal mission

Rural schoolchildren in front of home-front posters
(San Augustine County, Texas, 1943).
Photo courtesy of U.S. Government, Public Domain

of every citizen. Government agencies, businesses, and private organizations issued an array of poster images linking the military front with the home front—calling upon every American to boost production at work and at home. Deriving their appearance from the fine and commercial arts, posters conveyed more than simple slogans. Posters expressed the needs and goals of the people who created them. By definition, wartime posters are naturally propagandistic, but most posters were merely patriotically so. Some, however, resorted to extreme racial and ethnic caricatures of the enemy, sometimes as hopelessly bumbling cartoon characters, sometimes as evil, half-human creatures. The National Archives, Northwestern University, and the University of Minnesota all have extensive collections of World War II posters accessible online that contain many examples of posters of the era in regard to the use of propaganda, both subtle and patriotic, and blatantly anti-German and anti-Japanese.

One of the most noteworthy areas of civilian involvement during the war was in the area of recycling. Many everyday commodities were vital to the war effort, and drives were organized to recycle such things as rubber, tin, paper, lumber, steel, and many other items. Popular phrases promoted by the government at the time were "Get into the scrap!" and "Get some cash for your trash" (a nominal sum was paid to the donor for many kinds of scrap items). Such commodities as rubber and tin remained highly important as recycled materials until the end of the war, while others, such as steel, were critically needed at first, but in lesser quantities as damaged war supplies were returned from overseas for scrapping, lessening the need for civilian scrap metal drives. Once again, war propaganda played a prominent role in many of these drives.

A strong aspect of American culture then, as now, was a

fascination with celebrities, and many stars of Hollywood and radio gave service above and beyond the call of duty in the donation of their time for everything from being civilian defense marshals to making personal appearances at war bond drives. The sale of bonds produced the money that financed the war, and bond drives where celebrities appeared were always very successful. The public paid three-fourths of the face value of a war bond, and received the full face value back after a set number of years. While this may have represented a rather unspectacular interest rate, the government has never defaulted on payment of any bond. Entire factories of workers earned a special "Minuteman" flag to fly over their plant if all workers belonged to the "Ten Percent Club." There were seven major war bond drives, all of which exceeded their goals. An added advantage was that citizens who were putting their money into war bonds were not putting it into the home front wartime economy. There was a job for anyone who wanted one during the war, and most of them paid well. Personal income was at an all-time high, and more dollars were chasing fewer goods to purchase. This was a recipe for runaway inflation that was largely avoided because Americans—encouraged daily by their government to do so—were also saving money at an all-time high rate.

Hollywood studios also went all-out for the war effort, as studios allowed their major stars, such as Clark Gable (*Gone with the Wind*) and James Stewart (*It's a Wonderful Life*), to enlist, and they also created propaganda films to remind American moviegoers of their heritage. Many of the finest films of the era were about the war, such as *Casablanca, Mrs. Miniver,* and *Going My Way,* while others, such as *Yankee Doodle Dandy,* focused on patriotism. Even before active American involvement in the war, the popular *Three Stooges* comic trio were lampooning the Nazi German leadership, and Nazis in general, with a number of short-subject films, starting with *You Nazty Spy* in January 1940. This was nearly two years before the United States was drawn into World War II, and the very first Hollywood-produced work to ridicule Hitler and the Nazis.

Cartoons and short subjects were a major sign of the times, as Warner Brothers Studios and Disney Studios gave unprecedented aid to the war effort by creating cartoons that were both patriotic and humorous. Their contributions reminded moviegoers of wartime activities such as rationing and scrap drives, war bond purchases, and the creation of victory gardens. Warner shorts such as *Draftee Daffy, Russian Rhapsody,* and *Daffy— The Commando,* are particularly remembered for their biting wit and unflinching mockery of the enemy (particularly Adolf Hitler, Hideki Tōjō and Hermann Goering). Their cartoons of Private Snafu, produced for the military as "training films," served to remind many military men of the importance of following proper procedure during wartime for their own safety. Hanna Barbera also contributed to the war effort with their pro-U.S. short cartoon, *The Yankee Doodle Mouse,* with "Lt." Jerry Mouse as the hero and Tom Cat as the "enemy." Comic books such as *Sad Sack and the Sarge* became popular as propaganda tools for the youth of the day.

Walt Disney's studio also helped the war effort, as almost every cartoon produced by Disney in this period dealt with some aspect of the war. Each Disney cartoon began with a head shot of Mickey Mouse, Donald Duck, or Goofy; and during this time, each wore an army or navy cap. Disney produced a B-feature based on the book, *Victory Through Air Power,* and several promotional and comical short scripts on the importance of rationing, buying bonds, and paying one's income tax *(Taxes Against the Axis)*. *Education for Death* was a Disney short documentary based on the book of the same name, on the making of a Nazi. It demonstrated the cruelty of Hitler's Third Reich (which was devoid of compassion) against even its own citizens, weeding out the "weak or inferior" and breeding hatred and obedience in its people. *Der Fuehrer's Face* aka *Donald Duck in Nutziland,* starring Donald living a nightmare in a German province and working in a munitions plant, was one of the most popular and famous cartoons of the period. The song from the cartoon—*Der Fuehrer's Face,* recorded by Spike Jones & the City Slickers—also became very popular for its contempt of Nazi leaders.*

LOCAL HOME FRONT RECALLED (By Author)

Most Americans who lived through the World War II era recall vividly the many changes of life that were necessary for the success of the war itself. The unity of the American public, the media, and the military were a bond for one effort that has not been repeated since. It was not Democrats fighting Republicans, nor the opposing party trying to trip up the President, but it was a unified nation with one goal—defeating world corruption through winning the war. The additional taxes, economic controls, rationing, and the like, found an unselfish people willing to pay whatever price was required. War bonds were purchased as a witness of the public's willingness to do more than their fair share to finance the war. Farmers worked the factories to provide military necessities while still carrying

*Wikipedia Web site, "American Homefront," Public Domain.

on their farming to provide food for the American public. Women and teenagers pitched in to take up the slack of the missing male workforce. Although the draft was implemented, many teens volunteered immediately as they became of age (and often before), with many women joining noncombatant military positions.

Only the "Tower of Babel" could be compared to the unified efforts that were exemplified in America. Families were in one accord as they hovered around their old box radios to listen to the daily war reports from the front lines by such great reporters as Ernie Pyle who captured the true emotion of the war from such Allied positions as North Africa, Italy, and the Pacific. Pyle was awarded the 1944 Pulitzer Prize for Distinguished War Correspondence. The media, the government, the schools, and every other effort pushed a propaganda that was pro-USA and pro-war effort in hopes and prayers for a victorious and speedy conclusion to a war that had been forced upon the American people.

America was so unified that Congress was alarmed that the people had elected a president for a fourth consecutive term. Fear arose that America might conform to a dictatorship much like the German one they were fighting—one that was trying to conquer the world. As a result, legislation was passed that limited the tenure of the President of the United States to two terms.

CHAPTER 6

Service Men's Home

MRS. MARGARET HEFFINGTON

MRS. MARGARET LATIMORE HEFFINGTON was born in Madisonville, Tennessee, where her father, C. F. (Fred) Latimore, was the local county court clerk. He was also influential in local and state politics; and over the years, he entertained many dignitaries in his home, including Tennessee governors. When Margaret was growing up in Madisonville, she was friends with Estes Kefauver (United States Senator); and in later years, he would visit her in Lawrenceburg. Fred Latimore later moved to Tellico Plains, Tennessee, where he was a banker and farmer.

Margaret met her husband, C. L. Heffington, in Tellico Plains where he worked as a banker with her father. Mr. Heffington was originally from Lawrence County; so in later years he, his wife, and family moved to Lawrenceburg where he ran the Standard Oil service station. Margaret was widowed at a young age when her husband died of complications from a blood clot. In later years she would marry Jim Stricklin.

Margaret loved to play tennis in her younger years and spoke often of family fun times at their cabin up in the Smoky Mountains. After she moved to Lawrenceburg, she was involved in the Lawrenceburg community where she started a study club and donated many books to the library. She helped plant some of the trees around the old Lawrence County court-house and was a loyal member of the First Presbyterian Church. After the start of World War II, she was asked to run the Lawrence-burg area Service Men's Home (USO) located on West Gaines Street near the intersection of Highways 43 and 64 (Cyclone Corner).

Two soldiers standing on "Cyclone Corner."
Photo courtesy of Layde Ezell

A group of ladies decided that they wanted to help the servicemen, so the USO was created. Luzonne McKelvey Couch helped with the organization of the Service Men's Home and was the president. Her son, Lon H. McKelvey, served as a sergeant in the 50th Signal Battalion.

Heffington became known as "Mother" to many soldiers throughout the years. A registry was kept at the Service Men's Home, and soldiers from far and near stopped in at the home as they traveled from camp to camp. The men were allowed to spend the night at no charge as they passed through the area where Margaret, their hostess, provided the soldiers with lots of food and hospitality.

Left: Margaret and her "boys" in front of the Service Men's Home.
Right: Margaret and another serviceman at the home.
Photos courtesy of Layde Ezell

Margaret was hostess, or chaperone, to the parties that were held at the Service Men's Home. Local girls came to the dances to socialize with the young men. They added a little feminine company to these events, a custom that was popular throughout the United States during World War II. The girls came from Lawrence, Giles, and Maury Counties as evidenced by the signatures in the register.

Margaret was affectionally known as "Bubba" to her family, many of whom still reside in Lawrence County. Her daughter, Blanche, married Arthur Hardy; and their three children, Al and Mike Hardy, and Layde Hardy Ezell, all still live in Lawrenceburg.

Al and his wife, Gaye, live on part of the property that once housed the POW camp. Underneath their house is a steel rod that was used to anchor the guy wire for the utility pole for the camp. Al's mother and father, Arthur and Blanche Hardy, built the house in the late 1960s. They wanted to keep the steel rod in the ground to preserve a part of the history of the camp. The house is situated on Pine Bluff in Lawrenceburg, Tennessee.

Arthur Allan Hardy and his son, Al. Arthur is in his service uniform, and Al is wearing his daddy's hat.
Photo courtesy of Al and Gaye Hardy

Author's note: This guest register to the Service Men's Home gave much insight into the vastness of the operation of the POW camp located on the outskirts of Lawrenceburg during the latter years of World War II. Many additional names were derived as enlisted servicemen who assisted with the overseeing of the local POW camp. Military personnel from all states are shown as visitors to the Service Men's Home. Originally there were to be fifty guards and four maintenance men (one guard for each fourteen POWs). However, there was a total of three hundred thirty-one POWs listed in one newspaper article.

The register that was used for sign in at the Service Men's Home in Lawrenceburg. Following are some of the pages where soldiers and others signed in when they visited the home.

Unless otherwise noted, photos here and on the following pages are courtesy of Layde Hardy Ezell, daughter of Arthur and Blanche Hardy

Pages 2 and 3 show the name, rank, service, and address of each person. The first person who signed in was Aviation Cadet Arthur A. Hardy, of the U.S. Army Air Corps, San Antonio, Texas. Arthur was actually a local man who later married Margaret Heffington's daughter, Blanche, in May of 1943

Blanche Heffington Hardy and Sara Gallaher (Sharpe) with soldier. Blanche was daughter to Margaret Heffington and wife of Arthur Hardy, who was the first soldier to sign in at the Service Men's Home.
Photo courtesy of Layde Ezell

RANK	NAME	SERVICE	HOME ADDRESS

Pages 26 and 27 show Pvt. George E. Boston, who was the father of Cindy Boston Peters and Lynn Boston Pettus. Boston was orginally from Lawrenceburg; however, he was living in Florence, Alabama at the time he joined the military. He married Martha Jewell Denson of Lawrenceburg.

Private George Edward Boston in World War II battle uniform.
Photo courtesy of Curtis Peters

Christmas Eve

RANK	NAME	SERVICE	HOME ADDRESS
Sgt.	Jack Fox	Army		134-19 *(illegible)* Ave. Richmond Hill, N.Y.
Cpl.	Al Martin	Army		8123-12 St. Woodhaven, N.Y.
PVT.	WILLIAM H. MATTOX	U.S. ARMY	SIGNAL CORPS	FLORENCE, ALABAMA
Air Corps	Luther Willingham			
	Johnnie Walters			
	George Clayton	Navy		
Ensign	Annie Laura Lawrence	Navy	Nurse Corps	Lawrenceburg, Tenn. R.I.
2nd Lieut	Ellen Crowder	Army	Nurse Corps	Lawrenceburg, Tenn.
1st Sgt.	Frank V. Barton	Army		
Cpl.	Joe Tomalyne	INF.		LORAIN, OHIO
Pfc.	*(illegible)*	Army		
Cpl.	Lester L. McCool	Inf.		4406 Third Ave. Altoona, Pa.
Sgt.	William H. Tyler	I.N.F.		976 Marion Rd. Akron, O.
Cpl.	James M. Smith	Ren. Corps		700 Brownwood Ave. Akron, O.
	(illegible)			New York City, N.Y.
	Chas. *(illegible)*	Army	Corps	Florence, Alabama
	Walter *(illegible)*	Air Corps		New Philadelphia, Ohio
Pvt.	Richard C. Malone	Air Corps		Alliance, Ohio
	Billy *(illegible)*	Air	Corps	Portland, Oregon
	William E. Thorpe	Air	Corps	Spokane, Washington
Pvt.	Jim H. *(illegible)*	Air	Corps	Brownson, Texas
Sarge	*(illegible)* Wright	Air	Corps	*(illegible)*
	Wilmer C. *(illegible)*	Air	Corps	*(illegible)*
Private	John W. Yount	Air Corps		Pittsburgh, Pa.
PRIVATE	Guy C. Glover	ARMY		Camp Rucker, Ala.
PVT.	*(illegible)* Kelly	ARMY		Camp Rucker, Ala.
Cpl.	G.P. Moon	Army		G.P. Forest, Tenn.
PFC	*(illegible)* Cavanaugh	Army		RR #2 Connellsville, Pa.
Pvt.	L.C. Anderson	Army		*(illegible)*, Pa.
Sgt.	Carl De Groat	Army		Rusby, Wyoming
Pvt.	*(illegible)*	Army		Camp Forest, Tenn.
Sgt.	Robt. Crowley	Army		Camp Forest, Tenn.
	George Mitchell		" "	" " "

There were two women (who signed this register) from Lawrenceburg who were in the military—Annie Laura Lawrence and Ellen Crowder. Lawrence lives in Washington, D.C., with her daughter; and Crowder lives in Lawrenceburg (at the time of this publication). Both women were members of the nurse corps: Lawrence was in the navy and Crowder was in the army. In 1947 or 1948, the army air corps became the air force (a separate entity). Crowder was given the option of staying with the army or going with the air force, she chose to go with the air force and stayed with the air force until her retirement. Lawrence and Crowder went to high school together and joined the military at the same time.

Two soldiers standing outside the Service Men's Home.

BILL McCRORY

Capt. William "Bill" McCrory, son of Mr. and Mrs. B. W. McCrory of this city, was killed in action on Iwo Jima in the Pacific theater of war on February 25, 1945. He was a graduate of L.C.H.S., and a star football player there. He also attended State Teachers' College at Murfreesboro. He was 29 years old and had been in service for more than three years. He was overseas 26 months. After graduation, he taught school at Isaac Litton in Nashville. He was also a stellar football player at Teachers' College. He received his basic training at Parris Island, S. C., and his officer's training at Quantico, Va.

Bill always led his men. He did never send his men where he would not go himself. That is, no doubt, the way he died—leading his men. He has two brothers in the service, Ramon, in France, and Lewis, in New Orleans.

William McCrory from Lawrenceburg signed in as private first class from Camp Breckinridge with the 391st Infantry. He later earned the rank of Captain but was killed at Iwo Jima in the Pacific. His brother, Ramon McCrory, was principal of the Lawrence County High School and was later superintendent of Lawrence County schools.

← *Captain Bill McCrory's obituary: He was killed in action on Iwo Jima in the Pacific Theater on February 25, 1945.*

Photos courtesy of Lawrence County Archives and Old Jail Museum, Lawrenceburg

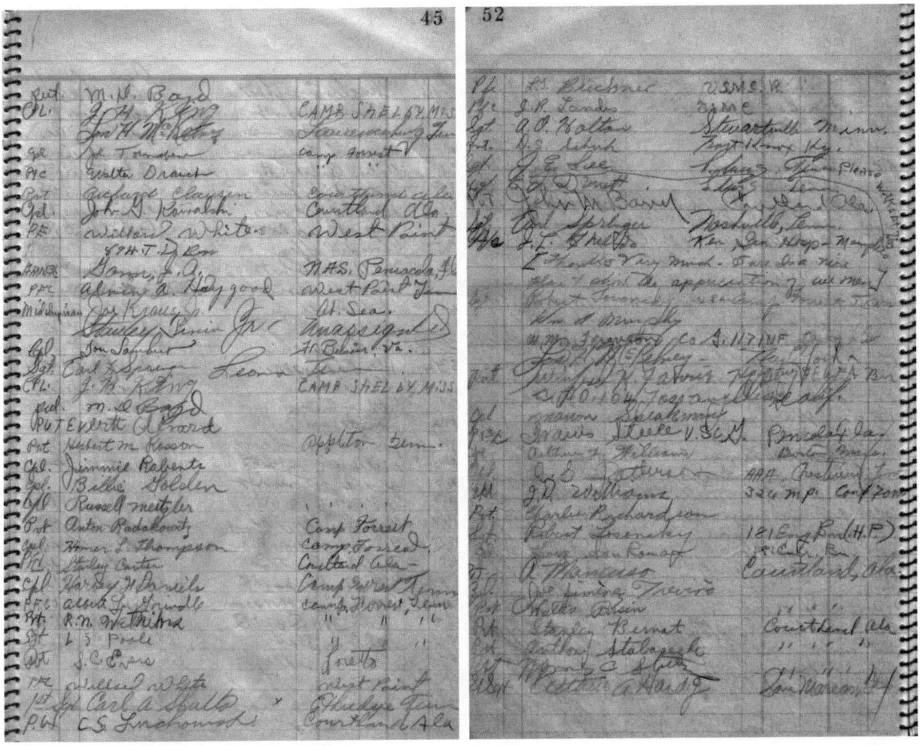

Page 45 (left): Several local communities are represented—Lawrenceburg, West Point, Leoma, Appleton, Loretto, and Ethbridge; also regional military bases—Courtland, Alabama, Camp Shelby, Mississippi, and Camp Forrest, Tennessee. Page 52 (right): Sgt. Arthur A. Hardy.

A few of the soldiers standing on the corner. Notice the old Pure sign in the background.

Page 59 (left): Several POW guards listed as visiting the Service Men's Home. They are (as signed in): Pvt. Curtis Boone, S/Sgt. John Tweedy, Robert E. Solino, Pvt. A. H. Washam, Pvt. Warren B. Spivey, Pvt. Francis Curtin, Cpl. John King, S/Sgt. Arthur Greene, Pfc. R. Izzo, Pvt. Mike Reyes, Pvt. John Turner. Page 60 (right): Ralph T. Kelley, Lawrenceburg POW camp, Miami, Florida.

A soldier sitting on a woodpile.

Page 65 (left): S/Sgt. Arthur A. Hardy. Page 67 (right): Pfc. P. N. Kahn—Lawrenceburg POW camp—New York, New York, Pfc. John J. Cerone—Lawrenceburg POW camp—Chicago, Illinois, and Sgt. Mike A. Carnevale—Lawrenceburg POW camp, New York, New York.

Pfc. John J. Cerone and Sara Sharpe with others at the Service Men's Home.

Page 70 (left): Pvt. Francis Orton—Lawrenceburg POW camp.
Page 71 (right): Sgt. James Tweedy—Lawrenceburg POW
camp, Courtland, Alabama.

A soldier and girl at the Service Men's Home.
Their names are not known.

Page 72 (left) is dated November 30, 1944—Thanksgiving Day. This Thanksgiving Day was on the fifth Thursday although President Roosevelt (FDR) had signed a bill on December 26, 1941, that Thanksgiving would be observed on the fourth Thursday of November. However, for several years some states continued to observe the last Thursday date in the years with five November Thursdays. Page 73 (right): Sgt. Earl F. Springer—Leoma, Tennessee.

Two soldiers and a girl on the street corner.

Page 79 (left): *Visitors, most of whom were women, were local women who probably were on hand as volunteers. There were several pages of these visitors. Page 82 (right) shows Marise Parrish of Mount Pleasant, Tennessee. Marise later married Jack Lightfoot who was a high school coach, principal, and city mayor in Mount Pleasant. An annual award is given in Marise's memory to the one—who like Marise—portrayed the greatest community service effort. Her dad and husband were both military men which probably explains her patriotism of prior years to the USO in Lawrenceburg. She also wrote several books regarding Maury County history and was considered to be one of the great local historians of Maury County.*

Marise Parrish Lightfoot,
Maury County historian.
Photo courtesy of Bob Duncan,
Maury County Archives

The Service Men's Home closed and an auction was held on September 29, 1945, to sell off the contents of the home. The home served its purpose throughout the years of World War II, providing a sanctuary for soldiers passing through the area. The following articles were published in *The Democrat-Union*, a Lawrenceburg newspaper.*

The Democrat-Union
February 13, 1942

War Mothers Make Rapid Headway

Two Recreational Centers Arranged For In New Plan

Lawrence County's "war mothers" make headlines this week in the announcement of plans to establish two recreational centers in this county for men in the service of the United States.

Several weeks ago a small group of Lawrence mothers who had sons in the service met in Lawrenceburg and perfected an organization. Since that time they have worked untiringly toward a goal—a goal of contributing their part in doing whatever they can for the boys in the service.

Today their dream has materialized and now they will not only be able to provide one center, but two headquarters of hospitality.

Arrangements were completed last week with J. H. Stribling for the centers. One will be the Old Ladies' Home on the Christian Home property west of this city, and the other will be located on Groh Street, in Lawrenceburg.

Both centers will be completely equipped with furniture, emergency beds, day-rooms for reading and indoor games, programs, etc. Mr. Stribling told the ladies that electric lights, water, telephone, furnishing—everything—would be provided without cost. (Note: An article that appears at a later date in *The Democrat-Union* states that the Home was furnished by G. A. Dugger rent free, verifying that Stribling's proposal was not accepted.)

Arrangements are also now being made for a recreational center for Lawrence County colored boys in the service.

---

*These articles are reprinted by permission, courtesy of Jim and Marie Crawford and family and *The Democrat-Union*.

The ladies are going right ahead with the work incident to the opening of the centers and their facilities will be available to the boys for seven days a week.

Thus, Lawrence County women say to Uncle Sam: "Here's our part, Uncle—and we're going to do more."

The Democrat-Union
1943
Story Behind Flag at Service Men's Home

Perhaps, if you have been a visitor at the War Mothers Service Men's Home, up on East Gaines Street, you've noticed a large and strikingly beautiful American Flag on the wall.

The Flag is unusual, in its texture, design and accoutrements. It was given to the War Mothers Home by Mrs. Clyde Newby, of this county, who has two sons now in the service of Uncle Sam.

But here's the unusual and the touching part of the story about the flag.

It was draped over the casket of her husband—who fought in World War I.

The Democrat-Union
June 26, 1943
Service Men's Home Widely Mentioned

Splendid Work Is Being Done; All Boys Praise It.

Lawrence County's "Home For Service Men" is gaining popularity all over Middle Tennessee, as one of the most welcome and hospitable centers within a radius of 100 miles.

The Service Men's Home, located on East Gaines Street in Lawrenceburg, was established by the War Mothers Organization, embracing ladies from all over the county, and the center is maintained by them.

It offers recreational facilities, reading rooms, writing desks, comfortable sleeping quarters, and is also careful to liberally distribute small gifts of usable necessities to its soldier-boy guests.

Mrs. Margaret Heffington is regularly on duty at the Home as matron, and is doing a splendidly efficient job in personal supervision.

Reports come to this office that the soldiers, sailors, and Marines who have been entertained here are high in their praise for the fine hospitality that has been extended, and that they will travel miles, just to come to Lawrenceburg.

The effort, which was begun by the War Mothers, with no available funds, and little encouragement on the part of the public, has grown to be one of the most proud possessions of Lawrence County.

The Democrat-Union
War Mothers To Hold
Auction Sale

An auction sale will be held at the Service Men's Home in this city on Saturday, September 29, [1945] at 1:00 o'clock, p.m., it was announced by the War Mothers today. The ladies are disbanding the organization, following the termination of the war. Articles to be offered will include bed springs, mattresses, bed clothes, pillows, linens, chairs, stoves, linoleum rugs, tables, mirrors, large music box, divans, lamps, smoking stands, pictures, dishes, silverware, vases, lawn chairs, curtains, shades, books, and other items.

The proceeds of the sale will go to the American Legion Memorial Fund.

The Democrat-Union
(No Date)

Lawrence County War Mothers Leave Splendid Heritage of Deep Devotion and Infinite Courage

Four years ago a small group of women banded together in Lawrenceburg, and in their minds and hearts there burned an all-consuming purpose.

That purpose was to contribute of their time, money and ability toward bringing happiness, comfort cheer, and moral support to our men in the armed forces.

The group was indeed small, and they "started from scratch," yet an unswerving will and a flaming patriotic loyalty gave them a magnificent courage, and saw the fruition of a noble accomplishment.

These good ladies simply called themselves "the war mothers." They established for the men a home—one with all the comforts of home, and the associations of home. And it was good.

They secured some financial assistance from the USO, the building was furnished by G. A. Dugger, rent free, County of Lawrence contributed $15 a month, the City of Lawrenceburg, $10— and the rest had to depend upon the generosity of those who cared.

The ladies spent more than a thousand dollars on the home building; they furnished it completely, and the net result was that more than 9,000 boys who were away from home were given that which they so generously offered.

Backed by these valiant women, among whom was a five-star mother, Mrs. C. L. Heffington undertook the arduous task of remaining permanently as matron—and this fine lady did a splendid work.

And among all those 9,000 men, every one was given a Bible who did not already have one of his own.

Never in all the four years was it necessary to call an M.P., on account of the slightest disorder. That in itself speaks for the high plane upon which the home was maintained.

Now that the war is over, the work of the ladies is done. They are now disbanding. They can look back with a surge of justifiable pride on the contribution they have made.

We of Lawrence County look to them with a feeling in our hearts that we cannot adequately find words with which to express our pride and appreciation.

God bless you all.

CHAPTER 7

POW Camp at Camp Stribling

WHILE AMERICANS WAGED a war overseas in Europe and the Pacific during World War II, the enemy came to stay right in their backyards. Reactions to the thousands of German and Italian prisoners of war were mixed on the American home front. Some Americans were appalled at the thought of the enemy living not more than a few miles from

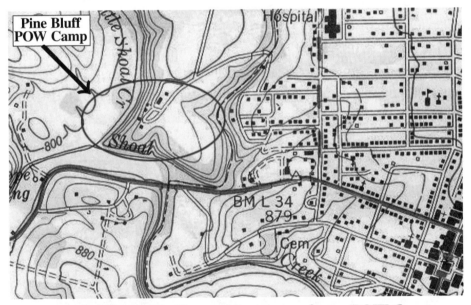

Pine Bluff: TOPO Map of Lawrenceburg POW Camp.
Available data show that this map was created from aerial photographs taken from 1946 and 1949. This map shows the permanent buildings of the POW camp.
Provided by Wallace Palmore

their homes, and they were worried about prison escapees. But others, knowing that the prisoners would help alleviate a severe labor shortage, grudgingly accepted the situation.

Since the war began in 1939, Great Britain had amassed a huge prison population, one that the tiny country could barely handle. By the fall of 1942, the United States finally agreed to help alleviate the situation and authorized the arrival of 50,000 Axis POWs from England. The Office of the Provost Marshall General organized the Prisoner of War Division and began the process of building POW camps throughout the United States.

Using abandoned Civilian Conservation Corps camps built during the Depression offered the best option for the POW camps. Fairgrounds, unused sections of military bases, auditoriums, and even tent cities were also considered. The Civilian Conservation Corps camps were perfect for housing POWs since they were built as barracks near rural work projects, were empty and available, and were located mainly in the American South and Southwest, far removed from the war industries of the Midwest and the Eastern seaboard.

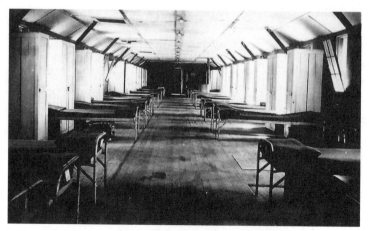

Inside of a POW barrack.
Photo courtesy of Ray Morris, CCC camp alumnus

But many camps were built from the ground up. The Department of War drew up a basic plan for the construction and layout that all camps followed. Built of wood frame construction on concrete piers, the sidewalls and roof were covered with black battened tar paper. Each barrack was designed to hold twenty to twenty-five bunks and was heated with three coal-burning stoves. (Note: One of the buildings used by the guards was converted into a four-apartment complex after the war. The CCC house was also rented.)

Camps usually included a hospital, chapel, and showers with unlimited hot and cold running water, a post office, warehouse, and utility area. Many also included a bakery, library, a recreation area for sports, and a theater for variety shows and theater productions.

Unfortunately, the "luxury" of these accommodations did not escape the attention of the American public. Many locals started calling the camps the "Fritz Ritz." The camps were certainly much better than anything Allied POWs could expect to find.

AFRIKA KORPS BECOMES POWs

By the beginning of 1943, General Erwin Rommel's faith in Germany's ability to win the war was crumbling, as was his estimation of Hitler. Touring Germany, Rommel was appalled at the devastation of the Allied bombing raids and the erosion of the people's morale. He also learned for the first time of the death camps, slave labor, the extermination of the Jews and the other atrocities of the Nazi regime. Rommel became convinced that victory for Germany was a lost cause and that prolonging the war would only lead to his homeland's devastation. He came in contact with members of a growing conspiracy dedicated to ousting Hitler and establishing a separate peace with the Western allies.

In March of 1943, Rommel had flown to Germany to plead with Hitler for reinforcements. Instead Hitler demoted Rommel, replacing him with General Jurgen von Arnim.

One year later, British aircraft attacked Rommel's staff car with machine gunfire, severely wounding the field marshall. He was taken to a hospital and then to his home in Germany to recuperate. Three days later, an assassin's bomb nearly killed Hitler during a strategy meeting at his headquarters in East Prussia. In the gory accusations that followed, some suspects implicated Rommel in the plot.

Although Rommel may not have been aware of the attempt on Hitler's life, his "defeatist" attitude was enough to warrant Hitler's wrath. The problem for Hitler was how to eliminate Germany's most popular general, without revealing to the German people that he had ordered Rommel's death. The story that Hitler told was that Rommel had died as a result of his injuries in the attack on his vehicle.

Rommel was given a choice: to face trial and watch his family suffer alongside him, or to commit suicide. If he chose suicide, his family would not be punished and would be given his pension; and he would be awarded a state funeral. The "suicide plot" was later revealed by Rommel's son who stated that his father had told him that he, Rommel, had only fifteen minutes to bid his family farewell and to put his affairs in order. Rommel was escorted from his home by two of Hitler's comrades where, within a short distance of his home, he was given a cyanide pill and died.

The famous "Afrika Korps," made up of German and Italian tanks and trucks, was surrounded in Tunisia. On May

12, 1943, the Afrika Korps became prisoners of war of the United States and Great Britain. General Jurgen von Arnim, Rommel's replacement, went into captivity as a prisoner of war along with 275,000 German and Italian soldiers. They were housed in tents surrounded by barbed wire. Food, water, and other essentials had to be transported to the German and Italian prisoner-of-war compounds. A shipping shortage plagued the Allies. How could they feed and house the German and Italian prisoners in Africa, while the United States and Great Britain needed all ships to bring troops and equipment from America for the Normandy invasion? After unloading their cargoes in Great Britain, many of these ships returned empty to the United States.

To help alleviate the shipping problems, a decision was made by the U.S. government to bring the German and Italian prisoners of war from North Africa to prisons in the United States. It would be less burdensome and less costly to house and feed the captured men in the United States. Additionally, the prisoners of war (POWs) could be put to work in non-military jobs. A German soldier who fought in North Africa kept a diary from his surrender on May 12, 1943, until his arrival some months later at Camp Clinton, just outside Jackson, Mississippi. He and his fellow veterans of the now-defeated Afrika Korps were marched and trucked to the city of Algiers in Algeria, North Africa, where they were put on ships that carried them to the Algerian port of Oran. They were then marched to a POW compound in the desert where they were housed in a "cage" (the name used by American soldiers for a barbed-wire enclosure). The POWs were trucked from the cage back to Oran on the North African coast. There they boarded ships for the journey across the Atlantic Ocean to the United States. In the last four months of 1943, German and Italian prisoners of war began arriving in the United States from their compounds in North Africa. After two weeks at sea, the ship docked at the Port of Norfolk, Virginia, on August 4, 1943. At Norfolk the prisoners were assigned to camps.

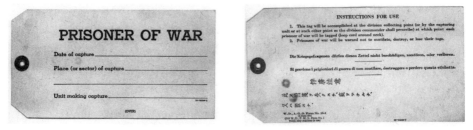

Prisoner of war tags (front and back).
Photos courtesy of Curtis Peters

These base POW camps in the United States had most of the facilities and services that could be found in a small town—dentists, doctors, libraries, movies, educational facilities (English language was the most popular course), and athletics (soccer was the most popular sport). POWs were guaranteed by an international treaty called the Geneva Convention to be provided with food, clothing, and medical care equal to that of their captors.

POWs were housed in barracks that held up to fifty men in the major camps and in heavy duty tents in smaller camps. They had a mess hall with cooks, waiters, silverware, and—by all accounts—very good food. Food was not a complaint for the prisoners. In fact, most of the food was prepared by German cooks with ingredients furnished by the U.S. Army. A sample breakfast was cereal, toast, cornflakes, jam, coffee, milk, and sugar. A typical lunch was roast pork, potato salad, carrots, and ice water. Supper might be meat loaf, scrambled eggs, coffee, milk, and bread. Beer could be bought in the canteen.

POWs were allowed to keep their uniforms for ceremonial

occasions such as funerals and holidays. These uniforms, however, had already seen much wear. For everyday wear, POWs wore black or khaki shirts and pants with the letters "PW" stenciled in paint on each leg. Winter clothes were wool jackets and pants. Athletic shorts and shirts were issued for games.

Notice the "PW" on the knees of the pants.
Photo courtesy of Stribling Estate

Under the Geneva Convention, officers could not be forced to work. However, soldiers could be required to work if the tasks did not aid their captor's war efforts. If the POWs worked outside the compound, they received a payment of eighty cents a day. That was enough money to buy cigarettes and other items that were available in the prison PX. Most chose to work. The kinds of work done by these POWs depended on the region in Tennessee where they were housed.

The POW camps in Tennessee during World War II included:

- Crossville (Camp), Crossville, Cumberland County, Tennessee (base camp).
- Forrest (Camp Nathan B.), Tullahoma, Coffee and Franklin Counties, Tennessee (base camp).
- Forrest (Camp) Hospital (POW General Hospital #2), Tullahoma, Coffee and Franklin Counties, Tennessee.
- Huntsville, Scottville County, Tennessee (branch camp under Forrest, Tennessee).
- Jackson, Madison County, Tennessee (branch camp under Forrest, Tennessee).
- Kennedy General Army Hospital, Memphis, Shelby County, Tennessee (later known as the Kennedy Veterans Administration; was closed in 1967).
- Lawrenceburg, Lawrence County, Tennessee (branch camp under Forrest, Tennessee—Tullahoma).
- McKeller Field, Jackson, Madison County, Tennessee (branch camp under Forrest, Tennessee).
- Memphis ASF Depot, Memphis, Shelby County, Tennessee (base camp).
- P.W. General Hospital #2, Camp Forrest, Coffee and Franklin Counties, Tennessee.
- Pigeon Forge, Sevier County, Tennessee (restricted listing, interrogation center).
- Tellico Plains, Monroe County, Tennessee (branch camp under Forrest, Tennessee).
- Thayer General Hospital, Nashville, Davidson County, Tennessee (branch camp under Forrest, Tennessee).
- Tyson (Camp), Routon, Henry County, Tennessee (base camp).*

---

*Curtis Peters, Historical Collection Summary.

*The following pages show articles from **The Democrat-Union** in Lawrenceburg. These articles were written periodically to give updates from the time it was announced the German POWs were coming to Lawrenceburg until they departed the area.**

The Democrat-Union
March 17, 1944

German War Prisoners
May Be Nearby Guests

This Area May Be "Host" to German Prisoners of War

Officials of the Tennessee Products Corporation and representatives of the War Production Board were in Hohenwald recently endeavoring to work out plans to locate 200 to 300 German prisoners in the county of Lewis to cut chemical wood at Wrigley. The proposed plans for locating the prisoners in Lewis have not been worked out yet and it will be some time before it is known if the project will reach fruition.

The plans are to erect barracks at the site of the work for the prisoners and quarters for officers and guards who will be in charge.

The Democrat-Union
March 24, 1944

German War Prisoners To This County

Going To Make Them Cut Wood For War Effort

According to information released last week at City Hall, a concentration camp of German prisoners will be established at the former CCC camp site at "Pine Bluff," about one-half mile west of this city. It was said that approximately 250 Nazi prisoners of war would be located there.

Barracks will be constructed and an electrified barbed wire barri-

---

*These articles are reprinted by permission, courtesy of Jim and Marie Crawford and family and *The Democrat-Union*.

cade will be built. The men are to work as wood cutters, being transported to Lewis County to cut chemical cordwood for the Wrigley plant.

The establishment of the camp for the 250 prisoners was announced by Raymond Skillern, superintendent of the Tennessee Products Corporation at Rockdale.

No corroboration of the announcement was forthcoming at the Columbia offices of WMC, but surveys have already been made, and it is understood that priorities for necessary materials have been secured.

(*The Democrat-Union* Editor's note: It seems that this changing world has brought about unusual turns. "Pine Bluff" is where we all learned to swim. Now, they're putting Nazis over there.)

The Democrat-Union
March 31, 1944

Prisoners To Be Located At Pine Bluff

Barbed Wire For Fencing, Barracks; Material Moves In.

Barbed wire fencing. prefabricated barracks and incidental material has been moved in by Army trucks for the construction of a prison camp, located just west of the city limits, on the J. H. Stribling property, the former site of the Government CCC camp, commonly known as "Pine Bluff."

It was indicated that from 250 to 400 Nazi prisoners would be located here and that they would be put to work cutting wood for the Wrigley Chemical Plant, the operations to be in the edge of Lewis County.

If this paper is correctly informed, the German prisoners are paid the identical base pay they received while in the service, plus, of course, meals and maintenance.

The City of Lawrenceburg has already made the necessary installations as to electricity, sewerage and other details. Army engineers will have charge of construction of the stockade and barracks.

It was erroneously stated in this paper that the barbed wire enclosure would be electrified. It will not be so connected.

Large trucks have been bringing in equipment for several days. Officers' quarters will be built along with the barracks for the men.

If this paper is permitted to do so, we may be privileged to publish some interesting interviews with the individual prisoners. (But we must brush up on our German.)

The Democrat-Union
April 7, 1944
Nazis To Be Here Soon

Heavy Guard To Be On Woodcutters

Work is rapidly progressing at Pine Bluff, just west of this city, where a Nazi prison camp is being constructed, to barrack, we are told, between 250 and 400 German prisoners of war.

The prisoners will probably be here in two or three weeks.

According to information given this paper, there will be an armed guard for each fourteen prisoners, however this is not official. In that case, however, accommodations for quite a sizeable number of American guards will have to be constructed.

The prisoners, as stated in last week's paper, will be worked as woodcutters, drawing their original German base pay according to grade, whether private, corporal or sergeant. It was not learned up until the first of the week, whether any German officers would be interned here.

The camp is being made into a modern prisoner-of-war stockade, with barbed wire fences, floodlights and machine gun towers. The prisoners will be transported to their work in the edge of Lewis county in trucks.

Preparations for the camp are expected to be completed by April 15th.

The Democrat-Union
April 14,1944
Nazis To Be Here Soon

Prison Camp Will Soon Be Complete

Lawrenceburg's newly acquired Nazi prison camp will be complete within a few days, it was stated Monday of this week by the construction bosses in charge.

Located at "Pine Bluff," just west of this city, it will house between 250 and 400 German prisoners of war.

The prisoners will cut wood for the Tennessee Products Corporation, operators of Rockdale furnace, and for the company's distillation plant in Hickman county. The woodcutting will actually be done in Lewis county.

Under international law, the prisoners will not be directly concerned in war production and will be paid for their work, although the Government stands to make a profit since TPC will pay the Government the full amount usually paid woodcutters in that section, which is considerably above the prisoner-of-war rate of pay.

It is expected that the Nazis will be here by April 15th.

The Democrat-Union
April 21, 1944

Nazis Have Arrived

Prison Camp Setup Is Completed

Between 250 and 400 Nazi prisoners of war are here. They are interned in a stockade at "Pine Bluff" about one-half mile west of this city. The men are to be employed in cutting wood for the chemical pulpwood plant at Wrigley, Tenn. The prisoners arrived Wednesday of this week, and were barracked immediately.

The prison camp is a miniature city with commissary, mess hall, kitchens, sewerage and drainage facilities, and the quarters are apparently as comfortable as a home.

The Democrat-Union
April 28, 1944

German War Prisoners Cutting Wood

250 Men At Local German Camp; Start Work Monday

Two hundred and fifty German prisoners of war have been installed at the newly constructed camp located on Pine Bluff about one-half mile east of Lawrenceburg. Forty-eight American soldiers are here as guards and four more as maintenance men, first aid directors, etc., under, command of Captain Sanland, Commanding officer.

Monday of this week the first contingent of 79 prisoners was set to work cutting cord wood for the Tennessee Products Corporation on land located near Napier and owned by the Christian Home.

Five guards were detailed to watch the men and those who saw them say the men are model prisoners and require but little overseeing by the guards, who allow them unusual privileges while they are at work. The prisoners have their own mess halls inside the barricaded area, their own cooks, and prepare their own food at camp, and their lunches, which they take with them to work.

The contract calls for them to work for six months after the cessation of hostilities.

The Democrat-Union
September 22, 1944

Two Nazis Walk Out

Escapees Still Being Hunted Over State

State, county and local police are cooperating with the FBI and military police in searching for two German prisoners of war who escaped a few days ago, it was said from the Lawrenceburg internment camp.

The two men were missed at final check after the day's work of woodcutting, D. S. Hostetter, head of the F.B.I.'s Memphis office said.

The two Germans, neither whom is believed to speak English, were dressed in prisoner of war fatigue uniforms with the letters, "PW" stamped on their backs.

The escapees were:

➤ Willy Graul, 20, 5 feet, 7 inches tall, 150 pounds, dark brown hair, blue eyes, fair complexion, with a scar on the left side of his chest. (and the little finger of his right hand amputated at the first joint.

➤ Berthold Schmidt, 20, five feet, six inches tall, 126 pounds, brown eyes, black hair, fair complexion, with a scar on the right hand.

The Democrat-Union

September 27, 1944

Two Nazis In "Vacation" Picked Up

Offer No Complaint Upon Capture By Wayne Barber

Two former members of Hitler's army who, as prisoners of war, escaped September 14 from a wood-cutting detail near Hohenwald, were captured early Thursday morning about six miles south of Waynesboro by a Waynesboro barber, Wayne County Sheriff Walter Brewer said.

Dressed in German army uniforms, the two, Willy Graul, 20, and Berthold Schmidt, 20, were caught by Jim Henson, the barber, as they trudged along Highway 13, about 25 miles from the Alabama state line, according to the sheriff.

Didn't Use Possessed Arms

Henson, the sheriff said, questioned the pair and then ordered them to get into his automobile and drove them to Waynesboro. Sheriff Brewer stated that Henson, who was en route from Collinwood to Waynesboro, was armed when he made the capture but the Germans made no attempt to resist.

The capture came while Sheriff Brewer, deputies, posse men and army men blocked the roads in the vicinity. The sheriff said he previously had received a tip that the escapees were in the vicinity. He stated they told him they realized they were trapped and had come out of a wooded area near the highway and headed for Waynesboro with the intention of giving themselves up.

Left Wood Cutting Detail

A widespread search for the two men began after a checkup at the end of the day's work on September 14 disclosed they were missing from the wood cutting detail after it returned to the prisoner of war camp at Lawrenceburg, where they had been confined.

Brewer said yesterday the two men stated they had had nothing to eat since their escape but some roasting ears, peanuts and tomatoes taken from truck patches. One of them speaks English fluently and the other speaks it with difficulty. They slept on river banks and wooded areas during their period of freedom, the sheriff added.

When captured, the Germans had with them maps of Tennessee and Alabama and a quantity of extra clothing, including raincoats and some civilian apparel. Sheriff Brewer said he was called after the capture, placed the prisoners in the Lawrence County jail and later turned them over to military authorities who carried them to the Camp Forrest prisoner of war internment camp.

The Democrat-Union
May 18, 1945

German Prisoner To Wear Repaired Allied Clothing

German prisoners of war in the southeast will, in the future, wear repaired clothing formerly worn by American fighting men in training, so says an order issued today by Major-General Frederick E. Uhl. The move is a part of the clothing reclamation program. The prisoners will be issued Class "X" garments, previously used by U.S. Troops as work clothes or for actual combat training.

The Democrat-Union
July 6, 1945

Rumors Unfounded About Escaped Men

Rumors by the scores have been circulated about the local German prisoner of war camp, located just west of Lawrenceburg. "I heard," were the repeated utterances "that men escaped. In one instance that a prisoner had killed another."

An investigation reveals that in not one single instance have the above rumors been founded.

At one time, a prisoner was lost in the woods. They said he had tried to run away. He hadn't. He was trying to find his way back to camp.

In another instance two men were reported to have bolted. They didn't.

We have the information not from the commanding officer, but from a very reliable source and one that can be depended upon.

What with good food, adequate recreation, comfortable quarters and efficient supervision, it doesn't add up that one of these men would want to run away. Besides that—what have they got to go back to?

The Democrat-Union
July 13, 1945

Local PWs Aid Maury Co. Farmers

There are 331 German prisoners of war now located at the Lawrenceburg camp, according to Maj.-Gen. Edward H. Brooks, Commanding General of the 4th Service Command at Atlanta, and the prisoners are finding numerous useful occupations, both in private contract work, and public work.

According to the *Mt. Pleasant Record* a number of prisoners are being used on Maury County farms, doing farm work as well as working for private corporations requiring labor.

The Democrat-Union
August 24, 1945

No Elections, War Is Over
So What Will Papers Print?

Your newspaper man is perplexedly scratching his cranium and casting about to find something to print which would be of news and interest to his readers.

Since the war is over, the dominating news in this field has dwindled like a snowball under a hot sun—if that could happen.

And, too, since 1945 is not an election year, the ballyhoo of politics will be missing until 1946. Some special election may come up, but according to B. J. Alford, chairman of the election commission, nothing is on the calendar.

The Democrat-Union
October 26, 1945

P.O.W.s Continue Work From Camp

Work of German Prisoners of War, interned at the Lawrence County P.O.W. camp, continues to go regularly forward, despite the fact that the war has been ended for some time. The prisoners are transported early each morning to the woods for cutting and preparing for shipment of timber. They are returned in the afternoon and placed in the stockades for the night.

No statement was made as to a specific date for release or transfer of the prisoners from the Lawrenceburg camp.

The Democrat-Union
November 28, 1945

Prisoners of War
Sent Back to Europe

Thirty Prisoner of War local camps in the seven southeastern states have been closed and twelve more are scheduled for closing in the next three weeks, reducing the PW population by some 21,000 from the peak figure of last June, it was stated today.

In the past 45 days almost 8,000 have been shipped out of the Fourth Service Command as requirements for their labor in harvesting crops have been reduced. The sick and wounded prisoners are being repatriated and, upon their arrival in Germany, will be sent directly to their homes. For the able-bodied prisoners it is simply a change from a prison camp in the United States to a prison camp overseas. Their work is not finished.

No release for publication has been made by the local POW camp as to whether the prisoners here will be moved. At present they have been engaged in pulpwood production.

The Democrat-Union
December 7, 1945

German Boys To Be Taken
To New Camp

Prisoners Of War To Be Taken Over To Camp Forrest.

There will no longer be a Prisoner of War Camp in Lawrenceburg. Disbanding of the camp and removal of prisoners and U.S. property has already been going on, and this probably marks the last wartime touch of a local nature.

It was said that the prisoners are being taken to the big POW camp at Camp Forrest, Tennessee for repatriation or further shipment to the countries from which they originally came. The local project is a part of a general disbanding of camps all over the southeastern area.

During their internment here the German prisoners were engaged chiefly in cutting wood to go into the manufacture of war time chemicals and other needs.

It was also learned that in a large number of instances, when prisoners are returned to Germany, it will not necessarily indicate that they will be released, but will be put to further work to fill in gaps caused by the war in their own country.

During their stay here for the past two or more years, no serious trouble ever occurred at the Lawrenceburg camp.

The Democrat-Union
December 14, 1945

Prisoners of War To Be Kept For Some Time Yet

A report in this paper may have sounded rather premature last week that the local prisoner of war camp was to be disbanded and the German prisoners taken to the larger concentration area at Camp Forrest, near Tullahoma. This information was given to the paper, though not officially.

We have later learned, through unofficial channels, that the date for moving has been prolonged for some time yet, possibly two or three months.

In the meantime it is understood the prisoners will continue to be engaged in cutting wood in Lawrence and adjoining counties.

The Democrat-Union
February 15, 1946

Prisoner of War Truck Burns

A Prisoner of War truck carrying 28 German war prisoners caught fire last Wednesday afternoon at the corner of Pulaski and

Locust Streets. Many civilians gathered at the scene of the blaze and mixed with the prisoners. Many of the prisoners were concealed from the view of the guards but none of them had any thought of escape. Their main desire appeared to be to get back to their quarters and they gratefully piled into a relief truck and were hurried back to their barracks on Pine Bluff.

The Democrat-Union
February 23, 1946
Prisoner of War Returning Profits

Prisoners of war from the camp in Lawrenceburg are returning profits, working under private contract, it was revealed by Hqrs. Fourth Service Command. The profit represents the difference between 80 cents per day each working prisoner receives in canteen coupons and the per day cash wage scale which would have been paid civilian workers for like tasks, it was explained.

PRISONERS OF WAR
AT THE LAWRENCEBURG SITE

The following is a list of known German POWs at the camp (331 total prisoners); the list may contain some prisoners whose last names are unknown or the spelling is questionable, but the author wanted the list to be as comprehensive as possible.

Willi Müller	Johan Ernat
Marlies Kiess	Edward Plathner
Erich Thimmann	Alois Quade
Johannes Hartmann	Otto Hensseler
Helmut Lau	Johann Vaculik
Gottfried M Rest	Tony Wimmer
Gustav Kiess	Franz Leibelt
Ernst Schacke	Alfons Mailhammer

Eugen Hirth (dentist and artist)
Emil Hirth
Johann Mayk
Leopold Klackl
Hans Hirth
Paul Bernert
Heinrich Mayk
Alfons Leeb
Simon Leeb
Rudi Lorenz
Alfons Schwab
Frank Lei
Kurt Lorenz

Herbert Simmchen
Emil (last name not known; camp cook)
Michael Reise
Karl Heinz Uble
Marlies Zwurgirt
Willy Graul—age 20, 5'7", 150 lb.
Escaped 9/22/1944
Captured 9/29/1944
Berthold Schmidt—age 20, 5'6", 126 lb.
Escaped 9/22/1944
Captured 9/29/1944

The POW camp was located on Stribling property and the POWs did work on the property and other properties owned by the Striblings. Being around the young POWs, the Striblings became fond of some of the young men, as was attested to through the correspondence that was kept up for many years after they returned home.

The last night the POWs were in camp (the POWs were being sent back to Europe), some of the POWs slipped out of camp to tell the Brocks good-bye. This shows evidence of the closeness of the Brocks and the POWs who worked on the Stribling farm.

The young men sent letters regarding marriages, children being born, and of needs for their own families. The following pictures tell the story of the impact the Stribling family made on these POWs, who were so far from home without their own families.

Letters from Germany

April	25-47	Letter from			Heinrich
"	27	"	"	"	Helmut
"	"	"	"	"	Erich
May	1	"	"	"	Michael Rew
"	2	"	"	"	Anna Hutter
April	30	"	"	"	Leopold
May	3	Card from Herbert Sunnisen in France
"	6	Letter from		Johom u Hartman
"	10	"	"	Eugen
"	"	"	"	Helmut
"	11	"	"	Gustav
"	13	"	"	Anna
"	14	Package for birthday from Gottfried
"	16	Letter from		Ad Plathner
"	17	"	"	Leopold Klautel
"	26	"	"	Gottfried Rest
"	"	"	"	Heinrich Mayls
"	"	"	"	Erich Thuman
"	"	"	"	Gustav Kiess
"	28	"	"	Anna Hutter
"	"	"	"	Marie Zwingit
"	"	"	"	Marie Kiess
June	3	"	"	Anna Hutter
"	"	"	"	Johanes Hartmann

This sheet, page 140, came out of a railroad ledger that belonged to Mr. Stribling. The beginning date on this page is April 25, 1947. It lists letters and packages received from former POWs. Note that several are listed by first name only . . . perhaps POWs who worked for Mr. Stribling on his farm in Lawrence County, Tennessee.

Photo courtesy of Stribling Estate

POWs working on the Stribling farm. Pictured above (back row, left to right): Abe Potter (Stribling farm worker), Delma Brock, POW, POW, POW, Jim Stribling Brock. (Front row, left to right): Sam Buchanan (Christian Home employee who is holding Lucky the dog), POW, POW, POW Eugen Hirth (dentist and artist).

The POWs eating lunch at the Stribling farm.
Photos courtesy of Stribling Estate

POWs—These six men worked on the Stribling farm.
Notice the pleasant expressions on their faces.

The POWs listening to a band.
The occasion is unknown.
Photos courtesy of Stribling Estate

Another picture of the POWs listening to the band.

POWs working at the Stribling farm.
Photos courtesy of Stribling Estate

Having a little relaxation time—the POWs are wearing original German uniforms and hats.

POWs working at the Stribling farm. Notice "PW" stamped on the back of the pants.
Photos courtesy of Stribling Estate

MILITARY GUARDS AT THE LAWRENCEBURG WORLD WAR II POW CAMP

Known U.S. soldiers at the camp:

Capt. Sanland—camp commander (from newspaper articles)

Capt. Andress—camp commander—Texas (from letters and former guard)

Master Sgt. Henrick—West Virginia

Sgt. Farrar

Sgt. Sias

Ralph T. Kelley (in charge of dispensary)

Edward A. Wernet—Ohio (spoke German; married a local girl)

Lawrenceburg Camp PX built for U.S. soldiers by POWs in 1945. The building was still there in 1956 according to a letter written by Edward Wernet to Ralph Kelley.
Photo courtesy of Juanita Kelley Shiver via Robert Alvin Noack

?* Hill

? Bogie

Lt. Luders (married a local girl)

Robert Alvin Noack—New Jersey (duty clerk at camp and amateur photographer; married a local girl)

J. W. Krick—Leoma, Tennessee (married a local girl)

American guard riding through camp tents.
Photo by Robert Alvin Noack; Photo courtesy of Wallace Palmore

Additional U.S. soldiers at the camp as recorded in the register of the Service Men's Home:

Pvt. Curtis C. Boone

Sgt. James P. Tweedy—Courtland, Alabama

Robert E. Solino (?)

Pvt. A. H. Washam (?)

Pvt. Warren B. Spirlin (?)

Pvt. Francis R. Curtin

Cpl. John King—Butner, North Carolina

Staff Sgt. Arthur Greene—Fort Payne, Alabama

PFC. R. Izzo—Boston, Massachusetts

*Note: ? Denotes that complete names and/or spelling of names may not be accurate.

Pvt. Mike Reyes

Pvt. John Turner

Pvt. Paul N. Kahn

Sgt. Michael A. Carnevale—New York

Pfc. John J. Cerone (later Cpl. rank)—Chicago, Illionis

Pvt. Clarence E. Canell

Jim Taylor

Pvt. E. Orton

Cleo Long

Truman Farris

Ruben L. Thomas—Camp Forest, Tennessee

William Vess—New York (married a local girl)

Captain Andress (left) and Ralph Kelley (right). Posing in front of the Meriwether Lewis Monument near the Natchez Trace in Lewis County.
Photo by Robert Alvin Noack; photo courtesy of Juanita Kelley Shiver

Ralph Kelley working on a jeep.

The Four Heavies*—U.S. Soldiers—Hendrick, Hill, Wernet, and Bogie; POW Camp Lawrenceburg—July of 1944.
Photos courtesy of Juanita Kelley Shiver

---

*"The Heavies" was a term used for some of America's most destructive bomber planes used during World War II. Several of these bombers seemed to bulge in the middle near the cockpit area. It appears these "four heavies" are bulging in the middle as well.

U.S. Master Sergeant W. V. Henrick.
Photo courtesy of Juanita Kelley Shiver

This combined image of two pictures of the camp gives a total view.
Photos by Robert Alvin Noack; photos courtesy of Juanita Kelley Shiver

Ed Wernet (notice cigar).

*Sgt. Farrar, Edward A. Wernet, and Sgt. Sias
inside Camp PX—1945.*
Photos courtesy of Juanita Kelley Shiver

POW (left) and a soldier taking a break.
Photo by Robert Alvin Noack; photo courtesy of Wallace Palmore

Ralph Kelley (right).
Photo courtesy of Juanita Kelley Shiver

A U.S. POW guard gets a letter from home.
Photo by Robert Alvin Noack; photo courtesy of Wallace Palmore

Lawrenceburg POW Camp, 1944. Notice fence and guard tower (left of photo).
Photo courtesy of Juanita Kelley Shiver

More views of the camp—POW living quarters.
Photo courtesy of Juanita Kelley Shiver

This picture was sent by Ed Wernet to Ralph Kelley with a note.
Photo by Robert Alvin Noack; photo courtesy of Ralph Kelley's daughter

Emil (POW) and Edward A. Wernet, camp mess hall, September 1944.
Photo courtesy of Juanita Kelley Shiver

The following four POW Camp guards married local girls:

William Robert Vess, POW camp guard. Vess was from New York and married Inez (not sure of her last name), who worked at the Lawrence County Hospital.
Photo courtesy of Alvie Pickford

Robert Alvin Noack,
duty clerk at POW camp, married
Dorothy Prokesh from Leoma,
Tennessee, on March 24, 1945, in
Lauderdale, Alabama. Edward Wernet
(guard) and Eva Davis (from
Lawrenceburg) were witnesses at the
wedding. Robert had seen Dorothy
sitting on a soda-fountain stool and
had told his buddy, "I'm going to
marry that girl right there." And he did.
Daughter Patricia (Noack) Palmore
was born June 24, 1946, back in
Newark, New Jersey, where Robert
was from.
Amateur photographer
(took pictures around camp); photo
courtesy of Wallace Palmore

Edward Wernet, POW camp guard.
Edward married local Lawrence
County girl, Eva Davis. Ed and Eva
came back to visit relatives in 1956.
Photo by Robert Alvin Noack;
photo courtesy of Wallace Palmore

*POW camp guard, Corporal J. W. Krick, from Leoma, Tennessee,
married Mildred Lurene Augustine in 1946 at the
Tennessee-Alabama state line. Krick was twenty-one years old
and Augustine was seventeen years old. Krick was a POW in
Germany during World War II. He survived horrendous
treatment during his time as a POW, yet his outlook on life has
always been positive. For more of his story see Chapter 12.*

Photo courtesy of Corporal Krick

Post-War Gratitude

LETTERS AND GIFTS

DURING THE TIME that the German prisoners of war were in Lawrenceburg, Tennessee, Jim Stribling and his daughter and son-in-law, Jim and Delma Brock, became close to some of the POWs. Stribling hired some of them to do work on his farm and other properties that he owned. During this time, he and the Brocks heard their stories about families and homes waiting for them in Germany. Although the Striblings and the Brocks were loyal to the World War II cause, they saw these German soldiers as men who were caught in a war that they did not want, much like our own men.

The POWs were grateful to the Striblings and the Brocks for treating them as equals and not as prisoners. Although the prisoners were only in Lawrenceburg about two years, they became lifelong friends with the Striblings and the Brocks. When it was time for the POWs to leave, the six men who had worked so hard for their new American friends, left the camp without permission to say good-bye to their friends.

Over the course of the next thirty years, some of the POWs kept in contact with the Brocks. They sent letters, pictures, wedding announcements, requests for supplies, and general information about their lives. They wanted their friends in the States to know how much they appreciated the kindness shown to them while in captivity.

The figurines below were carved by Eugen Hirth, a former German POW, and given to the Brocks as a "thank you" for all that the Brocks did for him while he was a prisoner of war in Lawrenceburg, Tennessee. Note on the bottom of the metal horse that reads "Prisoner of War—Eugen Hirth." These were carved from marble, wood, and lead. Hirth is also the artist who painted the scene from North Africa (see "The Painting" in Chapter 4).

Eugen Hirth and his family—1972;
68 Mannheim-Almezzhof
Niederfeldstrasse 68—
West Germany.

The following letters are just a small sample of the letters sent to the Brocks from some of the POWs after they returned home to Germany.* The majority of the POWs were returned to Europe early in 1946, but rather than being sent to their own country, they were sent to work in Britain or France until as late as fall of 1948. A third of the 3.5 million German POWs sent to Siberia at the war's end were literally worked to death; those who did return to Germany trickled back as late as 1956. (The war ended in August 1945.)

When they did return home, some found their families and homes gone. Some of the letters asked for shoes, clothing, medical supplies, and other necessities for everyday living, while other letters were filled with joyous occasions such as weddings and birth announcements. Some of the envelopes were addressed simply to "Mr. and Mrs. Brock, Lawrenceburg, Tennessee," and the Brocks received these letters with no other information in the address. Most of these letters were written in German, and the Brocks found someone who spoke German to translate the letters for them.

Most of these letters contain thanks to the Brocks and others, for their generosity in sending care packages to these former prisoners of war. The letters tell of the daily lives of these men and their adjustments to being home. These men had to endure captivity only to return home to houses that were bombed, family members gone, and no jobs in which to support their families. Some of them were unable to get jobs because there were no jobs available.

While reading through the letters (those written in English), we found ourselves immersed in their stories. The men

---

*There were over 250 letters from the POWs that were found after the Brocks had passed away.

became real to us. We hope that you will be as blessed by their writings as we were. All letters and pictures in this chapter were provided by the Stribling estate.

POW QUOTES FROM SOME OF THE LETTERS*
Leopold Klackl—Austria—January 7, 1947

Several times I was asked by visitors—who that was in the picture—but Anni answers before I get the chance, "that is the farmer and his wife from America where father, as a prisoner of war, was so well treated." Yes it was really so—I would not have dreamed when I was put aboard ship in Africa, that fate would bring me to such noble and good people. Many of our comrades in Camp Lawrenceburg envied us, for with you we prisoners had only happy, bright days.

Willi Müller—Germany—September 3, 1948

I think there would be no war and no enemies in the world if the members of the different nations could understand so well as we did. We paid dear for starting and leading the war. I wished everybody could forget the war and the bad things which happened in it and to try to live in peace and respect his neighbor, the whole world would benefit from that.

Alfons Mailhammer—December 14, 1946

The finest time I had at Lawrenceburg was when I worked in the wood command when 10 men worked for Mr. Stribling. Eugen and Erich who were my room-mates worked for you. I often recall the words Mr. Stribling said, "You'd better work a few other months in America and get a direct discharge than be handed over to the French to work for them" which really came true.

---

*Letters submitted by Curtis Peters.

Alfons Schwab—November 25, 1946

At that time we were shipped near New York and crossing over the ocean lasted 9 days when we reached Le Havre. There we had to stay about 8 days and nobody knew what would happen, and we were afraid that the French would overtake us and a new period of captivity would begin. But fortune had good intentions towards us. I was astonished that we were really transported home, and you will imagine the joy when I stood suddenly before my parents.

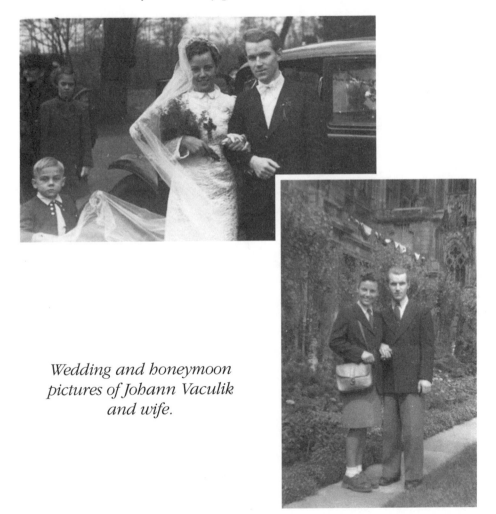

Wedding and honeymoon pictures of Johann Vaculik and wife.

Malsch, 11.April 1948

Liebe Frau Brock !

Heute sende ich Ihnen recht herzliche Grüße und zu
Jhrem Geburtstag herzliche Glückwünsche.Gott möge
Jhnen die vielen Wohltaten die Sie uns erwiesen haben
mit Gottes reichem Segen und guter Gesundheit lohnen.
Jch hoffe,daß das Geschenk rechtzeitig bei Jhnen ein=
trifft.
Liebe Familie Brock, es ist bei uns nun auch wieder
Frühling geworden, die Saat ist schön und die Bäume
blühen, aber wir wollen hoffen ,daß es uns in diesem
Jahr nicht wieder so ergeht wie in den vergangenen
Jahren.Ohne Hilfe von Amerika hätten wir verhungern
müssen.Die größten Sorgen sind uns aber momentan die S
Sorgen vor dem Osten.Sollte das nicht aufgehalten wer=
den dann wollten wir lieber sterben als diesen in die
Hände fallen.Wir müssen beten,daß Gott uns den Frieden
wieder schenkt und wir mit unsern Kinder wieder glück=
lich sein dürfen.Die Freude auf ein Wiedersehen mit
Jhnen ist uns vielleicht noch lange vergönnt,aber wenn
Gott es will wird es schon einmal war werden.
Liebe Familie Brock wir sind jeden tag in Gedanken bei
Jhnen und das erste Wort ist von Eugen wenn er nach
Hause kommt ist Post da von Amerika. Sie glauben nicht
wie Sie uns mit Jhren Briefen glücklich machen.
Nun nochmals recht liebe Grüße und herzliche Glück=
wünsche zu Jhrem Geburtstag.

Jhre
Fr. Hirth

*A letter from Johann Vaculik and his wife, dated April 11, 1948.
The drawing is from Eugen Hirth.*

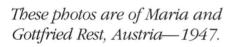

These photos are of Maria and Gottfried Rest, Austria—1947.

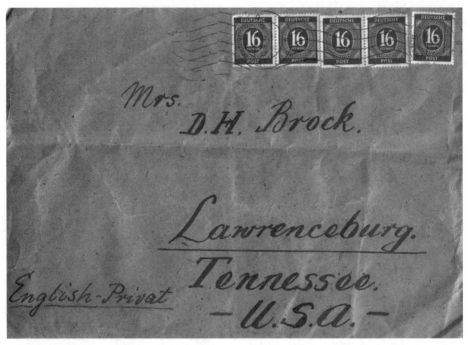

This large envelope was addressed simply as "Mrs. D. H. Brock, Lawrenceburg, Tennessee, USA." This letter was delivered with no more than this address. Most of the letters sent to the Brocks were addressed in the same manner.

Jim Lois Brock enjoyed receiving letters from the former POWs.

11. 19. 1948

Dear Mr. and Mrs. Brock!

all the best to Christmas and New
Year to you and your husband from
your friends in Austria, and we wish
that the comming year bring you both
much luck.

Just a little parcel we send and
hope you enjoy yourself. we canol send
something else, because everything is so
much money and impossible to buy.

Our kindest regards
you freind form Austria
Gottfried and Maria

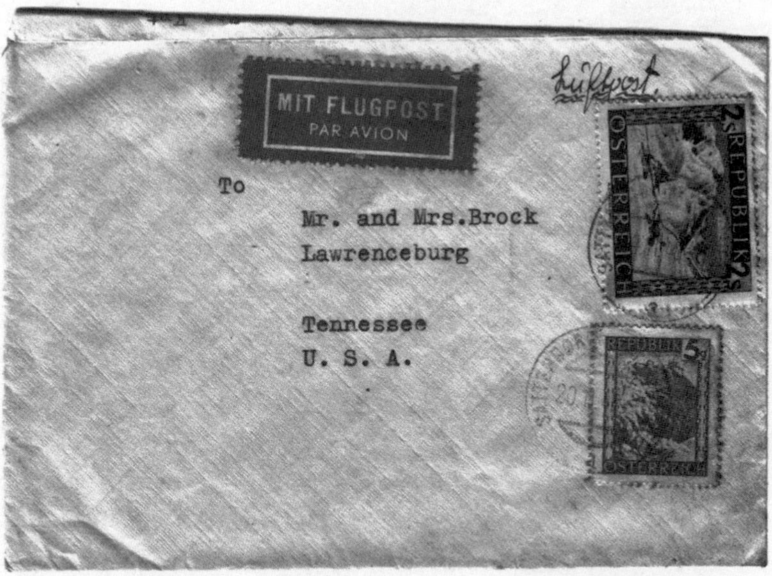

MIT FLUGPOST
PAR AVION

Luftpost

To

Mr. and Mrs. Brock
Lawrenceburg

Tennessee
U. S. A.

A note from Gottfried and Maria Rest wishing the Brocks a Merry Christmas. They also mention a package that they sent to the Brocks.

Johannes Hartmann

This letter, written by Johannes Hartmann and dated January 19, 1947, is filled with pain from losing his wife to another man. Read how she sold everything they had and then he "had nothing of which to take care of his elderly mother."

But life goes on and four years later Johannes Hartmann found a new bride. He sends pictures to the Brocks so they may share in his newfound happiness. Johannes Hartmann's wedding picture, November 17, 1951.

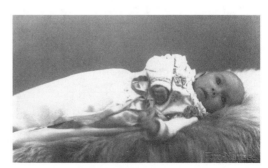

Erich Thimann and his family.

Aschersleben den 18. Juli 1948

Meine Liebe Familie Brock!

Heute am Sonntag komme ich endlich dazu, für Sie einiege Zeilen zu schreiben.
Wie geht es ihnen Frau Brock und Herrn Brock? Mir geht es gesundheitlich
gut. Ich hoffe es auch von Ihnen.
Ihren Brief vom 23. Mai habe ich erhalten. Ich danke aufs herzlichste für
die Liebe Zeilen. Ich hätte ja schon Längst ihren Brief beantworten müßen,
aber ich wollte Sie ja in diesen Brief mit etwas überraschen. Sie werden
es ja sofort gesehen haben. Ich meine das Foto. Erkennen Sie mich noch?
Es hatt einen fehler, Sie werden es bestimmt sofort bemerken die eine
Gesichtshälfte ist zu stark belichtet worden, daher etwas undeutlich.
Aber noch eines wird Ihnen (oft) auffallen, denn es fehlt etwas bei mir.
Sie kennen mich doch ganz anders Frau Brock oder was sagt Herr
Brock dazu? Es ist das immer Lachende Gesicht, ja das fehlt und wo ist
es geblieben, die Zeit, die trariege Zeit hatt es mir gestohlen.
Aber ich werde versuchen nochmal eine aufname machen zu lassen, ich
hoffe, das die schöner wird. Dabei werde ich an Sie meine Liebe Frau und
Herrn Brock denken und an die schone Zeit die ich bei Ihnen in Amerika
gehabt habe.
Sie sind ja nun schon Lange wieder zurückgekehrt nach Lawrenzeburg
ich glaube ja, in wenigen Tagen einen Brief von Ihnen zu erhalten.
An Heinrich u. Gustav hatte ich geschrieben, es hatt sich aber keiner auf meinen
Brief gemeldet. Erhalten Sie noch immer reichlich Post von meine Kameraden?
Schreibt Eugen noch fleizieg? Nun muß ich Ihnen noch eine unangenehme
mitteilung machen.!! Ich bin arbeitslos und so geht es jetzt viele hier,
An an arbeit fehlt es nicht, aber niemand kann zahlen, weil unser Geld <u>entwertet</u>
worden ist.

Letter from Eric Thimann.

Feb. 2, '47

Dear Uncle and Aunt:–

Your dear letter from Fla. with the scenic pictures I received with much joy. It must certainly be pretty there; and I wish you much pleasure and good recovery. Here we have a sure-enough winter. We have had snow for several days. It is reported that it is quite cold in Germany, which is regrettable. It is to be hoped that the cold will not continue a long time. Received a letter from Eugen several days ago, and today a card from Willi Müller. From my parents I have still not had any word. From day to day I hope to get some sign of life from them, but ever in vain. Dear Aunt, that package I received on Feb. 11. – As to health it is well with me, + hope the same for you. There is much talk of going home, + I hope my turn may come sometime soon, for we are tired of this prisoner-life. Many hearty greetings from England sends

Helmut.

FROM.
MITTENTE.
ABSENDER.
NOME.
VOR UND ZUNAME

PRIG. DI GUERRA NO.
GEFANGENENNUMMER

P.o.W. Camp No. 702(202) R.A.F. King's Cliffe
Peterborough, Northants Gt. Britain
Helmut Lau B 224 200

Notice that the letter is addressed to "Uncle and Aunt" and is from Helmut Lau, a former POW in Lawrenceburg. The return address shows he is in a POW camp in Great Britain and he hopes to go home soon. The letter is dated February 2, 1947.

Lieber Onkel und liebe Tante!   d. 4.2.1947

Euren lieben Brief aus Florida mit den Ansichts-
karten habe ich mit vielen Freuden erhalten.
Es muß dort bestimmt sehr schön sein, wünsche
euch nochmals viel vergnügen und gute Genesung
Hier ist jetzt schon richtig Winter geworden,
es liegt schon seit einigen Tagen Schnee, in
Deutschland soll es ja auch ziemlich kalt
sein, was ja sehr bedauerlich ist, hoffentlich
hält die Kälte nicht zu lange an. Von Eugen
bekam ich vor einigen Tagen auch einen Brief,
und von Willi Müller erhielt ich heute eine
Karte. Von meinen Eltern habe ich immer noch

keine Nachricht, man hofft immer von einen Tag
auf den andern mal ein Lebenszeichen von ihnen zu
erhalten, aber immer vergebens. Liebe Tante das
letzte Päckchen habe ich am 2.11. erhalten.
Gesundheitlich geht es mir noch immer gut und
hoffe von euch dasselbe. Es wird ja jetzt wieder
viel gesprochen vom nach hause senden, hoffe
wir doch das die Reihe auch bald mal an
uns kommen wird, denn man ist das Leben in
der Gefangenschaft schon so über. Viele herzliche
Grüße aus England sendet euch Helmut.

This letter from Helmut Lau is written in German (see English version on previous page). The Brocks had a local translator who converted letters to English.

Feb 23.

Received you package day befor christmas & received with pleasure. thanks It arrived at the right time. Cigarettes are very short here. Otherwise things go good with me I am still well and hope you are same. I am now at a different camp, Here we are working in a ware house. It has its advantage because we are sheltered from the weather. In England the weather is always unpleasant. The nice days we can count on our fingers. I am hoping to get home this summer. Several from here have already arrived at home. Maybe it wont be so long and even if things are bad in Germany we would at least be free. I received a card from Willi Müller. Have Gustav & Erich written? From my parents I still have had no word. Maybe I will receive something soon. A comrade whose home is not so far from my home received a few days ago his first message from home.

Greetings Helmut

This letter from Helmut Lau, dated February 23 (no year shown), states that he is still in England and hopes to "get home this summer." He has had no word from his parents. He mentions that he has received a letter from Willi Müller.

Passau, 14 Dec. 1946

MY DEAR BROCK FAMILY:-

I take the liberty of letting you have a few lines from
my home place today. I guess you remember the PW Camp where
I worked for a year. I and my pals were discharged on 21 June;
I arrived at home quite unexpectedly and thank God met all my
dear ones in good health. I hope you, too, are fine which is
the most essential thing. The finest time I had at LAURENZBURG
was when I worked in the wood command when 10 men worked for
Mr. STRIPPLING, EUGEN HIRT and ERICH who were my room-mates
worked for you. I often recall the words Mr. STRIPPING said,
"You'd better work a few other months in America and get a
direct discharge than be handed over to the French to work for
them." Which really came true.

I don't know whether I might trouble you by asking you
for a little favor, but perhaps you might be able to kindly
let me have a few articles for which I'ld be extremely grateful.

Now I finish up my letter. Will you please accept my best
regards.

Very sincerely yours,

Alfons Mailhammer
(Alfons Mailhammer)

an
Familie Brock
Lawrenzeburg
Tennessee
U.S.A.

This letter, dated December 14, 1946, is from Alfons Mailhammer, former POW. He tells the Brocks that he and his buddies were discharged June 21 and that he arrived home unexpectedly. His family is in good health and he is asking for a "few articles." The address is Germany. (Note the censorship strip by the German government along the left side of the envelope.)

This letter, dated April 13, 1947, is from Heinrich Mayk. He is still in a POW camp, but it is not known where. He mentions several of the men with whom he spent time in Lawrenceburg. He also writes that he knows the Brocks receive letters almost daily from Germany. He hopes that "this will all end soon and will be just a bad dream" as Mrs. Brock has said it will be (except for the happy memories of his time spent in Lawrenceburg). He also mentions Lucky, the dog (who is pictured with the POWs in Chapter 7). Lucky had died the previous October. The woman in the picture is Mayk's girlfriend.

May 18, 1947

Dear Family B r o c k !

I should like to send you herewith a few
lines again. In the meantime I have received
your 2 letters for which I am very much obliged
to you. Especially I shall enjoy at the parcels
you have sent and I hope that they will reach
us safely.

And now I must inform you of the latest and
most important news. I am meanwhile married.
I know my present wife for long years already.
During the time of my captivity she has waited
for me, and now we have concluded to meet the
struggle of life side by side. The start is very
hard indeed, because we could purchase the ab-
solutely necessary furniture under the greatest
difficulties only. I am no longer living with
my parents at Klein-Krotzenburg, but I have an
own home in the house of my parents in law at
Hainstadt. I am very content and happy, but the
conditions of life in Germany must turn better,
as it is impossible to live by the love only.
There is no stopping with regard to hunger, but,
as I am still young, I don't give up the hope
for a better future and I am sure that the day
of an amelioration for Germany will come.

Dear Family Brock! You write you will
regularly get mail of all your ancient prisoners
who have become friends to you in the course of
time. From this you may see that nobody has forgotten you and they all like to remember the
beautiful time they spent with you.

My youngest brother, who was in America too,
but had then to stay in France, is now working
in a coal-mine. He is very unhappy and is longing
for returning home, for he is not feeling so well
there as I did with you in America.

Now, I shall finish my letter with the best
wishes for all your family and all your friends.
With kind regards of my beloved wife and my parents
I am

Your thankful
Alfons

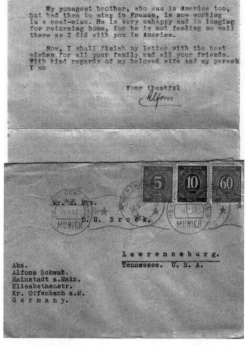

*Letter from Alfons Schwab,
former POW, dated May 18,
1947, informs the Brocks that
he has gotten married to a
girl he has known for a long
time. He also mentions his
brother, who was also in the
army and had been a POW
in America but had to stay
in France. He is working in a coal mine and very unhappy.
Schwab also mentions that his brother is "not feeling so well
there as I did with you in America."*

FROM: Johann VACULÍK, FÜRSTENBERG 44
ABS: über FRANKENBERG/EDER
(16) HESSEN, DEUTSCHLAND
GERMANY.

Former POW Johann Vaculik.

Hildesheim, Germany,
December 13, 1947.

Dear Mr. and Mr. Groh:

I thank you very much for all your assistance in getting a visa. I got your letter contained the papers of immigration from Washington and the letters which were changed intending to assistance me. It was hard to translate all these papers, because there were so many phrases, which I never heard before. But your present, the big dictionary helped me in translating all that properly. Now I know the straight way, and if you send me the documents I need we will progress.

My application was sent to Frankfort after that day I got the newspaper-cutting of the Nashville Tennessee. I sent the cutting with my application and asked for formularies. Before long I got them, and one day later I sent back them, by mail, answering all the many questions and added three free-envelopes — addressed to myself. I was writing to the consulate, that I intend to work for you on the farm and in the forest. — That was right. — You see, that I did, what could be done. Because the consulate office ordered no documents and no letters to send without to be asked for them, so I was waiting for this order. All the records and certificates which are needed, I have in my pocket and there is none of them what could bring me in difficulty. That's all in this matter what I could do.

My health is much better and I hope it will be before long still better. When I have again my old constitution — that will be fine.

I am very sorry for I still did not get the books for Selma and you. I only got the reply to be waiting till January. That is a pity, because I hoped to make a little joy to Christmas for you. So I only can send my heartily wishes for a Merry Christmas. That nice picture of you both with the white horse again will be standing under our Christmas tree and we all like you so very much, that we all wish you could be among us on Christmas.

I would like, when you would say to Mr. Luke, that I also wish him and his family a "Merry Christmas" and when you would pronounce my many thanks for writing that letter to his friend. I don't know whether is the Luke the same who sent some clothes last winter. Therefore I don't write direct to him — because I don't like to make a mistake. Otherwise I can not write now to Mr. Luke about a "Merry Christmas", — if it should be the same family. Can you give my greetings to all of them?

Now I will close this letter and hope you still will get it to Christmas.

Yours friend
Johann Hartmann.

A letter received from one of the former POWs after he returned home. Note the drawing of a foot. The POW was asking Jim Brock to send him a pair of shoes.

THE FIRST NATIONAL BANK

LAWRENCEBURG, TENN.

Dear Howard ― Stribling: the bearer of this boy—

I am a one time war prisoner. the last 9 months I worked for you. I am hoping that you can remember me. you + your honored wife were very good to us + that is the reason I take the liberty to write to you.

I came from America to England + have been free since March 8th. I would like to come back to the states but I don't know how to make arrangements. May be you can tell me how. you can't imagine the bad conditions in Germany. we are all very poor. If you would send me some tobacco I would certainly appreciate it. Heartiest greeting to you + Mrs. Stribling

This letter (originally written in German) was translated to English and written on Mr. Stribling's First National Bank letterhead.

Frohe Weihnacht und ein
glückliches neues Jahr

we wish you a merry Christmas
and a happy new year

*A Christmas card sent to the Brocks
from Henrich Mayk, former POW.*

Willi Mueller
(21b) Dortmund-Marten
Froschlake 18
Germany

                                        9th April 1947.

    Dear Mrs. Brock!

    As promised I will write you a detailed letter. In case that you
did not get my last letter from England I thank you again for the nice
parcel I received from you, that was very kind of you.
Well, now I am about three weeks back in my country. I am still glad
that I am back again and will always be glad. But on the other side
everything is so hopeless. I tried without success to get back to my
old trade (I was employed as clerk before the war) . If I had a kind
of recommandation about my work in America I could try to find employment
with the Military Government (British) May be you can tell me the adress
of Capt. Andress or you could write to him and ask in my name for that,
may be it will help and I hope I don't trouble you too much.
As I wrote you already my home was a little damaged by two bombs but
nobody was hurt.My father is seriously ill and I don't think we will
get him through. Right now I am living with my brother, he was prisoner
of war too but returned one year ago. I lost all my clothes but that
does not matter. The living conditions are really deperately bad but I
am satisfied as long as I am healthy , I never expected to find everything
that bad.
    How are you and your husband, I hope everything is still alright.
I often remember the time I spent over there , it was not so bad after
all we were treated so well. I will never forget you and your husband
may be we will meet again.
Well, Mrs. Brock, that is all for to-day.
With the best wishes for you and your husband I am

                              Yours truly

                              Willi Müller

*Letter from Willi Müller, dated April 9, 1947. Müller lets the
Brocks know that he is home; however, his home was "damaged
by two bombs but nobody was hurt." His father is seriously ill.
Müller has been unable to find work and wants the address for
Captain Andress in hopes that the captain can write a letter
of recommendation for him. Captain Andress was camp
commander at the POW camp in Lawrenceburg.*

Dortmund-Marten September 3, 1948.

Dear Mrs. Brock:

To-day I received your most welcome letter from August 22, I thank you. I am pretty astonished to read that you did not hear from me since June in the meantime I wrote several times to you and I presume that my letters got lost somehow. The last letter I received from you was written In Dallas, Texas and I was always waiting for a letter to tell me that you were back again in Tennessee and since no letter arrived I presumed that anything was wrong. But I am very glad that everything is alright . How come that you can't do as much work as you used to do, don't you feel so well or were you too busy with other things that you could not take care of your farm properly. Can you get enough workers for your farm? I think our boys were real good in farm work though they were not all skilled workers, I had the impression that the they liked the work on your farm and worked as it were their own. I remember that the whole camp wished to work with your detail and they envied the boys who worked with you. I am quite sure that the boys will never forget you and when it comes to speak of the good days spent as Prisoner of War you will be mentioned first. You treated them very good and you did more than you were allowed to do. I think there would be no war and no enemies in the world if the members of the different nations could understand so well as we did. We paid dear for starting and leading the war. I wished everybody could forget the war and the bad things which happened in it and to try to live in peace and respect his neighbour, the whole world would benefit from that . –

My wife is not doing so well. To-day she finished the course of treatment and I wonder whether it will do her any good. I think the heart is the most important thing of the body like a motor and when the motor is not working properly the other parts of the body can't work properly neither. Well, we will hope the best.

I have not heard from the other boys who were with me in Lawrenceburg, I don't know their adresses. We promised each other to write when we said good-bye but since I don't know their adresses I can't keep my promise.

I wonder what our camp looks like by now. I wished I could go to the States for a few weeks and see all the places I have been during my captivity or at least see good old Lawrenceburg again, but I know for sure that it will never happen, it is a pitty. –

This letter from Willi Müller, dated September 3, 1948, speaks of how he would like to come back to the States and see some of the sites he saw while here as a prisoner of war, especially the campsite. He also mentions that

"we paid dear for starting and leading the war. I wished everybody could forget the war and the bad things which happened in it and to try to live in peace and respect his neighbour; the whole world would benefit from that."

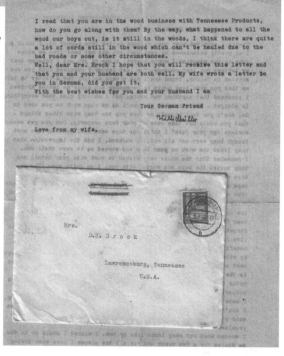

I read that you are in the wood business with Tennessee Products, how do you go along with them? By the way, what happened to all the wood our boys cut, is it still in the woods, I think there are quite a lot of cords still in the wood which can't be hauled due to the bad roads or some other circumstances.

Well, dear Mrs. Brock I hope that you will receive this letter and that you and your husband are both well. My wife wrote a letter to you in German, did you get it.

With the best wishes for you and your husband I am

Your German Friend

Willi Müller

Love from my wife.

Mrs.
D.H. Brock

Lawrenceburg, Tennessee
U.S.A.

CHURCH OF CHRIST
14 Niederräder Landstrasse
Frankfurt a.M., Germany

February 26 , 1948

Dear Brethren:

Because of Post Office regulations most churches have been sending packages in the names of individuals. Consequently we do not know which packages are from churches and which are from individuals, and the task of notifying senders is much more difficult. Many return addresses are not legible and so the reports are not always accurate. For these reasons we are asking you to help us. We are sending you the list of senders in your city from where we have received packages, and are requesting that you see that these people receive our report.

To many of you Jesus will surely say: "I was hungry and you fed me, I was naked and ye clothed me." The noble way in which you have responded to the call when you saw the opportunity to help directly in the name of Christ is evidence that your Christianity is a reality. The hearts of many have been turned heavenward in thanksgiving because of your generosity.

Inclosed you will find a brief summary and explanation of our work here. We feel that you will want to help us to make the work as effective as possible.

Sincerely,
OTIS GATEWOOD
ROY V. PALMER

We have received packages in November, December, and January from the following individuals:
We received one clothing package from you during November 1947.

During December 47 we received three (3) clothing packages from:

J.G.Crews	1 ea
H.W.Mitchell	1 ea
Salem Church	1 ea

During January 48 we received twenty-one (21) clothing pkgs from:

Ray Narris	1 ea
Herman Marrow	1 ea
Mia.Mathis	1 ea
C.L.North	1 ea
J.Dugger	1 ea
Chris Lawrence	1 ea
S.Kelly	1 ea
Pack Rikmar	1 ea
P.F.Zocke	1 ea
Ch.M.Jones	1 ea
M.V.Goollin	1 ea
C.W.Moore Sr.	1 ea

turn over

clothing packages received during January 48 (Cont'd)

Earl Turner	1 ea
Gibson Barber	1ea
R.O.Downey	1 ea
G.A.Dugger	1 ea
Stanley Crews	1 ea
W.A.Moody	1 ea
Edna J.Milly	1 ea
Walter Layton	1 ea
M.L.Watson	1 ea

CHURCH OF CHRIST MISSION
c/o. Lina Lueters
Gutleutstr.77
Frankfurt a.M., Germany

Salem Church of Christ VIA AIR MAIL
Lawrenceburg, Tenn.

This letter, dated February 26, 1948, was written by the Church of Christ in Frankfurt, Germany, to the Salem Church of Christ in Lawrenceburg, thanking many people in Lawrenceburg for the packages sent.

Nov. 26, 1947

Dear Mr. & Mrs. Brock:

I am sending this package to you, which my husband brought back from Germany. I hope you receive it in good condition. Wishing you both very pleasant holidays. I remain —

A friend
Mrs. Anna Weinberger

Plattling, am 23.10.47

Dear Mrs. and Mr. Brock

A little souvenir from German friend

F. Alfons Loos
Plattling
Stäudingerstraße 348½
Niederbayern – Germany

Two notes received.

Passau, August 7, 1947

Dear Brock Family:

To-day I'll try again to send you a few lines. I imagine you've not got my first letter I wrote in December 1946. You'll be sure not to remember my name but the P.O.W.-Camp at Laurenzburg where I stayed for a year. I lived with Eugen Hirth and Erich in a room. I have got several letters from Eugen and I think he has already written you. He is going on learning his profession. But Erich did not write me yet. I often think of the logger-party with Mr. Strissling, where we worked 10 men of us. Then we had the only trouble to see again our native country and our dear families. But now there are still more troubles.

At the end of my letter I should like to ask you for a little favor: maybe you could oblige me by sending me a few cheap articles.

Yours very sincerely,

/ALFONS MAILHAMMER/

An
Familie Brock

Lawrenzeburg

Tennessee USA.

Another letter from Alfons Mailhammer, dated August 7, 1947. He referenced the POW camp at Lawrenceburg where he stayed for a year. He also asks for a "few cheap articles."

Unsee am 21.1.1948

Diesen Brief lege ich auch ein Foto
bei, wo Anni mit der schönen Puppe von
Frau Brock darauf ist. Bei Anni und
auch bei uns vergeht kein Tag, wo nicht
von Familie Brock gesprochen wird,
hoffentlich seid Ihr immer schön gesund,
was zum glücklichen Leben viel bedeutet.
    Bei uns ist der Winter dieses Jahr
sehr mild, Schneefälle und Regen wechseln
sich immer ab, von Lawinen und Über-
schwemmungen kann man jetzt täglich in
der Zeitung lesen, um was es im Sommer
zu trocken war, scheint die Natur jetzt
ausgleichen zu wollen.

    Nochmals vielen Dank für
Euer schönes Foto und die
allerherzlichsten Grüsse von mir
    und Familie, Euer dankschuldiger
                        Leo.
    Viele Grüsse an Mr. Stribling,
Mr. North und Peter.

*This letter, written in German,
is from Leopold Klackl and has
an address from Austria.*

MIL. CEN.-CIVI

MISTER
D.H. BROCK
LAWRENZEBURG
TENNESSEE
U.S.A.

ABS. LEOPOLD KLACKL
UNTERSEE 66
POST: STEEG.
AM HALLSTÄTTERSEE
OBER-ÖSTERREICH
AUSTRIA

A letter from Johannes Hartmann, dated December 3, 1947. His address is shown as Germany.

Hildesheim, Germany
December 3, 1947.

Dear Mr. and Mr. Groek, I got your nice letter written on Nov 23rd, and thank you very much for it. In the near future I intend to make some pictures and will send them to you.

If you can get no address for sending the bedspread, I shall try it on the next, Export-show in Hannover. But that will take a very long time. Our next, Export-show will start in April and finished in May 1948. It is possible Belmor knows the one or the other of the merchants, who intend to do this trip to Germany. Then I could bring your bedspread to the Export-show. At the last, there were many American to visit our show. From Mrs. Knox I got no answer to my letter — we have in Germany proverbs too. One of it says: 'out the eyes — out the sense'. It means the same as yours.

I received a letter from Gustav. Eugen did not answer. Gustav wrote, he feels ashamed for not writing to me, and he promised to visit me on one of the next sundays.

I thank you very much for your words to the matter, horses', and for you are willing to teach me in riding on a horse-back.

I am glad to hear, that your friends in Florida are not injured by the storm. I was in our movie-show, because there was showed pictures of that storm. I saw the hard blows of the storm and the dangerous waters.

I hope the rain stopped now in Tennessee, and you can do, what must be done in your farm-work.

I hope this winter will be not as cold as the last. We are very happy because my brother in law got some fire-wood. That will help us all in the coming winter. We have had still snow here; but it was soon smelted again.

It is raining here, and because I am very tired, I shall close this letter, now.

I and all members of my family send our best wishes and regards to you.
Your friend
Hans Hartmann.

FROM JOHANNES HARTMANN
(20a) HILDESHEIM, HAGEMANNSTR. 9
GERMANY (BRITISH-ZONE)

Dear Family Brock:—

Many thanks for your dear letter of Nov 22. We all have been very happy over the arrival of the little package, especially because it pleased you so much. That plate was not carved by me. As soon as I have time I will carve something for you – but only when I have time! That will be a wonderful moment for us. At present there is so much work. But after the reform [Währungsreform – an unknown word to me, and not in the lexicons] that will all be different. But then it is to be hoped that one can hold his occupation. It is estimated that we have 5 million unemployed. It will be difficult for me also, after that, to find work. Times will get so bad that the present will seem like golden times. When I think back to '30 – 33 a fear comes over me of how much worse it will be this time. There is less room, more people, and this multitude of unemployed – all coming together. It is to be hoped that there will be some sort of solution. — Thanks much for the new address of Erich. I'll write to him

A letter from Eugen Hirth, undated, talks about the new reform coming to Germany that will have conditions worse than they are at the time of this letter. He also thanks them for the address for Erich (Thimann) and he requests the address for Johannes Hartmann. (Hirth is the POW who carved the figurines at the beginning of this chapter and also created the painting shown in Chapter 4.)

this week yet. I have lost the address of Hartman. Kindly inform me what it is.
With best wishes & many cordial greetings
Your
Eugen Hirth

Amerique   U.S.A.

— KRIEGSGEFANGENENPOST —
Correspondance de Prisonniers de guerre

Absender
Expéditeur

Name *Herbert Simmchen*
Nom

Vorname
Prénom

Dienstgrad *Gefr.*
Grade

Erkennungs-N° *889977*
N° Mle

Adresse *Hesdin (P.d.C.)
Section Nord Kdo 1144*

(1) Nichtzutreffendes durchstreichen
Rayer les mentions inutiles

Name *Meister Brok*
Nom

Ort *Lawarenzeburk*
Lieu

Straße   **N°**
Rue

Kreis

Provinz *Tennesee U.S.A*
Province

Zone Französische   Nord — Nord
Française   Süd — Sud
                          Österreich — Autr.
Amerikanische — Américaine
Englische — Anglaise
Russische — Russe

**Dieser Teil ist für den
Kriegsgefangenen reserviert**
Partie réservée au
Prisonnier de guerre

Den *24 Feb 1948*
Le

KORRESPONDENZ
Correspondance

(Leserlich schreiben, nur
auf die Linien schreiben in
lateinischen Buchstaben.)

25 Worte
25 Mots

*Lieber Meister Brok ich arbeitete 1945 bei Ihnen mit
Gustav. Ich bin nun hier in Frankreich im
5ten Jahr Gefangen. Meine Mutter ist schon
vor lauter Kummer über mich gestorben,
es würde mich freuen wenn sie mir ein
paar Zeilen schreiben würden od. ein
Zeugnis über mich nachträglich ausstellen.*

Unterschrift *PW Herbert Simmchen*
Signature

*This postcard (front and back) from POW Herbert Simmchen is
written in German but shows different zones from which this
card could have originated.*

Dear Mr. & Mrs. Boock!   2. May 1948.

First I will send to you hearty Greetings and hope you are always yet in good Health. On April of 31st I got the package which you mailed on March 31st. This time it takes only four weeks. Many thanks I say for all the good things. My mother has been very happy about the lard. It is a ~~~ ~~~ when she is missing one often in her kitchen. We must help us with very little rations. The papers say, that we should get more soon. We hope it is true.

Since yesterday the broadcasting say we can send letters by air mail. In seven or eight days you should get this letter. Much easier it is for our correspondence.

Today a week ago when I go together with my girl for a walk I meet a Lawrenceburg fellow. His name is Karl-Heinz Uble and live on one third together with Eugen and Erich. It is a big fellow, but I doesn't think you remember him. Then we have had to talk about the time in Lawrenceburg. Just a short time before he got letter from Eugen and Erich and we speak about them. He is working near my work place and we should see us more now

a long time we are going the same ways and streets yet in a lucky moment that we see each other. Very often we find things like this in our life. The same luck I wish to meet our you anywhere.

Now I have a other wish to tell you. I need a pair of black shoes for daily, to work. I try to get a coupon since I am here, but I doesn't get any. Not yet for a handkerchief. I always have to answer, see again in a other four week. If you get a pair take size 8½ please. For same sox and a pair of stockings I would say many thanks, too. Always if I write, I speak about wishes. Most I would not like to write, now we get all the things without coupons in Germany, too. We hope it doesn't take more such a long time.

I am really happy you now write by air mail and I hope I to get a answer soon on this letter, for I like to know how long a letter takes to and from America.

Again I wish you all the best and send you many hearty greetings and best wishes from all of us.

                    Your Heinz

cs. Heinrich Mayk - Ha Gelsenkirchen-Horst
    Reichenbergerstr. 2
    Brit-Zone
    Germany

A letter from Henrick Mayk, dated May 2, 1948. He tells of taking a walk with his girl and meeting a "Lawrenceburg fellow" whose name was Karl Heinz Uble. They were both at the Lawrenceburg POW camp. They find that they are working in the same work place and will be able to see each other more often.

Letter and envelope from Johannes Hartmann, dated December 13, 1948. Johannes is thanking Mrs. Brock for sending him an application which he completed and sent to Frankfurt, Germany, along with newspaper clippings from Nashville, Tennessee. He does not clarify the purpose of the application.

Alfons   Schwab
Hainstadt / Main
Elisabethenstr.

Hainstadt, 14th July 1947

Dear Family Brock ,

        I am glad to be able to confirm herewith the receipt of
2 parcels you have sent. I am still missing the advised »Care »
parcel which will surely arrive yet. First of all I should like
to say my best thanks for your kindness. I was much surprised at
the good things which I was in urgent want for. The food parcel
reached us first. I was just en route in the country with a view
to ask for foods at the farmers, but I returned home without success,
for I had not got a piece of bread. Totally discouraged I came back
and found your parcel there. Immediately I was in good humour, as
the greatest distress was overcome. You don't know how often I remember of the time of my captivity for I had always enough to eat
but now I must really hunger. With your first-class flour my wife
could bake the first cake and then the good coffee. That was really
a festival for us, as we have seen these things the last time before
the war.

        The parcel containing the clothes was a heaven's gift. When
I had returned home from the captivity I got a slip for the purchase
of a suit, but it is impossible to get one, as there are no cloths
available. In our region many refugees from the east have been settled
who are much poorer than ourselves, as they had to leave their home
and were expulsed by the Russians and Polards. It is self-evident
that these people must be supported at first and we have to refrain
on their behalf.

        I go daily after my profession, but it is not a pleasure to
work. One earns money and there is no possibility to spend it. In a
new-founded household as mine there are a lot of things to be purchased, but nothing can be bought. Daily I put the question before me
when it will turn better for us. 2 years have passed that the war is
over, but there is not yet peace in the world.

        I will finish my letter for to-day thanking you once more
for all the good things and with my kind regards for you and all
your family, I believe,

                        Your thankful

                            Alfons !

OPENED BY

Mr. & Mrs.

D.H. Brock,

Lawrenceburg.

Tennessee. U.S.A.

Alfons Schwab
Hainstadt a.Main.
Kr. Offenbach a.M.
Elisabethenstr.

OPENED

*A letter and envelope from Alfons Schwab, dated July 14, 1947.
His address is Elisabethenster, Germany. He speaks of the good
times as a prisoner where he had enough to eat but now he must
"go hunger" because they are unable to get food. Mrs. Brock had
sent flour and coffee, so he and his wife had a cake and coffee,
the first since before the war. (Notice the censorship strip along the
left side of the envelope.)*

Untersee July 28, 1947

Dear Mr & Mrs Brock:-

My family & I greet you most heartily & trust
that you are always quite well, as is the case
with us also. On the 24th I received your letter
mailed on the 13th; and on the 25th of this month
came the package which you sent April 30. For
both we thank you most heartily. Anni wants
to thank you personally for the nice candies. My
family & I can use the provisions mighty well,
for living-conditions are getting no better here.
I don't think such good people as the Brock family
are often found, who have such a heart of compassion
for sorely tried fellow-beings. Erich has also written
me such a friendly, chummy letter, which gave
me much pleasure, & he hopes soon to be released. Although he will not (or can not) go back to his old
home, he hopes that some way will open that he
may find a half-way means of existence. I
take it that the boys in England are already on the
way home, & I probably will not write there any more. Surely
Erich will be heard from when he has a definite abode.
To Eugen I'll write later, when his exams are over
& he'll have more time to write. I note from your
letter that Alfons, the "Schwab" [Buchian] got married
& Gottfried is about to do the same. Erich mentioned
in his letter how he had found such good folk in

you, & that often & often he is in his thoughts
with you in Lawrenceburg. I get much pleasure
out of looking at the photos which Mr Brock
had made at that time. I see, dear Mr Brock,
that you intend to make Anni's heart glad with
a pair of shoes for next winter. Anni & the rest of
us thank you for this in advance most heartily.
My wife has a great request – if it were possible
for you to send some wash-goods – soap and
thread. Many greetings from
me & my family
Your grateful
Leo
Many greetings to Mr Stribling & Mr North.

*Letter and envelope from
Leopold Klackl, dated July 28,
1947, from Austria, thanking
Mrs. Brock for her package
which contained candies. He
tells her of the terrible
conditions in Austria. He also
says that his wife would like to
make a great request for "some
wash goods, soap,
and thread."*

LEOPOLD KLACKL
UNTERSEE 66
POST: STEEG
IM HALLSTÄTTERSEE
OBER-ÖSTERREICH
AUSTRIA

MRS. D. H. BROCK
LAWRENCEBURG
TENNESSEE,
U.S.A.

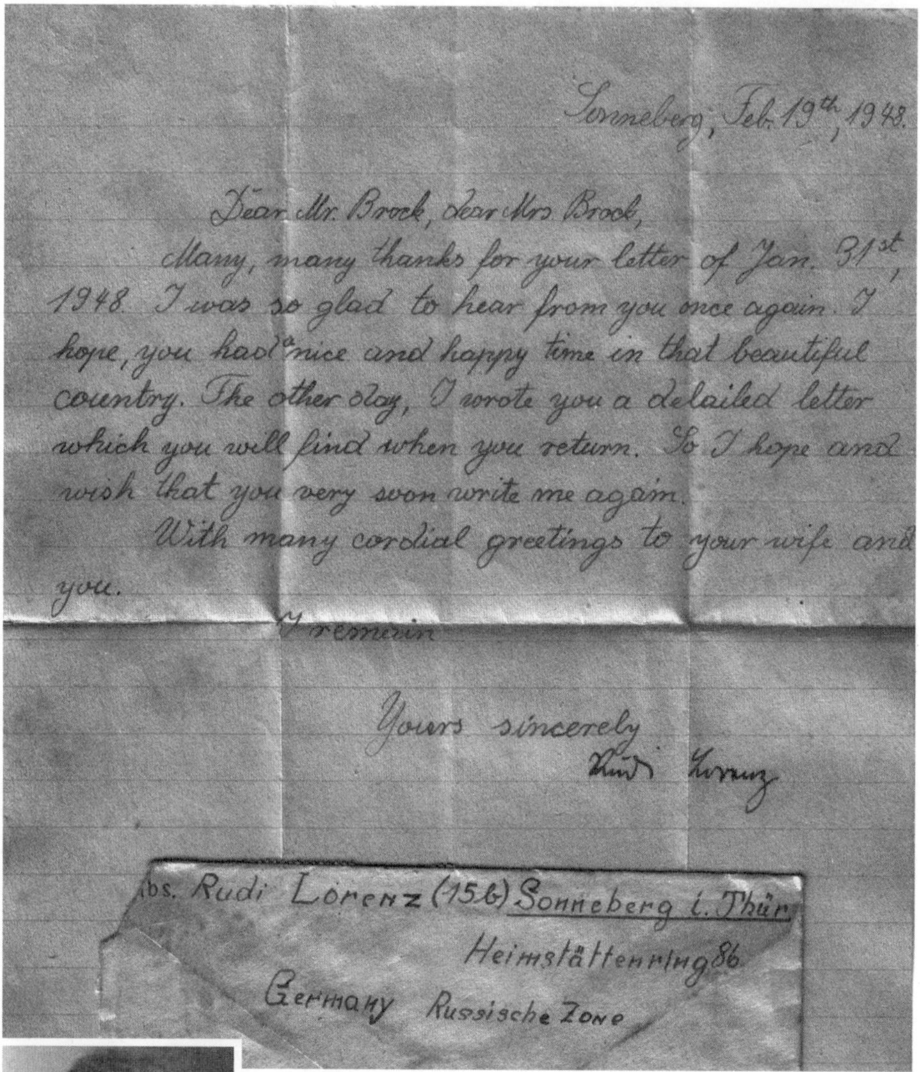

Sonneberg, Feb. 19th, 1948.

Dear Mr. Brock, dear Mrs. Brock,

Many, many thanks for your letter of Jan. 31st, 1948. I was so glad to hear from you once again. I hope, you had nice and happy time in that beautiful country. The other day, I wrote you a detailed letter which you will find when you return. So I hope and wish that you very soon write me again.

With many cordial greetings to your wife and you.

I remain

Yours sincerely
Rudi Lorenz

Abs. Rudi LORENZ (15b) Sonneberg i. Thür.
Heimstättenring 86.
Germany   Russische Zone

Letter from Rudi Lorenz, Germany, dated February 19, 1948, thanking Mrs. Brock for her recent letter.

Untersee Austria
Feb. 27, 1947.

Dear Mr. and Mrs. Brock:

My wife and I send you our heartiest greeting. We hope that you both are well.
We are well with the exception of my little daughter Anna. It is sad but true that
one half of the children in Austria are sick and absent from school be cause of
mal-nutrition.

On Feb. 25th I had notice from "CARE" in Salzburg that I had a package there which
the Salem Church of Christ had been so kind to send to us. The next morning at
6 o'clock I started on my journey which was about fifty miles from my home to get
it. Because of bad traveling conditions I arrived back at Untersee at one O&clock
then had to walk three miles to my home in the country.

As my wife heard me open the door she jumped out of bed and immediately awoke my
little daughter and my elderly father so we could all be together as we opened the
package. This was a very special day for when I arrived home from Salzburg my
wife put on the table two packages from you, Mr. and Mrs. Brock. As I unpacked them
my wife was crying for joy to the extent she was unable to help me. In both of your
boxes there was nice bacon and much good living provisions of which we are in
great need. Immediately I gave Anna a piece op the chocolate candy . It had been
so long since she had had any candy that she hardly remembered how it tasted.

When the packages had been unpacked and everything was spread on the table My
wife offered a prayer for the good people in America who had been so kind to us.

The "CARE" package contained 48 pounds of concentrated food which will be of great
help to us.

We thank and thank and thank both you and the Salem Church of Christ at Lawrence-

*In this letter dated February 27, 1947, the unknown writer talks
about receiving notice that he had a package in Salzburg from
the Salem Church of Christ. Salzburg was fifty miles from his
home in Untersee, Austria. His wife, daughter, and elderly father
came running to help open the box. He thanked Mrs. Brock for
bacon and chocolate. The church had sent forty-eight
pounds of concentrated food.*

CHURCH OF CHRIST MISSION
c/o. Line Lueters
Gutleutstr. 77
Frankfurt a.M., Germany

Salem Church of Christ VIA AIR MAIL
Lawrenceburg, Tenn.

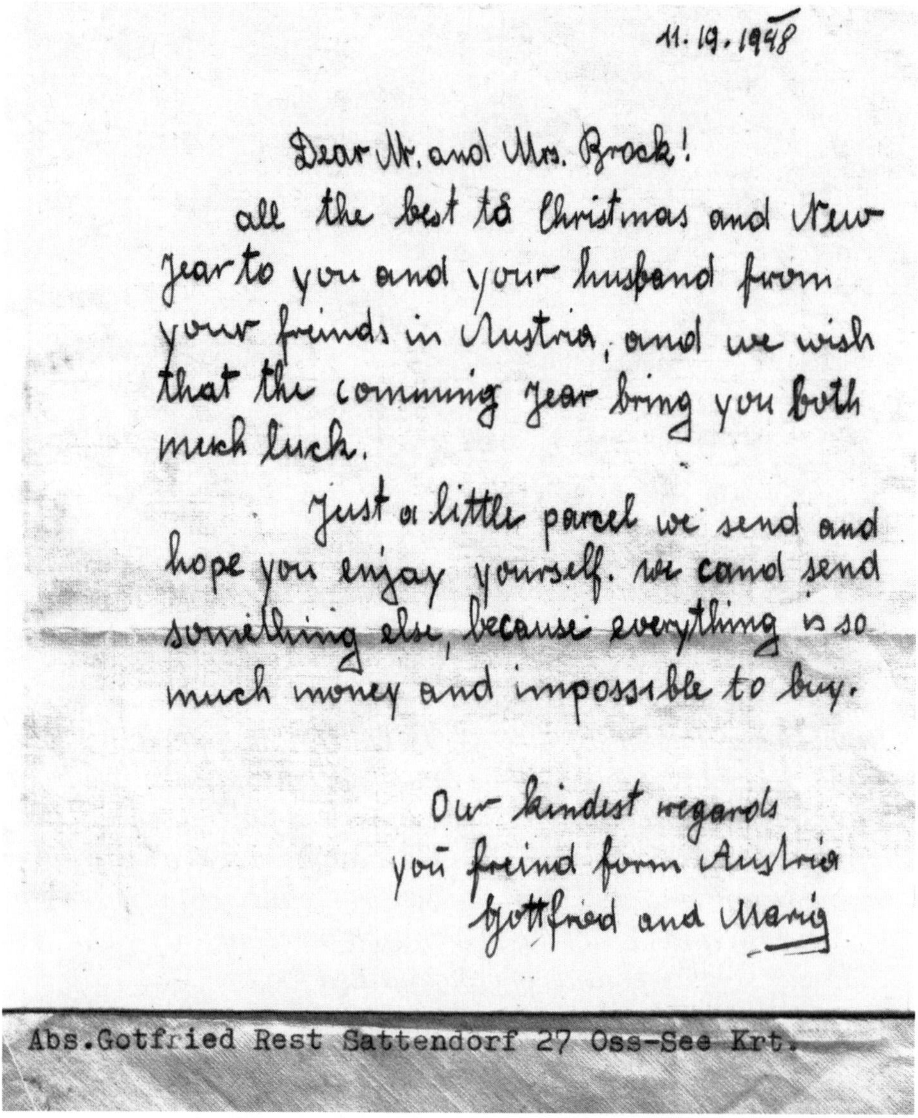

11.19.1948

Dear Mr. and Mrs. Brock!

all the best to Christmas and New Year to you and your husband from your friends in Austria, and we wish that the comming year bring you both much luck.

Just a little parcel we send and hope you enjoy yourself. we cand send something else, because everything is so much money and impossible to buy.

Our kindest regards
you freind form Austria
gottfried and Maria

Abs.Gotfried Rest Sattendorf 27 Oss-See Krt.

Letter from Gottfried and Maria Rest, dated November 19, 1948, wishing the Brocks a Merry Christmas and informing them that they are sending a package to them. Their letter comes from Austria.

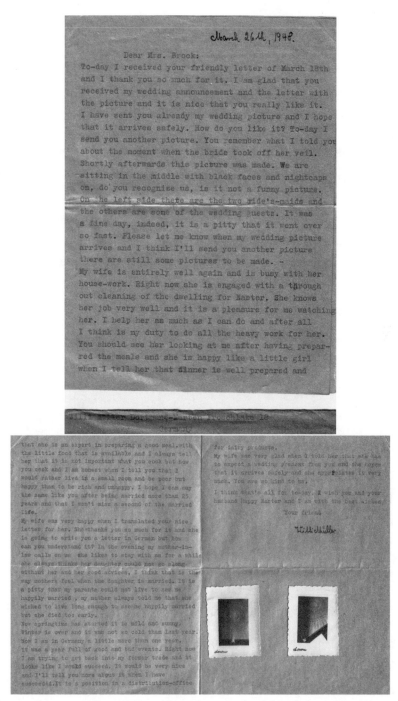

March 26th, 1948.

Dear Mrs. Brook:

To-day I received your friendly letter of March 18th and I thank you so much for it. I am glad that you received my wedding announcement and the letter with the picture and it is nice that you really like it. I have sent you already my wedding picture and I hope that it arrives safely. How do you like it? To-day I send you another picture. You remember what I told you about the moment when the bride took off her veil. Shortly afterwards this picture was made. We are sitting in the middle with black faces and nightcaps on, do' you recognise us, is it not a funny picture. On the left side there are the two bride's-maids and the others are some of the wedding guests. It was a fine day, indeed, it is a pitty that it went over so fast. Please let me know when my wedding picture arrives and I think I'll send you another picture there are still some pictures to be made. -

My wife is entirely well again and is busy with her house-work. Right now she is engaged with a through out cleaning of the dwelling for Easter. She knows her job very well and it is a pleasure for me watching her. I help her as much as I can do and after all I think is my duty to do all the heavy work for her. You should see her looking at me after having prepar- red the meals and she is happy like a little girl when I tell her that dinner is well prepared and

that she is an expert in preparing a good meal with the little food that is available and I always tell her that it is not important what you cook but how you cook and I am honest when I tell you that I would rather live in a small room and be poor but happy than to be rich and unhappy. I hope I can say the same like you after being married more than 25 years and that I won't miss a second of the married life.

My wife was very happy when I translated your nice letter for her. She thanks you so much for it and she is going to write you a letter in German but how can you understand it? In the evening my mother-in- law calls on us she likes to stay with us for a while she always thinks her daughter could not go along without her and her good advices, I think that is the way mothers feel when the daughter is married. It is a pitty that my parents could not live to see me happily married , my mother always told me that she wished to live long enough to see me happily married but she died too early.

Now springtime has started it is mild and sunny. Winter is over and it was not so cold than last year. Now I am in Germany a little more than one year, it was a year full of good and bad events. Right now I am trying to get back into my former trade and it looks like I would succeed. It would be very nice and I'll tell you more about it when I have succeeded. It is a position in a distribution-office

for dairy products.

My wife was very glad when I told her that she has to expect a wedding present from you and she hopes that it arrives safely and she appreciates it very much. You are so kind to us.

I think that's all for to-day. I wish you and your husband happy Easter and I am with the best wishes,

Your friend

Willi Müller

A letter from Willi Müller, dated March 26, 1948. He talks of his wedding day and how happily married he is. He says it is better to be "poor and happy than to be rich and unhappy."

February 15th 1949.

Dear Mrs. Brock:

To-day I am going to drop you a few lines which shall tell you that I am still alright. I hope you got my letter in the meantime I enclosed a letter for Capt. Andress I am anxious to get his answer. How are you and your husband doing, I hope fine. I read in the papers that you have lots of ice and snow over there even in sunny Tennessee? Well, that's all for to-day, the next time you'll get a letter again.

With the best wishes for you and your husband I am

Yours Willi Müller

Willi Müller

(Vor- und Zuname)

(21 b) Dortmund-Marten
Froschlake 18
Germany

Straße, Hausnummer, Gebäudeteil, Stockwerk oder Postschließfachnummer;
bei Untermietern auch Name des Vermieters

Postkarte
Carte postale

DORTMUND-KIRCHLINDE
16.2.49 - 18
b

Mrs.
Delmar H. Brock

Lawrenceburg, Tennessee

U.S.A.

*A postcard from Willi Müller, dated February 15, 1949, saying
that he had sent a letter for Captain Andress, a guard
at the POW camp.*

CHAPTER 9

The War—Its Toll and Effects

HOME FRONTS OF THE WORLD DURING WORLD WAR II

THE HOME FRONT* covers the activities of the civilians in a nation at war. World War II was a total war; homeland production became even more invaluable to both the Allied and Axis powers. Life on the home front during World War II was a significant part of the war effort for all participants and had a major impact on the outcome of the war. Governments became involved with new issues such as rationing, manpower allocation, home defense, evacuation in the face of air raids, and response to a takeover by an enemy power. The morale and psychology of the people responded to leadership and propaganda. Typically women were mobilized to an unprecedented degree, yielding great success to the economic output in supporting combat operations.

OVERVIEW

The major powers devoted 50 to 61 percent of their total gross domestic product (GDP) to war-related productions. The Allies produced about three times as much in artillery as the

---

*This entire chapter is based on information gathered from multiple contributors to Wikipedia "American Home Front," Public Domain.

Axis powers. From 1939 to 1944, the United States did a combined $106.3 billion in war production efforts compared to $41.5 billion for Britain and $56.6 billion for Russia. The Axis powers, Germany and Japan, in turn had $53.4 billion and $16.9 billion respectively (figures based on 1944 U.S. artillery prices).

ALLIES

The Allies called themselves the "United Nations" (even before that organization formed in 1945), and pledged their support to the Atlantic Charter of 1941. The Charter stated the ideal goals of the war: No territorial enhancement of power, status, or wealth; no territorial changes made against the wishes of the people; restoration of self-government to those deprived of it; free access to raw materials; reduction of trade restrictions; worldwide cooperation to secure better economic and social conditions for all; freedom from fear and want; freedom of the seas; and abandonment of the use of force, as well as the disarming of the aggressive nations.

China

China suffered the second highest number of casualties of the entire war. Civilians in the occupied territories had to endure many large-scale massacres, including the Nanking Massacre. In a few areas, Japanese forces also unleashed newly developed biological weapons on Chinese civilians, leading to estimated casualties from two hundred thousand to over one million dead. Tens of thousands are thought to have died when Chinese Nationalist troops broke the levees of the Yangtze to stop the Japanese advance after the loss of the Chinese capital, Nanking. Millions more Chinese died because of famine during the war. The city of Chongqing became the most frequently bombed city in history. (The number of Chinese dead is difficult to estimate. The figures range from as low as one hundred thousand to over one million. The range of the atrocities combined with the overall rurality of the people make it difficult.)

Though China received aid from the United States, China did not have sufficient infrastructure to properly arm or even feed its military forces, let alone civilians. Much of the aid was also funneled away through corruption.

France

After the stunningly quick victory in June 1940, France was knocked out of the war and became an informal ally of the Germans. A powerful Resistance movement sprang up, as the Germans fortified the coast against an Allied invasion and occupied the northern half of the country. The Germans captured two million French soldiers and kept them in prisoner-of-war camps inside Germany for the duration of the war, using them as hostages to guarantee French cooperation. The French government, called the Vichy Regime, cooperated closely with the Germans, sending food, machinery, and workers to Germany. Several hundred thousand French men and women were forced to work in German factories, or volunteered to do so, as the French economy itself deteriorated. Nevertheless, there was a strong Resistance movement, with fierce anti-Resistance activities by the Nazis and the French police. Most Jews were rounded up by the Vichy police and handed over to the Germans, who sent them to death camps.

The Germans seized about 20 percent of the French food

production, which caused severe disruption to the household economy of the French people. French farm production was cut in half because of lack of fuel, fertilizer, and workers; even so the Germans seized half the meat, 20 percent of the produce, and 2 percent of the champagne. Supply problems quickly affected French stores which lacked most items. The French government answered by rationing, but German officials set the policies and hunger prevailed. Some people—including German soldiers—benefited from the black market, where food was sold without tickets at very high prices. Farmers diverted meat especially to the black market, which meant less meat for the open market. Counterfeit food tickets were also in circulation. Direct buying from farmers in the countryside and barter for cigarettes became common. These activities were strictly forbidden, however, and carried the risk of confiscation and fines. In the remote country villages, secretive slaughtering of farm animals, vegetable gardens, and the availability of milk products permitted better survival.

Netherlands

The Dutch famine of 1944, known as the "Hongerwinter" ("Hunger winter") was a man-made famine imposed by Germany in the occupied western provinces during the winter of 1944–1945. A German blockade cut off food and fuel shipments from farm areas. A total of 4.5 million people were affected, 18,000 of whom died from hunger despite an elaborate system of emergency soup kitchens.

Poland

The Nazi Hunger Plan was to quickly kill the Jews of Poland and slowly force the Poles to leave by threat of starvation, so that they could be replaced by new German settlers. The Nazis coerced Poles to work in Germany by providing favorable food rations for families who had members working in the Third Reich. The ethnic German population in Poland was given good rations and was allowed to shop for food in special stores. The German occupiers created a harsh and cruel system of food controls, including strong penalties for the ever present black market. There was a sharp increase in the death rate due to general malnutrition, and a decline in birth rates.

On September 1, 1939, Germany invaded Poland, conquering it in three weeks, as the Soviets invaded the eastern areas. During the German occupation, there were two distinct civilian uprisings in Warsaw, one in 1943, the other in 1944. The first took place in a section less than two square miles in area, which the Germans carved out of the city and called "Ghetto Warschau." Into the thus created Ghetto, around which they built high walls, the Germans crowded 550,000 Polish Jews, many from the Polish provinces. At first, people were able to go in and out of the Ghetto, but soon the Ghetto's border became an "iron curtain." Unless on official business, Jews could not leave it, and non-Jews, including Germans, could not enter. Entry points were guarded by German soldiers. Because of extreme conditions and hunger, the death rate in the Ghetto was high. Additionally, in 1942, the Germans moved 400,000 Jews to Treblinka where they were gassed on arrival. When the April 19, 1943, Ghetto Uprising occurred, the population of the Ghetto had dwindled to 60,000 individuals. In the following three weeks, virtually all died as the Germans fought to put down the uprising and systematically destroyed the buildings in the Ghetto.

The Warsaw Uprising by Poles began on August 1, 1944,

when the Polish underground—the "Home Army"—aware that the Soviet Army had reached the eastern bank of the Vistula River, sought to liberate Warsaw much as the French Resistance had liberated Paris a few weeks earlier. Stalin had his own group of Communist leaders for the new Poland and did not want the Home Army or its leaders (based in London) to control Warsaw. So he halted the Soviet offensive and gave the Germans free rein to suppress it. During the ensuing sixty-three days, two hundred fifty thousand Poles of the Home Army surrendered to the Germans. After the Germans forced all the surviving population to leave the city, Hitler ordered that any buildings left standing be dynamited and 98 percent of buildings in Warsaw were destroyed.

Soviet Union

During rapid German advances in the early months of the war, nearly reaching the cities of Moscow and Leningrad, the bulk of Soviet industry that could not be evacuated was either destroyed or lost due to German occupation. Agricultural production was interrupted, with grain harvests left standing, or burned, in the fields. That would later cause hunger similar to that of the early 1930s. (Russians used a "scorched-earth" policy and burned their own fields and crops so as not to leave the Germans any basic supplies.) In one of the greatest feats of war strategies, factories were evacuated on an enormous scale, with 1,523 factories dismantled and shipped eastward along four principal routes to the Caucasus, Central Asian, Ural, and Siberian regions. In general, the tools, dies, and production technology were moved, along with the blueprints and their management, engineering staffs, and skilled labor.

The whole of the Soviet Union became dedicated to the

war effort. The population of the Soviet Union was probably better prepared than any other nation involved in the fighting of World War II, to endure the material hardships of the war. This is primarily because the Soviets were so used to shortages and coping with economic crises in the past, especially during wartime—World War I had brought similar restrictions on food—but still, conditions were severe. World War II was especially devastating to citizens of the USSR because it was fought on Soviet territory and caused massive destruction. In Leningrad, under German siege, over a million people died of starvation and disease. Many factory workers were teenagers, women, and old people. The government implemented rationing in 1941 which applied to bread, flour, cereal, pasta, butter, margarine, vegetable oil, meat, fish, sugar, and confectionary all across the country. The rations remained largely stable in other places during the war.

Despite harsh conditions, the war led to a spike in Soviet nationalism and unity. Soviet propaganda toned down extreme rhetoric of the past as the people now rallied by a belief of protecting their motherland against the evils of German invaders. Foreign minorities thought to be collaborators were forced into exile. Religion, which was previously shunned, became a part of the Communist Party propaganda campaign in the Soviet society in order to mobilize the religious elements. The social composition of Soviet society changed drastically during the war.

The city of Leningrad endured more suffering and hardships than any other city in the Soviet Union during World War II. Hunger, malnutrition, disease, starvation, and even cannibalism became common during the siege of Leningrad from September 1941 to January 1944. Many Soviet citizens lost weight, grew weaker, and became more vulnerable to diseases. If malnutrition persisted for long enough, its effects were irreversible. People's feelings of loyalty disappeared if they got hungry enough, and they would steal from their closest family members to survive.

Citizens of Leningrad managed to survive through a number of methods with varying degrees of success. Since only four hundred thousand Russians were evacuated before the siege began, this left two and a half million in Leningrad, including four hundred thousand children. More managed to escape the city; this was most successful when Lake Lagoda froze over and people could walk over the ice road—or "road of life"—to safety. Those in influential political or social positions used their connections to other elites to leave Leningrad both before and after the siege began. Some factory owners even looted state funds to secure transport out of the city during the first summer of the war. The most risky means of escape, however, was to defect to the enemy and hope to avoid governmental punishment.

Most survival strategies during the siege, though, involved staying within the city and facing the problems through resourcefulness or luck. One way to do this was by securing factory employment because many factories became autonomous and possessed more of the tools of survival during the winter, such as food and heat. Workers got larger rations than regular civilians and factories were likely to have electricity if they produced crucial goods. Factories also served as mutual-support centers and had clinics and other services, like cleaning crews and teams of women who would sew and repair clothes. Factory employees were still driven to desperation on occasion and people resorted to eating glue or horses in factories where food was scarce, but factory employment was the most consistently successful method of survival, and at some food production plants not a single person died.

United States of America

The main contributions of the United States to the Allied war effort included money, industrial output, food, petroleum, technological innovation, and—especially during 1944 to 1945—soldiers. Much of the focus in Washington was maximizing the economic output of the nation. The overall result was a dramatic increase in gross domestic product (GDP), the export of vast quantities of supplies to the Allies and to American forces overseas, the end of unemployment, and a rise in civilian consumption, even as 40 percent of the GDP went to the war effort. This was achieved by tens of millions of workers moving from low-productivity occupations to high-efficiency jobs, improvements in productivity through better technology and management, and the move into the active labor force of students, retired people, housewives, and the unemployed, along with an increase in hours worked. It was exhausting with leisure activities declining sharply. People tolerated the extra work because of patriotism, the pay, and the confidence that it was only "for the duration" and that life would return to normal as soon as the war was won. Most durable goods became unavailable, and meat, clothing, and gasoline were tightly rationed. In industrial areas, housing was in short supply as people doubled up and lived in cramped quarters. Prices and wages were controlled, and Americans saved a high portion of their incomes, which led to renewed growth after the war instead of a return to depression.

Great Britain and the Commonwealth

In mid-1940, the Royal Air Force (RAF) was called on to fight the Battle of Britain, but it had suffered serious losses. It lost 458 aircraft in France and was hard pressed. This loss was more than current production. The government decided to concentrate on only five types of aircraft in order to optimize output. They were Wellingtons, Whitley V's, Blenheims, Hurricanes, and Spitfires. They received extraordinary priority with the supply of materials and equipment being diverted from other aircraft types to acquire the necessary parts, equipment, materials, and manufacturing resources. Labor was moved from other aircraft work to factories engaged on the specified types. Cost was not an object. The delivery of new fighters rose from 256 in April to 467 in September—more than enough to cover the losses—and Fighter Command emerged triumphantly from the Battle of Britain in October with more aircraft than it had possessed at the beginning. Starting in 1941, the U.S. provided war-related artillery through lend-lease programs that totaled $15.5 billion.

Canada

Canada joined the war effort on September 10, 1939. This was a week after Britain joined because of the Statute of Westminster, which meant Canada had to vote before entering a war. With the war going on in Europe and Asia, Canada did not have any major problems in building supplies for the war other than switching factories to make war equipment. Many factories were set up which helped increase the employment rate. More or less out of range of Axis attacks, Canada became one of the largest trainers of pilots for the Allies. Many Canadian men joined the war effort, so with the men overseas and industries pushing to increase production, women took up positions to aid in the war effort.

Shipyards and repair facilities expanded dramatically as over a thousand warships and cargo ships were built, along with thousands of auxiliary vessels, small boats, and other craft.

Since 20 percent of Canada's population was not of British or French origins, their status was of special concern. The main goal was the integration of marginalized European ethnics—as opposed to the First World War policy of internment camps for Ukrainians and Germans. The government watched the ethnics closely for signs of involvement with and loyalty to their homelands. The fears proved groundless. In February 1942, some 21,000 Japanese American Canadians were rounded up and sent to confinement camps that closely resembled the similar camps in the United States because the two governments had agreed in 1941 to coordinate their evacuation policies. Most Japanese Canadians had lived in British Columbia, but in 1945 they were released from detention and allowed to move anywhere in Canada *except* British Columbia—or they could go to Japan. Most went to the Toronto area.

Women took the initiative to recycle and salvage in order to come up with needed supplies. Volunteer organizations led by women also prepared packages for the military overseas or for prisoners of war in Axis countries.

With World War II came the dire need for employees in the workplace. Without women to step in, the economy would have collapsed. By autumn of 1944 the number of women working full-time in Canada's paid labor force was twice what it had been in 1939, and that figure of between 1 million and 1.2 million did not include part-time workers or women working on farms. Women had to take on this intensive labor; and while they did this, they still had to find time to make jams, clothes, and other such acts of patriotism to aid the men overseas.

Australia

The government greatly expanded its powers in order to better direct the war effort, and Australia's industrial and human resources were focused on supporting the Australian and American armed forces. There were a few Japanese attacks, most notably the bombing of Darwin in February 1942. There was widespread fear in 1942 that Australia would be invaded.

Australian women were encouraged to contribute to the war effort by joining one of the female branches of the armed forces or participating in the labor force.

Australia entered the war in 1939 and sent its forces to fight the Germans in the Middle East (where they were successful) and in Singapore (where they were captured by the Japanese in 1942). By 1943, 37 percent of the Australian GDP was directed at the war effort. Total war expenditures came to £2,949 million between 1939 and 1945.

The Curtin Labor Government took over in October 1941, and energized the war effort, with rationing of scarce fuel, clothing, and some food. When Japan entered the war in December 1941, the danger was at hand; and all women and children were evacuated from Darwin and northern Australia. The Commonwealth Government took control of all income taxation in 1942, which gave it extensive new powers and greatly reduced the states' currency exchange rate. Manufacturing grew rapidly, with assembly of high-performance guns and aircraft a specialty. The number of women working in factories rose from 171,000 to 286,000. The arrival of tens of thousands of Americans was greeted with relief, as they could protect Australia where Britain could not. The U.S. sent in $1.1 billion in a lend-lease program, and Australia returned about the same total in services, food, rents, and supplies to the Americans.

India

With the massive demands of manpower for the British Indian Army fighting in European, African, and CBI (China-Burma-India) theatres of war, there was a shortage of able-bodied men for agriculture. The British were also afraid the Bengali Plains might fall into Japanese hands, so cultivation of border areas was prevented, all rice stocks were moved back towards Kolkata, and there was forced harvest of rice for the war effort in Europe. This led to severe food shortages, made worse by poor and dishonest management, thereby yielding food prices that the poor could not afford. The end result culminated in the Bengal Famine of 1943 in which 3 million Indian civilians died.

With the British recruiting Indian soldiers in large numbers as well as the Japanese recruiting Indian soldiers living outside of India into the Indian National Army (INA), a state of civil war existed on the east Indian border with Indians killing Indians.

AXIS COUNTRIES (THE ENEMY)

Germany

Germany had not fully mobilized in 1939, or even in 1941. Not until 1943 under Albert Speer did Germany finally redirect its entire economy and manpower to war production. Nazi policy was not to burden the people on the home front because of the fear of another rebellion of its people that the Nazis truly believe happened to Germany in 1918.

Instead of expanding the economies of the occupied nations, the Nazis seized the portable machinery and railcars, requisitioned most of the industrial output, took large quantities of food (15 percent of French output), and forced the victims to pay for their military occupation.

The Nazis forced 15 million people to work in Germany (including POWs); many died from bad living conditions, mistreatment, malnutrition, and executions. At its peak, the forced laborers comprised 20 percent of the German workforce and were a vital part of the German economic exploitation of conquered territories. They were especially concentrated in war artillery and agriculture. For example, 1.5 million French soldiers were kept in POW camps in Germany as hostages and forced workers; and in 1943, a total of 600,000 French civilians were forced to move to Germany to work in war plants.

Although Germany had about double the population of Britain (80 million versus 40 million), it had to use far more labor to provide food and energy. Britain imported food and employed only a million people (5 percent of labor force) on farms, while Germany used 11 million (27 percent). For Germany to build its twelve synthetic oil plants with a capacity of 3.3 million tons a year, it required 2.4 million tons of structural steel and 7.5 million man-days of labor. Britain imported all its oil from Iraq, Persia (modern-day Iran), and North America. To overcome this problem, Germany employed millions of forced laborers and POWs. By 1944, they had brought in more than 5 million civilian workers and nearly 2 million prisoners of war—a total of 7.13 million foreign workers.

For the first part of the war, there were surprisingly few

restrictions on civilian activities. Most goods were freely available in the early years of the war. Rationing in Germany was introduced in 1939, slightly later than it was in Britain, because Hitler was at first convinced that it would affect public support of the war if a strict rationing program was introduced. The Nazi popularity was, in fact, partially due to the fact that Germany under the Nazis was relatively prosperous; and Hitler did not want to lose popularity or faith. Hitler felt that food and other shortages had been a major factor in destroying civilian morale during World War I which led to defeatism and surrender.

However, when the war began to go poorly against the Germans in Russia, and the Allied bombing effort began to affect domestic production, this changed; and a very severe rationing program had to be introduced. The system gave extra rations for men involved in heavy industry, and extremely low starvation rations for Jews and Poles in the areas occupied by Germany, but not to the Poles inside Germany.

According to a 1997 post by Walter Felscher to the "Memories of the 1940s" electronic mailing list:

> For every person, there were rationing cards for general food-stuffs, meats, fats (such as butter, margarine and oil) and to-bacco products distributed every other month. The cards were printed on strong paper, containing numerous small "Marken" subdivisions printed with their value—for example, from "5 g Butter" to "100 g Butter." Every acquisition of rationed goods required an appropriate "Marken," and if a person wished to eat a certain soup at a restaurant, the waiter would take out a pair of scissors and cut off the required items to make the soup and amounts listed on the menu. In the evenings, shop-owners

would spend an hour at least gluing the collected "Marken" onto large sheets of paper which they then had to hand in to the appropriate authorities.

The amounts available under rationing were sufficient to live, but they clearly did not permit luxuries. Whipped cream became unknown from 1939 until 1948, as well as chocolates, and cakes with rich cremes. Meat could not be eaten every day. Other items were not rationed, but simply became unavailable as they had to be imported from overseas. Coffee in particular was replaced by substitutes made from roasted grains. Vegetables and local fruit were not rationed, but imported citrus fruits and bananas were unavailable. In more rural areas, farmers continued to bring their products to the markets, as large cities depended on long-distance delivery. Many people kept rabbits for their meat when meat became scarce in shops, and it was often a child's job to care for them each day.

Germany had a very large and well-organized nursing service, with three main organizations, one for Catholics, one for Protestants, and the DRK (Red Cross). In 1934 the Nazis set up their own nursing unit, the Brown nurses, and absorbed one of the smaller groups, bringing it up to 40,000 members. It set up kindergartens, hoping to seize control of the minds of the younger Germans, in competition with the other nursing organizations. Civilian psychiatric nurses who were Nazi party members participated in the killings of invalids, although the process was shrouded in euphemisms and denials.

Military nursing was primarily handled by the DRK, which came under partial Nazi control. Frontline medical services were provided by male medics and doctors. Red Cross nurses served widely within the military medical services, staffing the hospitals that were close to the front lines and at risk of bombing attacks. Two dozen were awarded the highly prestigious Iron Cross for heroism under fire. They are among the 470,000 German women who served with the military.

The liberation of Germany in 1945 freed 11 million foreigners, called "displaced persons" (DPs)—chiefly forced laborers and POWs. In addition to POWs, the Germans seized 2.8 million Soviet workers to labor in factories in Germany. Returning them home was a high priority for the Allies. However, in the case of Russians and Ukrainians, returning often meant suspicion, or prison, or death. The UNRRA, Red Cross, and military operations provided food, clothing, shelter, and assistance in returning home. In all, 5.2 million were repatriated to the Soviet Union, 1.6 million to Poland, 1.5 million to France, and 900,000 to Italy, along with 300,000 to 400,000 each to Yugoslavia, Czechoslovakia, the Netherlands, Hungary, and Belgium.

In 1944–45, over 2.5 million ethnic Germans fled from Eastern Europe in family groups, desperately hoping to reach Germany before being overtaken by the Russians. Half a million died in the process, with the survivors herded into refugee camps in East and West Germany for years. Meanwhile Moscow encouraged its troops to regard German women as targets for revenge. Russian Marshal Georgi Zhukov called on his troops to, "Remember our brothers and sisters, our mothers and fathers, our wives and children tortured to death by Germans . . . . We shall exact a brutal revenge for everything." Upwards of 2 million women inside Germany were raped in 1945 in a tidal wave of looting, burning, and vengeance.

Japan

The Japanese home front was not well organized, as the government spent more attention on propaganda and not enough on mobilization of manpower, identification of critical choke points, food supplies, logistics, air-raid shelters, and evacuation of civilians from targeted cities. There was only a small increase of 1.4 million women entering the labor force between 1940 and 1944. The minister of welfare announced, "In order to secure its labor force, the enemy is drafting women; but in Japan, out of consideration for the family system, we will not draft them." The failure of maximum utilization of womanpower was indicated by the presence of 600,000 domestic servants in wealthy families in 1944. The government wanted to raise the birthrate, even with 8.2 million men in the armed forces, of whom 3 million were killed. Government incentives help to raise the marriage rate, but the number of births held steady at about 2.2 million per year, with a 10 percent decline in 1944–45, and another 15 percent decline in 1945–46. Strict rationing of milk led to smaller babies. There was little or no long-term impact on the overall demographic profile of Japan.

The government began making evacuation plans in late 1943, and started removing entire schools in 1944. There were 450,000 children moved—along with their teachers, but not their parents. When the American bombing began in earnest in late 1944, 10 million people fled the cities to the safety of the countryside, including two-thirds of the residents of the largest cities and 87 percent of the children. Left behind were the munitions workers and government officials. Civil defense units were transformed into combat units, especially the Peoples Volunteer Combat Corps, enlisting civilian men to age 60 and women to age 40. They were trained with bamboo pikes, since serious weapons were lacking. The media advocated "the Laureates Death of One Hundred Million" to defend the nation. Health conditions became much worse after the surrender in September 1945, with so much housing stock destroyed, and an additional 6.6 million Japanese were repatriated from Manchuria, China, Indochina, Formosa, Korea, Saipan, and the Philippines.

The American aerial bombing of a total of sixty-five Japanese cities took from four hundred thousand to six hundred thousand civilian lives, with over one hundred thousand in Tokyo alone and over two hundred thousand in Hiroshima and Nagasaki, combined. The Battle of Okinawa resulted in 80,000 to 150,000 civilian deaths. In addition, civilian deaths among settlers who died attempting to return to Japan from Manchuria in the winter of 1945 was probably around 100,000. Total Japanese military fatalities between 1937 and 1945 were 2.1 million with most coming in the last year of the war. Many of these were caused by starvation or severe malnutrition in garrisons cut off from supplies.

CHAPTER
10

Pictorial Review

CCC CAMP

THIS PICTORIAL CHAPTER is a compilation of pictures, maps, letters, wartime cookbooks, ration stamps, and a surplus of other items that are too relevant to the era to fail to share as a part of this publication.

Family heirlooms that are too expansive to be included in each individual chapter are recorded here, in addition to a family heritage for relatives and friends who choose this publication to enhance their own genealogical collection. Many of the rarities will never be found apart from this collection!

This chapter also includes pictures of CCC camps, the POW camp, the Stribling family, post-war POW families, relevant Lawrence County industry and buildings, and various related topics of the era.

These pages are rich with both local and national historical memorabilia not generally found in a book such as this. The history buff can find rare visuals, each one with its own story to satisfy the curious.

Those interested in women's rights will find the pictures of Jim Lois Stribling fascinating as she grew from precocious child to savvy businesswoman (see her full story in Chapter 4). Residents and former residents of the Lawrence County area will view the school and bank pictures with both interest and nostalgia.

Bull Session

CCC Cooks

CCC Repair Shop

CCC Truck Drivers

Tool Inspection—TVA Silt Basin, Roger Hays Farm.
(Left to right) Mr. N. B. Dunn, Mr. Gibson, Mr. J. G.
Eggleston.

CCC Tool Inspection

Soil Inspection

Company 448
District C
Lawrenceburg, Tennessee
Photos courtesy of the Old Jail Museum, Lawrenceburg

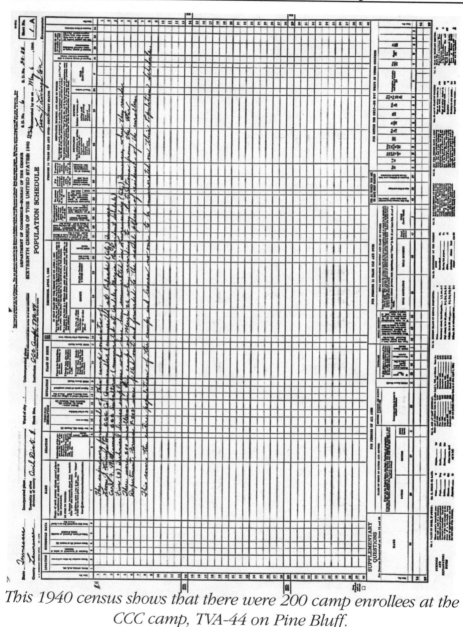

This 1940 census shows that there were 200 camp enrollees at the CCC camp, TVA-44 on Pine Bluff.

Photo courtesy of ancestry.com

The following pictures were provided by Ray Morris, Company 490, District C. He volunteered for the CCC camp in Brownsville (Dyer County), Tennessee. Morris, who turned ninety-one years old in May 2012, was the only living CCC enrollee that we were able to contact for information regarding the CCC program. See Chapter 12 for more information on Morris.

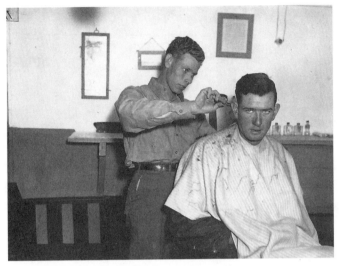

*CCC enrollee getting a haircut
by a barber-in-training.*

*Typical dining area used by the CCC enrollees.
Notice the tables are ready for a meal.*
Photos courtesy of Ray Morris, CCC camp alumnus

CCC enrollee getting medical attention at the nurse's station.

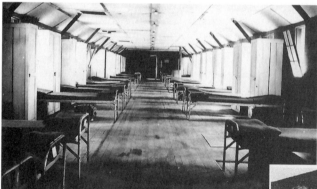

Typical barracks for CCC enrollees.

Ray Morris (right) takes on a good opponent.
Photos courtesy of Ray Morris, CCC camp alumnus

Ray Morris (right with guitar) enjoys some relaxation time with his buddies, Cascade Locks, Oregon, 1941.
Photo courtesy of Ray Morris, CCC camp alumnus

Civilian Conservation Corps honorable discharge papers for Homer D. Kelly, a night watchman, from the CCC 448/TVA-44 camp in Lawrenceburg, Tennessee on March 29, 1941.
Photos courtesy of Old Jail Museum, Lawrenceburg

District C—Company 490
Tenn. SCS-11
Brownsville, Tennessee
Pictorial View
Photo courtesy of Ray Morris, CCC camp alumnus

STRIBLING PICTURES

The Family

Dena L. Cobb Stribling

Mary Gladys Stribling

Jim as a young woman

Jim Lois Stribling

Photos courtesy of Stribling Estate

A tintype of James Henry Stribling (the date is unknown, however, the picture was taken nearly 150 years ago according to calculations).

Mother and daughter, Dena and Jim.

Dena Stribling at West Palm Beach, Florida.

*Envelope addressed to Col. J. L. Stribling (Jim's father).
Return address is J. H. Stribling & Co., Denton, Texas.*
Photo courtesy of Stribling Estate

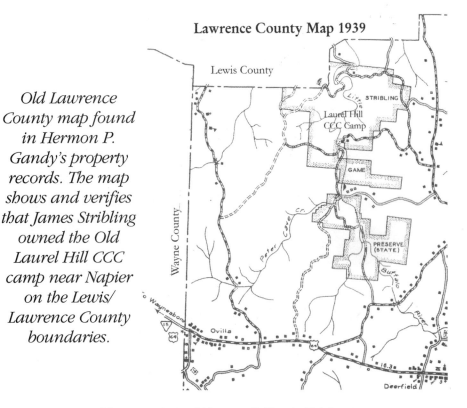

Lawrence County Map 1939

Old Lawrence County map found in Hermon P. Gandy's property records. The map shows and verifies that James Stribling owned the Old Laurel Hill CCC camp near Napier on the Lewis/Lawrence County boundaries.

Photo courtesy of Hermon P. Gandy Estate

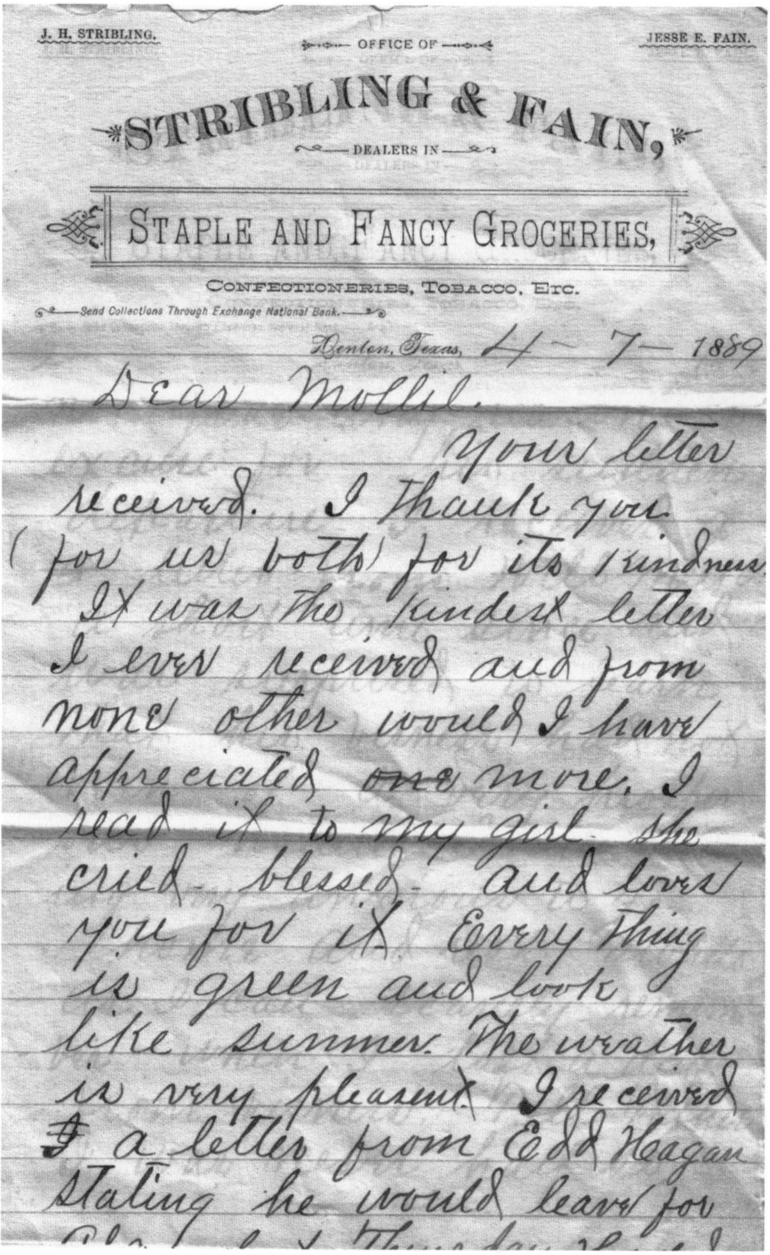

J. H. STRIBLING.

OFFICE OF

JESSE E. FAIN.

STRIBLING & FAIN,

DEALERS IN

STAPLE AND FANCY GROCERIES,

CONFECTIONERIES, TOBACCO, ETC.

Send Collections Through Exchange National Bank.

Denton, Texas, 4 – 7 – 1889

Dear Mollie.

Your letter received. I thank you (for us both) for its kindness It was the kindest letter I ever received and from none other would I have appreciated one more. I read it to my girl. she cried blessed. and loves you for it. Every thing is green and look like summer. The weather is very pleasant. I received a letter from Edd Hagan Stating he would leave for

A letter to Mollie thanking her for her letter earlier.
The letterhead is "Stribling & Fain"
Staple and Fancy Groceries
Denton, Texas
Dated April 7, 1889
Photo courtesy of Stribling Estate

Inside pictures of First National Bank
The calendar on the wall (far right) shows the month
and year as March 1918.

The First National Bank

The First National Bank was established in 1902 on the north side of the public square. It occupied a fine commodious building. It was equipped with every precaution for safety and had a modern fire-proof safe and vault. The first officers were: Judge D. Buchanan, president, James H. Stribling, vice president, James T. Dunn, cashier and J. E. Spence, assistant cashier.

The calendar on the wall (far left) shows
the month and year as January 1906.

Photos courtesy of Stribling Estate

Lawrence County High School, built in 1910 with funds furnished by Mr. and Mrs. J. H. Stribling. There was also a "Stribling Society" within the school. (Note the Stribling banners being held by several students.) The photo is from a 1913 "Sixth Annual Catalogue" for LCHS.

*In the February 1914 edition of the **High School Herald,** there is a call to the Stribling Society. This call states: "Fellow Striblings, 'When you find a noble cause, help it on. If you haven't enthusiasm, get it, and cultivate it because this is essential if you thrive in a Stribling atmosphere. Whether or not we make this the most pleasant and profitable year yet enjoyed rests with us. Then let us all work together and put forth every effort to make every program rendered by the Stribling Society a success.' "*

Officers elected to the Stribling Literary Society, Thursday, January 8, 1914, were: Edgar McGee, president; Mann Howard, vice president; Mergie Sims, secretary; Harold Thomas, chaplain; and Fannie Hurst, editor. Program committee: Lena Lamb, Ada Paris, and Polk LaCroix. Executive committee: Willie Forsythe, Lawrence Springer, and Dodge Old.

Photo courtesy of Old Jail Museum, Lawrenceburg

The old steam tractor is a prominent feature as it was an exciting day for Lawrenceburg to get a new steam tractor (model unknown). The W. E. Gunselman Wagon and Carriage Builder building is in the background. Some of the people listed on the back of the picture are (in no particular order): Charley Bentley, Jim Spence, Jim Stribling, Jim Dunn, Mr. Tobin, Oscar Davidson, George Bell, Marion Richardson, Jim Garrett, Will Massey, Jack Olive, John Gunselman, Mr. Sprouce, Lee Beakman, Abe Luna, and Sam D. Wiggins (date of photo unknown).
Photos courtesy of Old Jail Museum, Lawrenceburg

Richard B. Allen and Col. J. L. Stribling

The Allens and Striblings were close friends. Mary Alexander, granddaughter of Rev. John Hunter—an early minister in the area—was given a watch charm by William B. Allen, as he rode off to the Mexican War. He was killed in battle. Mary later married J. L. Stribling. The charm is still in the Stribling family.
On a professional note: *J. L. Stribling's father, Obidiah T. Stribling, was the first practicing physician in Lawrence County.*

The May Hosiery Mill (top picture taken in 1913) and the lower picture shows an inside view of the mill. Notice the two ladies working and the old steam tractor in the background that was used to operate the pulley system. The May Hosiery Mill closed in the late 1920s to early 1930s. Mr. Stribling bought the building and land in 1935.

Photos courtesy of Old Jail Museum, Lawrenceburg

The Potato House was built by the First National Bank in 1926. The building was designed to hold 70,000 bushels of potatoes.

The Lawrenceburg Square, date unknown. First National Bank is on the left. Perhaps the large crowd is due to a grand opening at the bank.
Photos courtesy of Old Jail Museum, Lawrenceburg

Swift & Company
Produce Plant
800 - 4th Avenue, North
Nashville, Tenn.

July 6, 1929

Mr. J. H. Stribling,
Lawrenceburg, Tenn

Dear Sir:

You will find attached to this letter the
lease properly executed by Swift & Company, which we are
sending to you for your files.

We have also received information from Chicago
that they received a letter which you signed authorizing them
to purchase the material for the building.

With kindest regards,

Yours respectfully,

SWIFT & COMPANY

By *J. P. Lasfey*

FCL:ML

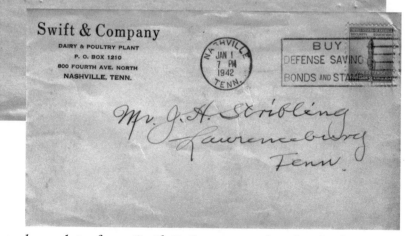

Letter and envelope from Swift & Company, dated July 6, 1929.
Photos courtesy of the Stribling Estate

PO Form C 3700

This Agreement, MADE and entered into this **Fifteenth**　　　day of
June　　　in the year One Thousand Nine Hundred and **Thirty-four**
by and between **J. H. Stribling**
hereinafter designated as Lessor, and **Swift and Company, a corporation,** hereinafter designated as Lessee,

　WITNESSETH: That the Lessor hereby demises and leases to the Lessee, the following
described property, situated in the city of **Lawrenceburg**
County of **Lawrence**　　　and State of **Tennessee**　　　to wit:

　　All that certain parcel of land known and
　　designated as Lots One Hundred Ninety (190),
　　One Hundred Ninety-one (191) and One Hundred
　　and Ninety-two (192)

　TO HAVE AND TO HOLD the said premises with the buildings and improvements thereon
and the appurtenances thereunto belonging for the term of **five (5)**　　　years,
commencing on the **First**　　　day of **September**
One Thousand Nine Hundred and **Thirty-four**　　and ending the **Thirtyfirst**
day of **August**　　　One Thousand Nine Hundred and **Thirtynine**
　AND IN CONSIDERATION thereof the Lessee agrees to pay rent for said premises at the
rate of **Fifteen hundred forty-five**　　Dollars ($**1,545.00**) per annum,
payable in equal monthly installments of **One Hundred Twentyeight**
　- - - - - - - -　　　Dollars **seventy-five - -** cents
($**128.75**　　) each and every month of said term.

*Lease between Mr. Stribling and Swift & Company
signed in 1934 for three lots.*
Photo courtesy of Stribling Estate

Mr. Stribling and ladies (occasion unknown).
Photo courtesy of Stribling Estate

Swift building (unsure of the year of this picture).
Photo courtesy of Lawrence County Archives

A view of the downtown area. First National Bank is on the left and the Gibbs & Belew building is on the right. The date is unknown; however, "1920" is written on the left side of the picture.
Photos courtesy of Old Jail Museum, Lawrenceburg

As the government folded and banks failed during the Depression, those banks having the resources produced scrip money guaranteed by the sovereign bank. Note the signatures of Jim Stribling and Delma Brock on the currency.
Photos courtesy of Curtis Peters

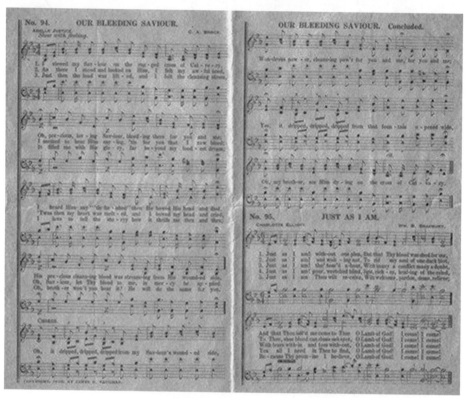

Our Bleeding Saviour
Written by Charles Albert Brock, Delma Brock's father.
Photo courtesy of ancestry.com

The spiritual song by Charles Albert Brock pictured above is a confirmation that singing was a true tradition of the Brock family. It should come as no surprise that Martha Jewell Denson Boston, niece to Delma Brock and great niece to Charles Albert Brock was such a profound hit with her musical talents. She was merely portraying what she had learned.

The following pictures are of ration stamps, books, an ad, even a cookbook, and recipes that were used during World War II. Some of these ration stamps and/or books are from Lawrenceburg, Tennessee, while others are from other states. These pictures were contributed by Curtis Peters.

The Ration Cookbook.
Photo courtesy of Curtis Peters

Recipe for quick breads.

Recipe for cakes and frostings.
Photos courtesy of Curtis Peters

An ad for using ration stamps.

A ration book for Duncan L. Peters, Milford, Ohio.
Photos courtesy of Curtis Peters

War ration book sleeve for Mildred Peters, Madeira, Ohio.

War Ration Book Two, James N. Gardner, Ethridge, Tennessee.
Photos courtesy of Curtis Peters

A ration check.

Front and back of War Ration Book No. 3. Notice the recommendation for recycling tin cans and waste fats on the back cover. The book belonged to Duncan L. Peters, father of Curtis Peters.

Photos courtesy of Curtis Peters

FUEL   FUEL

RATION DEPOSIT SLIP

The UNITED STATES of AMERICA
OFFICE OF PRICE ADMINISTRATION

FUEL OIL CREDITS

DEPOSITED IN

FIRST STATE BANK

F. R. 10   ELKHART, KANS.   83-1165

FOR THE RATION ACCOUNT OF

_____

_____

DATE_____194___

The depositor agrees that this bank will maintain all his ration bank accounts as an agency of and under the direction of the Office of Price Administration and will be responsible only to the Office of Price Administration as provided in General Ration Order No. 3; that the depositor waives all recourse against this bank except for wilful acts or omissions; and that all deposits are accepted subject to count and verification.

ITEMS DEPOSITED	GAL EACH COUPON	QUANTITY OF COUPONS	NO. OF SHEETS	GALLONS		
Coupons ___	1					
Coupons ___	5					
Coupons ___	10					
Coupons ___	25					
Coupons ___	50					
Coupons ___	100					
Coupons ___	250					
Coupons 1 Unit						
Coupons 5 "						
Coupons 25 "						
SUB TOTAL						
1. List separately the amount of each item deposited other than coupons.						
2. Indicate beside each amount the type of item deposited.						
3. The bank number, which appears on the ration check under the bank name to the right, must be written in beside the amount of each ration check deposited.						
TOTAL						

PREPARE IN DUPLICATE AND HAVE BANK STAMP OR INITIAL COPY FOR YOUR RECORDS.

Fuel ration stamp.
Photo courtesy of Curtis Peters

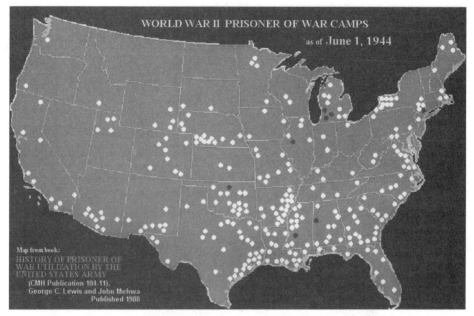

This map indicates the number of POW camps across the United States as of June 1944.

Henrich and sweetheart.

Former POW Henrich Mayk's family.

Helmut Lau's home and address.

Envelope and photo from Marlies Kiess, former POW.

Marlies K i e s s   Hannover, den 7. Mai 1947
                                      Tiefenriede 32

Meine liebe Frau Brock!

Daß Sie mir so schnell auf meinen Brief antworteten, erfreute
mich sehr. Es ist erstaunlich, wie Sie Ihrer "großen Familie"
gerecht werden können. Denn da gibt es doch manche Frage und
manchen Brief zu beantworten. Und daß Sie mich nun auch mit in
Ihrer Familie aufgenommen haben, macht mich recht glücklich.
Da es auch mein Wunsch ist mit Ihnen zu korrespondieren, will
ich auch Sie nicht länger warten lassen. -

Es ist bedauerlich, daß wir uns so schwer verständigen können.
Ich hatte vor einiger Zeit angefangen, englischen Sprachunter-
richt zu nehmen, den ich aber leider vorzeitig abbrechen mußte.
Meine Kenntnisse reichen nun noch nicht aus, Ihre Briefe zu
übersetzen. Aber ich hoffe sehr, daß ich sie doch einmal ver-
vollkommnen kann.

Beruflich bin ich sehr gut untergebracht. Solange ich im Be-
ruf bin, arbeite ich in der gleichen Firma. Es ist eine Mu-
sik-Radio-Elektro- und Fahrrad-Großhandlung. Ich bin dort als
Kontoristin angestellt. Alle Arbeiten, wie Kurzschrift, Schreib-
maschine schreiben, Verkauf usw. habe ich zu verrichten. Es
stellt mich sehr zu frieden, zumal ich ganz selbstständig arbeiten kann. -

Verheiratet bin ich noch nicht, aber ich habe einen sehr net-
ten Freund, den ich bald heiraten werde. Er ist vor 9 Monaten
von England aus der Gefangenschaft entlassen; aber leider kam
er nicht ganz gesund zurück. Noch heute muß er mit seinem Ma-
gen und seiner Leber in ärztlicher Behandlung sein. Seit dem
1. Mai hat er eine gute Stellung als Einkäufer einer größeren
Firma bekommen, die ihm sehr zusagt.

Nun werde ich Ihnen erklären, wie verheiratete Damen mit ih-
rem Namen unterschreiben. Auf jedem Fall ist der Name der

Letter from Marlies Kiess.

Frau durch des Mannes Namen bestimmt. Unterschreibt die
Schwester von Gottfried Rest mit Elisabeth R e s t , so
ist dieses falsch. Warum sie es tut, ist mir allerdings un-
erklärlich.

Ich kann mir vorstellen, daß Sie sich gern der Zeit erinnern
als Gustav bei Ihnen war. Auch bei uns ist es so, daß er immer Leben mit in das Haus bringt.

Seitdem draußen in der Natur alles an zu grünen und blühen
fängt, vergessen wir langsam den letzten grausamen Winter.
Auch erinnert man sich nicht gern an das Schwere, was wir mit-
erlebten, denn es steht doch jeden Tag in anderer Form und
Größe wieder vor einem.

Dafür, daß Sie ein Volk sind, das Sympathie für uns hat, geben
Sie doch gerade das beste Beispiel. Ich finde es rührend, wie
Sie um alle Jungen besorgt sind und mit welcher Mühe Sie alle
umhegen. Auch wir hätten es nie für möglich gehalten, daß man
jemals mit diesen knappen Lebensmitteln auszukommen hat. Ist
es Ihnen überhaupt ein Begriff, wenn einer Person monatlich
140 g Fett zustehen? Fleisch gibt es 600 g! Es ist heute schon
schwer für eine Mutter, alle sattzubekommen. -

Mit diesem Brief erhalten Sie auch zwei kleine Fotos von mir.
Leider sind sie nicht aus letzter Zeit. Unser Fotoapparat ist
schon seit langer Zeit nicht zu benutzen, da wir hier keine
Filme kaufen können. Darf ich Sie vielleicht um die Beschaf-
fung eines Filmes recht herzlich bitten? Er müßte die Größe
der Bilder (6 x 9 cm) haben.

Für heute soll dieser Brief genügen. Wenn wir uns jetzt öf-
ter schreiben, sollen Sie alles von unserer Heimat und unse-
rem Leben erfahren.
Ich grüße Sie, sowie Herrn Brock recht herzlich

                    Ihre

                    Marlies Kiess

German letter from Marlies Kiess (continued). Letters similar to
these were interpreted by a local translator.

*Former German POW
Simon Leeb.*

Simon Leeb family.

Simon Leeb house and stable.

Lounnet 1947.

A collage of pictures of Johannes Hartmann
(bottom picture is the backs of the top pictures).

Krible Family

Author's note: I believe the pictures* in this chapter, as in all other chapters, bring a unique depth to the stories told in these pages. There were so many more photographs and articles that could not be used due to space limitations. I hope you enjoyed viewing these treasures and learning more of the Lawrenceburg/Lawrence County history. Many of these pictures and hundreds more relating to local history can be seen at the Old Jail Museum in Lawrenceburg, Tennessee.

*Photos not otherwise attributed were provided by the Stribling Estate.

The Family Genealogies

JAMES (JIM) LOIS STRIBLING FAMILY BOOK SUMMARY

THE EARLIEST ANCESTOR of Jim Lois Stribling* through ancestry.com (and related public family trees) was **Thomas Stribling,** born in 1630 and probably in England. No spouse was recorded for Thomas, and his only recorded son was **Henry Stribling** who was born in Barnstaple, Devon, England, in 1655. Henry died in 1706 in England.

Henry Stribling was married on December 13, 1680, to Chiratie Seage, the daughter of John Seage. Chiratie was born in 1659 in Barnstaple, Devon, England. Chiratie died in England. Henry and Chiratie had five children: Mary who died in 1690; William who died in 1692; Henry who died in 1706; **Thomas Stribling** who was born on March 5, 1684, in Barnstaple, Devon, England, and died on March 25, 1755, in Frederick, Prince William, Virginia; and Joan who was born in 1686.

Thomas Stribling was married to Elizabeth Taliaferro (daughter of Francis Taliaferro III and Elizabeth Catlett) in 1715 in Virginia. Elizabeth was born in 1698 in Powhattan Plantation, Essex, Virginia, and died in 1775 in Frederick, Virginia. Thomas

---

*As is common in genealogies, when stating a location, the city is listed, followed by the county, then the state; in the absence of any of these elements, whatever information is known is stated in the order of city, county, state.

Stribling and Elizabeth Taliaferro had seventeen children: Margaret;* Francis who was born in 1716 and died in 1796; William who was born in 1718; Mary who was born in 1719; Daniel who was born in 1723; Taliaferro who was born in 1723 and died in 1774; William who was born in 1724 and died in 1748; John who was born in 1728; **Thomas Stribling** who was born on June 29, 1730 in Hamilton Parrish, Prince William, Virginia, and died on March 7, 1819, in Senaco River, Old Pendleton District, Anderson, South Carolina; Wilemont who was born in 1730; Conclough who was born in 1731; Benjamin who was born in 1733; Robert who was born in 1734 and died in 1800; Samuel who was born in 1735; Elizabeth who was born in 1739; Sigismund Stribling who was born in 1740 and died in 1816; and Millie who was born in 1748.

Thomas Stribling was married to Nancy Ann Kincheloe (born in 1734 in Hamilton Parrish, Prince William, Virginia, and died on December 2, 1822, in Anderson County, South Carolina). Thomas and Nancy had seven children: Francis who was born in 1756 and died in 1818; Elizabeth T. who was born in 1760 and died in 1839; Lucy who was born in 1769 and died in 1818; **Sigismund Stribling** who was born in 1772 in Browns Creek, South Carolina, and died on March 11, 1831, in Union, Union, South Carolina; Jesse who was born in 1775 and died in 1841; Nancy Ann who was born in 1779 and died in 1802; and Catherine who was born in 1798 and died in 1849.

Sigismund Stribling was married to Nancy Mary Birdsong (daughter of John Birdsong and Mary Armistead) who was born July 2, 1777, in Union, Union, South Carolina. Nancy Mary died September 15, 1852, in Pulaski, Giles County, Ten-

*No additional information available.

nessee. Sigismund Stribling and Nancy Mary Birdsong had ten children: Nancy Kincheloe;* John Birdsong who was born in 1790 and died in 1880; Miles Birdsong who was born in 1790 and died in 1875; Mary Meeks who was born in 1793; Mary Birdsong who was born in 1796 and died in 1863; Matilda who was born in 1797 and died in 1852; Thomas Farr who was born in 1803 and died in 1873; Francis who was born in 1804 and died in 1836; William M. who was born in 1805 and died in 1877; and **Obidiah Trimmier Stribling** who was born in 1800 in Pickens, Pickens, South Carolina, and died in 1833 in South Carolina.

In 1825 **Obidiah Trimmier Stribling** married Mary Frances Simonton, the daughter of John Henry Simonton and Jane Falls. Mary Frances was born in North Carolina in June 1799 and died on September 8, 1845, in Lawrence County, Tennessee. Obidiah and Mary Frances had three children: Mary Mitilda;* Nancy Jane;* and **James Lawrence Stribling** who was born on March 9, 1829, in Giles County, Tennessee, and died on February 25, 1914, in Lawrenceburg, Tennessee.

James Lawrence Stribling married Mary Jean Alexander and had six children: Edward Lawrence who was born on December 31, 1851, in Lawrenceburg, Tennessee; Mary Amelia Stribling who was born on June 6, 1856, in Lawrenceburg, Tennessee; Fanny Kimbell who was born in 1858 and died in 1898; **James Henry Stribling** who was born on September 21, 1863, in Tennessee and died on December 12, 1951, in Lawrenceburg, Tennessee; Emma Rose

---

*No additional information available.

who was born in 1866 in Tennessee and died in 1937; and Robert Lee who was born on May 23, 1872, in Lawrenceburg, Tennessee, and died on February 2, 1888. Mary Amelia Stribling married Isham O. Harvey (born in June 1850 in Tennessee, and died in 1910 in Lawrenceburg, Tennessee).

James (Jim) Henry Stribling married Ardelia Lois (Dena) Cobb (born on January 1, 1868, in Texas and died on June 24, 1931, in Lawrenceburg, Tennessee).

Jim and Dena had two children: Mary Gladys who was born in July 1897, in Lawrenceburg, Tennessee, and died on December 1, 1901, in Lawrenceburg, Tennessee; and **James (Little Jim) Lois Stribling** who was born on May 13, 1903, in Lawrenceburg, Tennessee, and died on February 2, 1988, in West Palm Beach, Florida.

James (Jim) Lois Stribling married Delma Huckabee Brock (born February 16, 1896, in Alabama) on January 3, 1923, in Lawrence County, Tennessee. Little Jim and Delma had no children. They owned several award-winning walking horses. Delma died on August 18, 1954. Little Jim later married Sidney Leonard of Lewisburg, Tennessee, on June 15, 1961. Leonard died in February, 1977. Both Delma and Sidney were World War I veterans.

JAMES (JIM) LOIS STRIBLING FAMILY

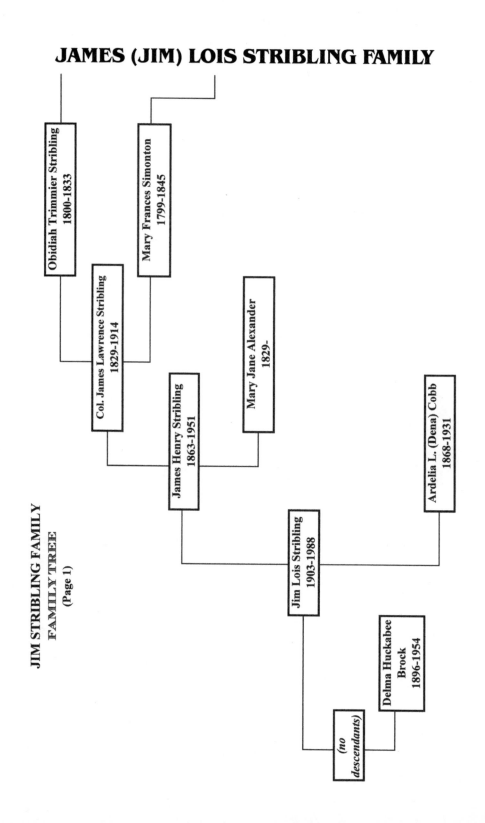

JIM STRIBLING FAMILY
FAMILY TREE
(Page 1)

Obidiah Trimmier Stribling
1800-1833

Mary Frances Simonton
1799-1845

Col. James Lawrence Stribling
1829-1914

Mary Jane Alexander
1829-

James Henry Stribling
1863-1951

Ardelia L. (Dena) Cobb
1868-1931

Jim Lois Stribling
1903-1988

Delma Huckabee
Brock
1896-1954

(no descendants)

JIM STRIBLING FAMILY
FAMILY TREE
(Page 2)

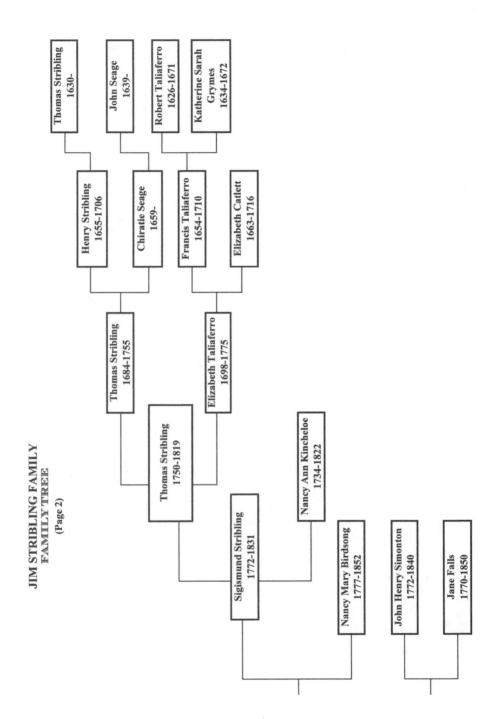

DELMA HUCKABEE BROCK
FAMILY BOOK SUMMARY

The earliest ancestor of Delma (also listed as Delmar) Huckabee Brock through ancestry.com (and related public family trees) was **Waddy Brock,** born in 1790 in Union, South Carolina (or Kentucky), and died on November 2, 1842. He married Sarah Easterwood on September 20, 1819, and they had five children: Elizabeth G. (Betsy) who was born in 1822 in Georgia and died in 1880 in Cleburne County, Alabama; Martha Patsy who was born in 1823 in Georgia and died in 1880; Jane Sparks who was born on September 2, 1824, in Georgia and died on June 12, 1900, in DeKalb County, Alabama; **David Nelson Brock** who was born on June 7, 1829, in Georgia and died on March 17, 1899, in Meredith, Henderson, Texas; and John W. who was born in May 1834 in Georgia and died in 1890 in Cullman, Alabama (buried at Mt. Vernon FCM Church in Winston County, Alabama).

    David Nelson Brock was married to Mary Elizabeth Davis (daughter of George R. Davis, 1804–1864, and Jane Thur-

man, 1809–1886). Mary Elizabeth was born on November 19, 1832, in Tennessee and died on June 6, 1910, in Tolbert, Wilbarger, Texas. David Nelson and Mary Elizabeth had thirteen children: George William who was born December 2, 1852, in Georgia and died on April 19, 1927, in Vernon, Wilbarger, Texas; John Cannon who was born on May 19, 1854, in Georgia and died in 1912 in Comanche County, Texas; Aaron Madison who was born on May 14, 1855, in Georgia and died on September 13, 1913, in Tolbert, Wilbarger, Texas; James Waddie who was born on April 5, 1857, in Villa Rica, Carroll, Georgia, and died on March 31, 1938, in Chillicothe, Hardeman, Texas; Sarah Jane who was born in 1861 in Villa Rica, Carroll, Georgia; Marion Jackson who was born on June 4, 1866, in Carrollton, Carroll, Georgia, and died on April 30, 1952, in Chillicothe, Hardeman, Texas; Marian J. who was born in 1867 in Georgia; Robert Lee who was born on March 9, 1869, in Alabama and died on April 30, 1935, in Wilbarger, Texas; Eli Walker who was born on December 12, 1870, in Carroll, Georgia, and died July 15, 1956, in Chillicothe, Hardeman, Texas; Sarah I. was born in 1870 in Georgia; **Charles Albert Brock** was born on March 17, 1872, in Carrollton, Carroll, Georgia, and died on July 14, 1933, in Lawrenceburg, Lawrence, Tennessee; Thomas Franklin who was born on September 20, 1873, in Macon, Bibb, Georgia, and died on June 8, 1930, in Lubbock, Lubbock, Texas; and Rufus Wilburn who was born on October 29, 1875, in Georgia and died on June 10, 1960, in Lubbock, Texas.

Charles Albert Brock married Margaret Clementine Martin on January 8, 1895, in Ruby, Alabama. Margaret (born September 6, 1871, died March 22, 1947) was the daughter of Dr. William Henderson Martin (1844–1905) and Martha Elizabeth Leake (1847–1896). Charles Albert and Margaret had seven children: **Delma Huckabee Brock** who was born on February 16, 1896, in Alabama, and died on August 18, 1954, in Lawrenceburg, Lawrence, Tennessee; Mattie Adel who was born on October 5, 1897, in Texas; Lena Darling who was born October 4, 1899, in Alabama and died on October 6, 1967, in Nashville, Davidson, Tennessee; Clyde M. who was born on February 20, 1902, in Alabama and died on

December 12, 1910, in Lawrence County, Tennessee; **Clemmie Calera Brock** who was born on October 17, 1904, in Ruby, Alabama, and died on April 12, 1976, in Lawrenceburg, Lawrence, Tennessee; Dwight M. who was born on July 27, 1907, in Gadsden, Etowah, Alabama, and died on March 4, 1988, in Midlothian, Ellis, Texas; and Christine B. who was born in 1915 in Tennessee.

    Clemmie Calera Brock married Jewel Roosevelt Denson (1902–1976) on June 24, 1923 in Lawrence County, Tennessee. Clemmie Calera and Jewel had four children: **Martha J. Denson** who was born in 1924 in Alabama and still resides in Lawrenceburg, Tennessee; Charles Elwood who was born on November 6, 1925, in Athens, Alabama, and died on December 12, 1992, in Nashville, Tennessee; and Elwood's twin brother, Leon Edwin, who died on March 8, 1999, in Nashville, Tennessee; Gail Brock Denson, born January 16, 1935, in Lawrenceburg, Tennessee, and still resides in Lawrenceburg. (Author's note: **Martha J. Denson Boston** is the mother-in-law of Tim Pettus and Curtis Peters who are the originators-in-thought of this publication.)

    Delma Huckabee Brock (also referred to as Delmar Brock) married James (Jim) Lois Stribling on January 3, 1923, in Lawrence County, Tennessee. There were no children born to Delma and Jim Lois. Delma Brock died in Lawrenceburg, Tennessee, on August 18, 1954. Delma and Jim Lois kept in touch with the POWs from the Lawrenceburg camp for several years following the close of World War II.

DELMA BROCK FAMILY

DELMA BROCK FAMILY
FAMILY TREE

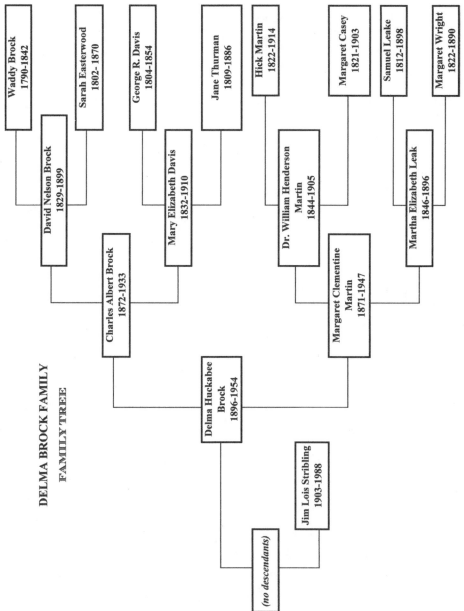

Waddy Brock
1790-1842

Sarah Easterwood
1802- 1870

George R. Davis
1804-1854

Jane Thurman
1809-1886

Hick Martin
1822-1914

Margaret Casey
1821-1903

Samuel Leake
1812-1898

Margaret Wright
1822-1890

David Nelson Brock
1829-1899

Mary Elizabeth Davis
1832-1910

Dr. William Henderson
Martin
1844-1905

Martha Elizabeth Leak
1846-1896

Charles Albert Brock
1872-1933

Margaret Clementine
Martin
1871-1947

Delma Huckabee
Brock
1896-1954

Jim Lois Stribling
1903-1988

(no descendants)

THOMAS SIGISMUND (T. S.) STRIBLING FAMILY BOOK SUMMARY

The earliest ancestor of Thomas Sigismund (T. S.) Stribling through ancestry.com (and related public family trees) was **Thomas Stribling** born in 1630 and probably in England. No spouse was recorded for Thomas, and his only recorded son was **Henry Stribling** who was born in Barnstaple, Devon, England in 1655. Henry died in 1706 in England.

Henry Stribling was married on December 13, 1680, to Chiratie Seage, the daughter of John Seage. Chirate was born in 1659 in Barnstaple, Devon, England. Chiratie died in England. Henry and Chiratie had five children: Mary who died in 1690; William who died in 1692; Henry who died in 1706; **Thomas Stribling** who was born on March 5, 1684, in Barnstaple, Devon, England, and died on March 25, 1755, in Frederick, Prince William, Virginia; and Joan who was born in 1686.

Thomas Stribling was married to Elizabeth Taliaferro (daughter of Francis Taliaferro III and Elizabeth Catlett) in 1715 in Virginia. Elizabeth was born in 1698 in Powhattan Plantation, Essex, Virginia, and died in 1775 in Frederick, Virginia. Thomas Stribling and Elizabeth Taliaferro had seventeen children: Margaret;* Francis who was born in 1716 and died in 1796; William who was born in 1718; Mary who was born in 1719; Daniel who was born in 1723; Taliaferro who was born in 1723 and died in 1774; William who was born in 1724 and died in 1748; John who was born in 1728; **Thomas Stribling** who was born on June 29, 1730, in Hamilton Parrish, Prince William, Virginia, and died on March 7, 1819, in Senaco River, Old Pendleton District, Anderson, South Carolina; Wilemont who was born in

---

*No additional information available.

1730; Conclough who was born in 1731; Benjamin who was born in 1733; Robert who was born in 1734 and died in 1800; Samuel who was born in 1735; Elizabeth who was born in 1739; Sigismund Stribling who was born in 1740 and died in 1816; and Millie who was born in 1748.

Thomas Stribling was married to Nancy Ann Kincheloe (born in 1734 in Hamilton Parrish, Prince William, Virginia, and died on December 2, 1822, in Anderson County, South Carolina). Thomas and Nancy had seven children: Francis who was born in 1756 and died in 1818; Elizabeth T. who was born in 1760 and died in 1839; Lucy who was born in 1769 and died in 1818; **Sigismund Stribling** who was born in 1772 in Browns Creek, South Carolina, and died on March 11, 1831, in Union, Union, South Carolina; Jesse who was born in 1775 and died in 1841; Nancy Ann who was born in 1779 and died in 1802; and Catherine who was born in 1798 and died in 1849.

Sigismund Stribling was married to Nancy Mary Birdsong (daughter of John Birdsong and Mary Armistead) who was born July 2, 1777, in Union, Union, South Carolina. Nancy Mary died September 15, 1852, in Pulaski, Giles County, Tennessee. Sigismund Stribling and Nancy Mary Birdsong had ten children: Nancy Kincheloe;* **John Birdsong Stribling** who was born in 1790 and died in 1880; Miles Birdsong who was born in 1790 and died in 1875; Mary Meeks who was born in 1793; Mary Birdsong who was born in 1796 and died in 1863; Matilda who was born in 1797 and died in 1852; Thomas Farr who was born in 1803 and died in 1873; Francis who was born in 1804 and died in 1836; William M. who was born in 1805 and died in 1877; and Obidiah Trimmier Stribling who

---

*No additional information available.

was born in 1809 in Pickens, Pickens, South Carolina, and died in 1833 in South Carolina.

John Birdsong Stribling married Hannah White (born in 1805 and died in 1865). John and Hannah had eight children: James Madison who was born in 1812 and died in 1885; **Andrew Hampton Stribling** who was born in 1816 and died in 1885; Mary Frances who was born in 1822 and died in 1913; Joseph Clayton who was born in 1827 and died in 1896; Elizabeth who was born in 1828; Thomas Jefferson who was born in 1830; Sarah Nelson who was born in 1831; and Lucinda who was born in 1833.

Andrew Hampton Stribling married Sarah Eaton and they had six children: James M. who was born in 1837 and died in 1910; **Christopher Columbus Stribling** who was born on November 24, 1844, in Lawrence County, Tennessee, and died on August 28, 1918, in Clifton, Wayne County, Tennessee; Clayton who was born in 1844; Elizabeth J. who was born in 1844 and died in 1885; Jim who was born in 1844; and

Mary Frances who was born in 1860 and died in 1930.

Christopher Columbus Stribling married Amelia Ann Waits (born in 1849 and died in 1927) and they had five children: **Thomas Sigismund Stribling** who was born on March 4, 1881, in Clifton, Wayne County, Tennessee, and died on July 8, 1965, in Florence, Lauderdale County, Alabama; Monetta Lee who was born in 1883 and died in 1965; Patricia who was born in 1885 and died in 1966; Rex Elton who was born in 1887 and died in 1972; and Roy Wilson who was born in 1887 and died in 1918.

Thomas Sigismund Stribling married Louella Kloss (born in 1899 and died in 1993) and they had one son, Thomas Edgar R. Stribling, who was born in 1922 and died in 1991. T. S. Stribling* was America's foremost author in the 1920s and 1930s, selling more works than any of the great writers of the day including Ernest Hemingway and William Faulkner. He won the Pulitzer Prize for Literature in 1932 for his novel, *The Store.*

---

*Author's note: The public library of Clifton, Tennessee, is named after T. S. Stribling, according to a local business owner of the Clifton area. The University of North Alabama at Florence claims strong bonds with Stribling, since he was a graduate of UNA.

THOMAS SIGISMUND (T. S.) STRIBLING FAMILY

T. S. STRIBLING FAMILY
FAMILY TREE
(Page 1)

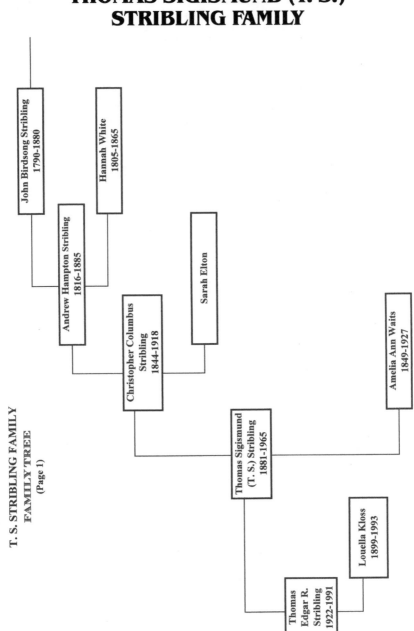

John Birdsong Stribling
1790-1880

Hannah White
1805-1865

Andrew Hampton Stribling
1816-1885

Sarah Elton

Christopher Columbus
Stribling
1844-1918

Amelia Ann Waits
1849-1927

Thomas Sigismund
(T. S.) Stribling
1881-1965

Louella Kloss
1899-1993

Thomas
Edgar R.
Stribling
1922-1991

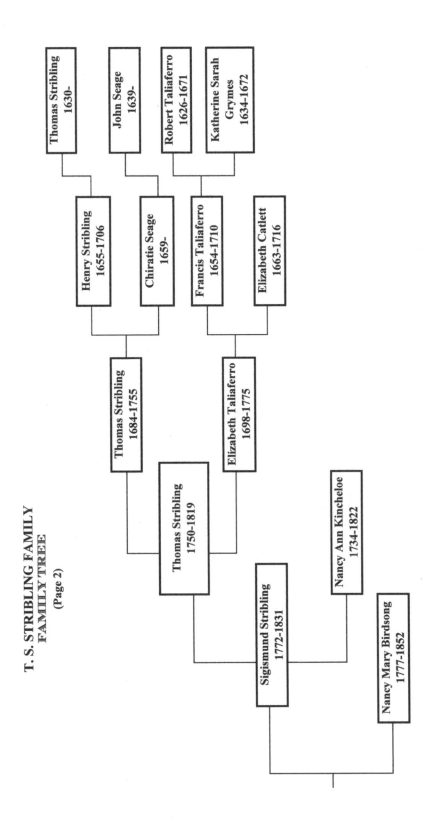

T. S. STRIBLING FAMILY
FAMILY TREE
(Page 2)

Thomas Stribling
1630-

John Seage
1639-

Robert Taliaferro
1626-1671

Katherine Sarah
Grymes
1634-1672

Henry Stribling
1655-1706

Chiratie Seage
1659-

Francis Taliaferro
1654-1710

Elizabeth Catlett
1663-1716

Thomas Stribling
1684-1755

Elizabeth Taliaferro
1698-1775

Thomas Stribling
1750-1819

Nancy Ann Kincheloe
1734-1822

Sigismund Stribling
1772-1831

Nancy Mary Birdsong
1777-1852

CHAPTER 12

Testimonials of Survivors and Descendants

THIS CHAPTER CONTAINS information that has been obtained by interviewing the following people. Some were interviewed in person while others were interviewed by phone. It has been a real pleasure to get to "meet" each of these people. Their stories* are what has made this book come alive. We appreciate them for giving of their time for this project.

A picture depicting German POWs.
Photo courtesy of Wikipedia, Public Domain

Jack Curtis

A native of Summertown, Tennessee—Curtis remembers seeing the German POWs when he was about six years old, around 1944 or 1945, when the POWs were in Lawrenceburg.

---

*These stories as relayed by each individual are their version of the incidents as they recalled them and cannot be sourced through any other means.

His dad ran a sawmill in the Summertown area, and they had a log truck that they used for the sawmill. On one particular morning Curtis, his dad, and several others were going fishing at about eleven o'clock. Curtis and a few others were riding on the back of the log truck when they came around a bend in the road on the Railroad Bed Pike, just below Baugus Church. (At that time the railroad had been converted to a very narrow dirt road. This location is right on the Lawrence/Lewis County Line. Curtis says that you can see for a mile after you round the curve.) As they rounded the curve, he saw that the road was full of POWs. He did not know if the POWs were going to another spot to cut trees, or why they were on the railroad bed at that particular time. Curtis said, "There had to be at least 100 POWs marching in the road. It looked like a 'sea of Germans.'" The men were spread out across the entire road. He remembers that a guard yelled a command and all the POWs moved aside so the truck could drive past.

The POWs were wearing dark gray cotton pants, and they all wore small, matching caps that looked like welding caps with bibs. None of the men looked happy, but they did not look as though they had been mistreated.

Curtis said, "This is a very vivid memory for me. I remember that I was not scared; I had no reason to be scared. Our family did not talk about the POWs that much."

Curtis said he did not feel threatened as they passed by the prisoners. Although the big POW camp was on Pine Bluff in Lawrenceburg, the POWs cut lumber somewhere in the vicinity of the railroad bed, and from there the lumber was shipped out from Lawrenceburg on railroad cars. Companies paid the government for the wood to use in various furnaces.

W. C. Johnson

Former coach and principal at Mount Pleasant High School, Mount Pleasant, Tennessee—Johnson and his family lived on a farm as sharecroppers. The farm was between Mooresville Pike and Highway 31 in Maury County. The property, owned by H. O. Petty, was about 150 to 200 acres. They raised alfalfa hay, corn, tobacco, and milk cows.

The farm had some hilly ground. The rolling ground had two big springs with a hill on each side. People who know about the water flow underneath this area speculate that there is a large stream of water, or maybe even a lake, under this area. One of the springs was used to water the cattle. The one up above the valley had all types of Indian artifacts, mostly arrowheads. (This area was a prime hunting ground for the Cherokee Indians, with Indians coming from North Alabama. The Shawnee came in from Nashville and northern Alabama.) On this particular farm on which Johnson lived, the two springs were about one-half mile apart, one on one side of the hill and the other on the other side. One of those places where they found Indian artifacts was where they raised tobacco. When they turned up the ground after a rain, they could find the arrowheads laying on top of the ground.

Somehow the farming activities came in contact with the POWs in Lawrenceburg. Johnson said, "I don't know if our boss man went to pick them up in Lawrenceburg, or if he picked them up close to Columbia where they were distributed out." They had five POWs who came to their farm but no guards. They were as nice as they could be and very trustworthy, doing whatever they were asked to do. Johnson's dad was very softhearted. The administrators of the camp wanted the POWs worked hard. Each day they came to the farm at about seven o'clock in the morning. They brought a small army canteen of water (holding about a quart of water) and a brown bag with their lunch, a small lunch that was supposed to last them for the day. Johnson commented, "The boss man told Daddy, 'Now you can't feed them and you can't give them water.' But Daddy said, 'I won't feed them and I won't give them water in front of you. But I'm not gonna work those men all day for only that small amount of water and that brown bag of food.' What he told the men, 'Now I understand what the regulations are and that I'm not supposed to give you anything, but I'm going to have lunch at the house either underneath the tree or on the front porch. You're welcome to join us.'"

Johnson continued, "Daddy made friends with those men by taking care of them and by feeding them and giving them water. They liked Daddy, and he liked them. They worked together mostly cutting tobacco. This was in 1944 or 1945 and I was thirteen years old. I remember that one of the men was a farmer in Germany. Somehow Daddy found out about that and put him in charge of driving the mules. (My daddy could not understand what the Germans said, and they could not understand him; so they used a lot of hand gestures to explain what they needed done.) The thing that amused me most is that the German farmer would talk to the mules in German and the mules would obey him as well as if Daddy was up there speaking to them in English. To me that was one of the big wonders of working with the POWs.

"We used those men several times that year. I don't remember if we used them a second year, but we used them a lot of the time the year that we had them. We became real good friends. After they went back to Germany, one of the men wrote Daddy, and they communicated with each other for several years. I believe those letters were written in English. Unfortunately, we do not have those letters today."

Johnson remembers that the farmer was short in stature and small in size, about one hundred sixty pounds and less than six feet tall. All the men were basically young men, although they seemed to be older than our servicemen. "They were good to us and helped us tremendously on the farm," Johnson said.

Johnson described the POWs as very neat, orderly, and eager to be compliant with what they were asked to do. They were interested in the work and showed no rebellion to his father. But, of course, his father made friends with them quickly when he told them, "If you are going to work here, I am going to feed you and give you water." You get people's attention when you tell them, "I am going to be good to you." Johnson said he was sure they could have been rebellious if they were mistreated, but the family found them to be trustworthy and they were allowed to go any place on the farm. "We didn't have to be with them all the time."

Johnson worked in the field with the men by dropping to-bacco sticks and carrying the tobacco to the wagons. They all worked alongside each other. Johnson said, "I don't know what they were paid for their work, but they worked very hard."

Mary Frances Davis Chaffin

A former resident of the Christian Home (Chaffin provided pictures and information regarding the Christian Home operations)—Chaffin went to the Girls' Christian Home when she was about eleven or twelve years old in 1942 and left in 1949, after graduating high school. She was the second girl at the home to graduate. Most girls did not finish school while living at the home. After graduating high school, Chaffin got a job in the Salant & Salant Shirt Factory in Lawrenceburg.

The girls at the home did cooking, laundry, sewing, cleaning, and canning (there was a cannery on the property). The laundry was done in a wringer-type washing machine, rinsed in a rinse tub, and then was hung out on lines to dry. They also fixed lunches for themselves and the boys to take to school. The sandwiches were wrapped in newspaper. They always worked in groups of three, and they rotated their jobs. One week they would work in the kitchen, another week in the laundry, or wherever they were needed.

Two girls cooking supper at the girls' dormitory at the "home." Boys and girls both ate at the girls' dormitory. The kitchen was under supervision of a dietician (information taken from back of picture).
Photo courtesy of Stribling Estate

The boys picked blackberries and sold them. The girls picked blackberries and harvested vegetables and canned them. After there were enough blackberries canned, the girls were able to pick and sell blackberries. They also had a chest-nut orchard, an apple orchard, and grapevines (they made lots of jelly). There was a basement in the girls' home that had shelves where the canned goods were stored. The old cannery was in the back of the building the boys used as a dormitory before a new home was built.

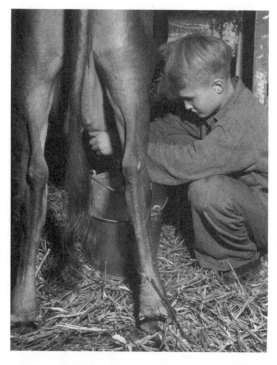

The farm raised hogs, chickens, and had a dairy which the boys tended. All the children picked the cotton in the fall.
Photo courtesy of Stribling Estate

Chickens were also raised at the home. Chaffin said, "Those chickens had to be killed, dressed, and cooked." She continued, "I never could kill a chicken, but I could dress it and cook it."

The boys' home did not have a kitchen, so their meals were prepared and eaten at the girls' home.

Chaffin remembers Mr. Stribling as a "plain old common person. You would never know he had a dime by looking at him. He was just a country person." At Christmas the children from the Christian Homes would go to Mr. Stribling's house to sing Christmas carols. He would give each child a coin (she believes that it was a fifty-cent piece).

The Girls Christian Home was built about 1936, with the first girls admitted in 1937. A new building for the boys was built in 1950. The homes are identical and across the road from each other.

Boys from the Christian Home: Front row bottom (L to R): Howard Turnbow (with dog, Two-Tone), Lynn Clifton, Tommy Owens, Ronnie Lohorn, Donnie Lohorn, Glynn Clifton. Middle row (L to R): Charles Martin, Robert (Buddy) Mashburn, Eddie Clifton, J. W. Clifton, Alvin Lohorn. Top row (L to R): Carl Wimbs, Raymond Luther, Clarence (Junior) Clifton, George Gray, and E. F. (last name unknown).
Photo courtesy of Mary Francis Davis (Chaffin)

Mr. J. H. Stribling was the president and founder of the Christian Homes. There were twenty-four directors. Mr. E. O. Coffman took over the homes in 1952 and retired in 1970. Mr. Jap Daniels was superintendent of the farm until about 1942. Mr. Marshall North took over and served until he died in 1961. Mr. and Mrs. H. A. Dewberry took charge of the new boys' building built in 1950. In 1971 Gary Polland took over the boys' home.

The Old Salem Church of Christ was on Granddaddy Road in Lawrence County. The children are from the Boys and Girls Christian Homes. Mr. Stribling was a firm believer that all the children should go to church (date of photo is unknown).
Photo courtesy of Mary Francis Davis (Chaffin)

Boys dormitory: This building of concrete and brick was originally built as an implement shed for the "home's" farm. However, it is divided into rooms and has a central heating system and is very comfortable. A dormitory similar to the girls' is on the construction program for next summer. The "home's" barn is in the background (information taken from back of picture).
Photo courtesy of Stribling Estate

In the girls department in June 1937, Miss Fannie Hurst and Miss Ella Alvia Hickman were there to start to work. Gretchen Gibbs came on August 15, 1939. Miss Fannie Hurst retired in 1953. Miss Essie Dodd came on April 16, 1953 and left December 1, 1961. Mrs. Cora Wilson came April 1, 1962. Gretchen Gibbs retired in October 1964.

Mr. and Mrs. Sam Rigsby were the first to work with the boys at the boys department.

There were 209 children in the home from its opening until March 1968.

Josie Hardiman was a blind lady who lived in a senior home with other women. That home was closed, and Ms. Hardiman was allowed to live at the Girls Christian Home. She would listen to her soap opera on the radio using headphones. She would then tell the girls all about the program when they came in. The girls thought the stories were true until they realized it was a soap opera. Ms. Hardiman liked to wash her own clothes, and she would spread them over the shrubs to dry.

The boys kept the grass mowed and the grounds in good shape around the girls' home. The tractor is a 1940s "H" John Deere with a factory front light.
Photo courtesy of Stribling Estate

Push mowing and pulling weeds was hard work.
Notice the old manual push mower.
Photo courtesy of Stribling Estate

*Even though the children had chores and worked hard, Mr.
Stribling, being a lover of fishing, saw to it that the
children had time to fish, too.*
Photo courtesy of Stribling Estate

The girls were taught to sing. Time spent around the piano was often done at night after the chores were done and before bedtime. It is not known who everyone in the picture is but Fannie Hurst is at the piano. Gretchen Gibbs was also one of the teachers at the home (upper right corner). Some of the girls are: Mary Newton, Christine Dunlap, Faye Allison, Pauline Clifton, and Geneva Newton.
Photo courtesy of Stribling Estate

J. W. Krick

Corporal, U.S. Army; author's personal interview with American POW survivor and camp guard for Lawrenceburg POW camp; photo courtesy of Mr. Krick—J. W. Krick volunteered for military service so his brother—who was married and had two children—would not have to go. After basic training he shipped out on the Queen Elizabeth to Le Havre, France, where he fought in the Battle of the Bulge (Belgium) in December of 1944. There were 21,000 men in his unit. Snow began to fall as his unit, the 106th Division, marched toward the  Rhine River in Belgium; and the snow continued to fall for two weeks. They were cut off from the artillery and could not get any air support, they had run out of ammunition, and they had gone six days without food. The Germans surrounded them and cut them off from other Allied forces. Krick's unit held the Germans off for four days and nights. There were turnip fields close by and the men would run out to the fields and get turnips. They got their water out of mud holes where trucks had run, and they scraped food out of the garbage. He was captured at the Battle of the Bulge (Belgium), along with the surviving 1,000 to 1,500 men in his unit. The rest were killed in the battle. He weighed 154 pounds when he was captured and weighed 94 pounds four months later. They were fed potato soup once daily at twelve o'clock. The potato soup had peelings and all. Sometimes they ate scrap Irish potato peelings they found in the garbage. "It was awful," Krick said.

The *Schutzstaffel* (or SS) troopers lined up a bunch of men, backed up their trucks in front of them, and killed them all. One of the young men fell before the bullets hit him and then he lay under other men who had been shot. The SS troopers, when they were finished, went along and kicked every man to ensure that he was dead. When they came to this young man, he made no noise or moved in any way, so they would think that he was dead. Later he was able to get away and find Krick's unit. Of course, he was taken prisoner along with the men in Krick's unit. The American prisoners were made to work in German factories, building artillery sleds for the Germans. The Americans bombed the building where Krick's group of POWs was working. They all hid in a small room; and when the bombing was over, that room was the only part of the plant still standing. They were put into groups of twenty, where they had to dig bodies from bombed-out buildings. Big trenches were dug to bury the bodies which were stacked like cordwood. One of the young men, a close friend of Krick's, found a gold spoon buried in the dirt. The Nazi soldier guarding the men demanded that the young man bring it over. When the young man brought the spoon to the Nazi soldier, the Nazi took the spoon and hit the young man in the back of his head with the butt of his rifle. It broke the young man's neck, killing him instantly. Krick was devastated that the soldier had killed his young friend.

One of the German guards had lived in America and had family here. He went to Germany to visit friends and was captured and forced to fight in the German army. This guard was over Krick's group of twenty men. The guard knew the Russians were coming in faster than the Americans, so he told the POWs he was going to move them toward the American forces (possibly hoping to be captured by U.S. rather than Russian soldiers). When they were within hearing range of the gunfire of the Americans, one sergeant from Westmoreland, Tennessee, asked the guard if he could go check on the fighting. The guard gave him permission. He came back a short time later riding on top of a half-track with a 50-caliber machine gun in his hands. The twenty in Krick's POW unit marched back and their "captured" guard rode the half-track back to meet the American forces. They came across a group of German soldiers; and when they saw the half-track and the machine gun, the Germans dropped their guns and surrendered. Not a shot was fired. "I never got the sergeant's name from Westmoreland who brought back the half-track where I could call him later and thank him. All we were concerned with was getting out and getting something to eat," Krick said. Their liberation took place on April 9, 1945.

When they had reunited with the Americans, they captured some Germans. One of the American boys who had a satchel on his back took all the watches from the captured Germans and put them in his bag. (When Krick and the others had been captured, the Germans took their wristwatches from them. Krick had a watch on him that cost about $80.) There was a solid gold pocket watch, in its case, in the bag of confiscated watches and Krick chose that one. He brought it home with him and would show it to people over the years. One day he took it to a jeweler to see what it was worth. The jeweler told him to never take the watch to have it worked on by someone he did not know. The pocket watch was estimated to be valued from $8,000 to $10,000. Krick said, "That gold watch had ten rubies in it, rubies that were large enough that one stone would have made a beautiful ring for someone; it was even prettier than a diamond." The watch was later stolen from Krick's house. Krick was heartbroken that someone had stolen the beautiful pocket watch since it had more sentimental value—priceless—than material value.

After a short stay in the hospital and some good meals in France, the men were shipped back to the United States. It took fourteen days to travel back to the States by ship. They ran into a typhoon; Krick thought, "We escaped the war only to be killed by a storm!" Yet they survived; and other than being seasick soldiers with shrunken stomachs, they were in high spirits. They were in the middle of the Atlantic when they heard the war was over. When they saw the Statue of Liberty, they knew they were home.

Krick was asked if he wanted to be an MP or a POW guard guarding German prisoners. He did not know that there were any German prisoners in the States, but he chose to guard the German prisoners. So they put him on a bus to Camp Forrest in Tullahoma. The General at Camp Forest asked him if he wanted to go to Lawrenceburg to guard prisoners at that POW camp. Well, since he was from Leoma, he jumped at the chance to go home. A truck with supplies was leaving Tullahoma for Lawrenceburg as they spoke, so Krick rode with the produce and was back home in short order.

Krick had been reported as MIA (missing in action). His family had not heard from him since before the Battle of the Bulge. People tried to tell his mother that he was gone, but she never gave up on the belief that he was alive. She said the Lord had not told her that her son was dead. When he returned home, his mother saw him in the distance; and she went running to meet him. Krick said with a smile, "There was a small ditch with a footbridge, but Mama's feet never touched the bridge . . . she jumped across that ditch to get to me." (Author's note: Krick's comments came with a tear, knowing that his mama's prayers were the sole reason he survived and was now home.)

When Krick reported for duty at the Lawrenceburg POW camp, he was assigned twenty prisoners to take out to cut chestnut trees. Two men would cut a cord of wood a day using crosscut saws and axes. There were two POWs who stayed near the fence and never helped cut wood or do any of the work. When Krick asked why they didn't work, he was told they were Nazis, SS troopers. (SS troopers were the men who killed his friend when they were POWs.) He said, "You put those two men with my group tomorrow. I'll take care of them. If they don't work, I'll leave them in the woods." He meant that if they gave him any trouble, he would kill them. The commander assured Krick that if he did have to kill them, he (the commander) would not sign the court-martial papers against him.

Krick told the translator to give them a saw and tell them to work, or he would leave them in the woods. The first day the men were out, Krick sat on a tree stump shooting squirrels while the men worked. (He had filled his pockets with ammunition before leaving the camp.) He piled up nine squirrels in front of him while the men worked, proving that he was an expert marksman. At the end of the day the two men had cut up a cord of wood just like the rest of them. He never had any more trouble with the two Nazis. He worked at the camp for four months. Later when Krick accompanied eighty POWs to Pennsylvania after their release, the two Nazis were part of his group.

Krick said of the POWs, "The German POWs in America ate what the people ate. They were taken care of much better than the American soldiers in the German camps. The German POWs did not want to go back. When it was time for them to go home, some of those men cried like little boys. They had plenty to eat here, and they did not know what they would find when they went home."

Author's note: It gave me great pride to meet and talk with a World War II soldier, a former POW himself, who never thought twice about giving his life for his beloved America. He did what he thought was right . . . he fought for his country. Mr. Krick volunteered to go into the army so his older brother would not have to go (his brother had a wife and two children).

Many years later my brother, Donnie F. Graham, volunteered for the army where he was sent to Viet Nam. Don earned the rank of Specialist E-5 for his hard work and determination. He also received the Bronze Star for his valor and meritorious service. These two men, along with the many, many more men, and women who have served our country, deserve our respect for what they did (and do). I salute you, Don and Mr. J. W. Krick, for your service to our country; may you be richly blessed for your unselfish acts of patriotism. These two men exemplify the true meaning of "Tennessee Volunteers."

William Earl Jones

Grew up in Lawrenceburg—Jones remembers when the POW camp was on the bluff, and he also remembers hearing about the CCC camp. Jones was reared on Piney Road near Lawrenceburg. His dad had an uncle, Oscar (O. A.) Clanton, who lived near them. (Mr. Clanton lived to be 102 years old.) Clanton had a two-ton, wooden flat-bed truck on which he hauled logs. He would go to the POW camp and get some of the POWs to go to Giles County, near Bodenham, to cut chestnut trees. (A guard would go with them since only one in the group could speak English.) The trees were huge, six feet in diameter. Jones said, "If you came up on one of those trees in the woods, it was so wide that you would think that it was a house." The trees were cut up into forty-eight-inch length sticks, busted up, and then taken to Lawrenceburg to the railroad.

One day Mr. Clanton found a tree with a knothole in it. Inside the knothole was a beehive. He told the guard that he was going to go get some buckets, washtubs, and knives. When he returned he had the guard tell two of the boys to cut down the tree. They used the crosscut saw to cut the tree back about forty-eight inches. The bees started flying out, stinging the two boys, and the men took off to the bushes to get away from the bees. After the bees settled down, they used the axe to bust up the forty-eight-inch section; and there was the golden honey. The bees started swarming again, so the boys took off running again. Mr. Clanton told them to run by the busted-up wood, grab a handful of honeycomb with their hands, and put it in the buckets. So they would run by, grab a handful of honeycomb, and go back to the bushes. Then they started eating the honey. Mr. Clanton got a kick out of watching those boys run by and grab the honeycomb, and then eat the honey.

Mr. Clanton worked with the POWs a couple of years and never had a problem with any of them. They never tried to run off. They were fed well, had a good place to sleep, and were treated fairly. Clanton had a rifle, but he never had to use it with them. He actually felt sorry for the boys. Jones remembers his uncle telling him that when the POWs were told they had to leave to go back to Germany, they broke down and cried. They did not want to go back (to Germany) because many of their families had been killed, and their homes destroyed.

Clarence (Junior) Clifton

Grew up at the Boys' Christian Home—Clifton remembers one German POW in the camp by the name of Conrad (he does not know his last name). Conrad was a blacksmith by trade in Germany, so he was in the shop at the camp shoeing horses and working on farm equipment. He also worked on the cannery's equipment. Conrad was a very smart man. He was not a Nazi . . . he had been drafted into the German Army.

Junior and Conrad became good buddies. They exchanged addresses but have since lost touch with each other. After he returned to Germany, Conrad wrote back to the Christian Home asking for food. He said that there was "no work and no food" in Germany. The home sent boxes of food to him, and Conrad sent back a letter of thanks. Conrad had a wife and three children in Germany, and the supplies were very helpful to his family.

Horace Hughes, who lived down the road from the Christian Home remembers that Conrad was a small man but very strong. He could bend a horseshoe with his bare hands.

Most of the German POWs could not speak English, but those who could, served as interpreters between the guards and the POWs. The interpreter was usually a German officer who spoke English.*

Joann Stotser Abbott

A native of Lawrenceburg—Abbott was born in 1929, just a few months after her parents moved from Iowa to Tennessee. Her father, G. M. Stotser (see next page), was the first manager at the Swift & Company Cheese Factory in Lawrenceburg. She remembers going swimming in the creek below Pine Bluff where the POW camp was located. She also worked as a volunteer rolling bandages.

Dr. Rufus Clifford

Remembering Mr. Stribling—Dr. Clifford was a young man in high school in Lawrenceburg when he first saw Mr.

---

*Submitted by Frances Davis (Chaffin).

G. M. Stotser at his desk at Swift & Company.
Photo courtesy of Old Jail Museum, Lawrenceburg

Stribling. He remembers Mr. Stribling as being a little on the eccentric side—an individualist. Mr. Stribling was a very religious man and was not opposed to others knowing how he felt about religion. Mr. Stribling would sometimes do peculiar things, but he used his money to help a lot of programs in Lawrence County, including starting a home for children. He remembers seeing Mr. Stribling a few times, and that his attire was not always proportional to his social stature. He remembers people talking about Mr. Stribling's wealth, and the fact that he used his money for many good things. Dr. Clifford did not remember having any direct interaction with Mr. Stribling, other than seeing him around town a few times and hearing the discussions about him from other people.

Dr. Clifford's father preached at the downtown Church of Christ in Lawrenceburg around 1950 or 1951. Shortly after Dr. Clifford's family moved to Lawrenceburg, he graduated from Lawrence County High School and left for college. His parents were in Lawrenceburg about eight or nine years. Dr. Clifford is a pediatrician with an office in Columbia, Tennessee. He is a member of the Columbia Noon Rotary Club and is past District Governor of the Rotary District 6760 that encompasses most of the clubs of Central and West Tennessee.

Dr. V. H. Crowder, Sr.

Interview with his son, Dr. V. H. Crowder, Jr.—Dr. V. H. Crowder, Sr., was camp surgeon for the CCC camp in Lawrenceburg. It was interesting how Dr. Crowder was appointed to the camp. Lawrenceburg, Lawrence County, and all of Middle Tennessee were heavily Democratic, and the Crowder family was Republican. When they got ready to name a camp sur-

Dr. V. H. Crowder, Sr., camp surgeon.
Photo courtesy of Old Jail Museum, Lawrenceburg

geon, one of the state CCC directors was Dr. Miles Crowder, from Maryville. He saw the name Crowder in Lawrence County; and he called Dr. Crowder, Sr., to see if he was interested in having the job. Of course, that was the middle of the Depression, and Dr. Crowder thought that the job sounded very attractive. Dr. V. H. Crowder, Sr., was sworn in as camp surgeon.

Some of the politicians in Lawrence County were beside themselves that a Republican had gotten the job. They tried every way in the world to get rid of him. They couldn't fire him because they did not appoint him. They brought charges against him that he was disloyal to the President of the United States and numerous other accusations, trying to get him out; but they could not. That was the politics of that day.

After the CCC camp closed, it was empty for a couple of years before it was reopened as a German POW camp. Dr. Crowder was appointed the civilian surgeon for the POW camp from 1944 through 1946. There was no military doctor in the camp, therefore he was the doctor for the whole camp. There was a German doctor in the camp, a POW who attended to some illnesses of the prisoners. Of course, the German doctor had little to no medical facilities, and Dr. Crowder supplied him with medicines that were not available to the German doctor. Dr. Crowder was over all the camp's medical needs. There was a sanitarium—a small facility in the county—that was run by the Seventh Day Adventist Church. If surgery was needed, it was typically performed at this facility.

V. H. Crowder, Jr., was born in 1935; like his dad, he too became a physician. He was still very young at the time the CCC camp was established. He does recall that the CCC camp had a very strict regiment, and the soldiers marched as they journeyed to their work. So the CCC became the backbone of the early military of the 1940s. They were already trained in drill and march, so the camps were organized to become very attractive to soldiers. A good many of the CCC young men went directly into the army. Of course, some of them did not come back.

Dr. Crowder, Jr., does remember that the POWs were blonde and tall. They were not Nazis but were German soldiers forced to fight the war. The POWs had a great dislike for the Russians and felt like they would probably end up fighting the Russians when, and if, they returned home. V. H., Jr., was not afraid of the POWs. He went out through the woods with the men, and they all had axes and saws; but he never felt threatened. He said, "They had no interest in doing harm to anyone. They had no reason." He remembers the POWs cut lots of timber. They were contracted through Mr. Jim Stribling, the property owner of the camp, to neighboring farmers and landowners. The POWs were paid a small amount of money for their work by those who contracted for their services. Dr. Crowder, Jr., remembers that the men did not mind working. They stayed in top physical condition. He recalls that Mr. Stribling owned a farm directly across from Dr. Crowder's (Sr.) farm. The POWs cleared some land on Dr. Crowder's farm that he had contracted with Mr. Stribling to do.

Paula Crowder

Sister-in-law to Dr. Crowder, Sr.—Paula Crowder and her husband, Kenneth, owned a farm in Globe, near Lewisburg; and they hired POWs from the camp in Tullahoma. Kenneth Crowder was brother to Dr. Virgil Crowder, Sr. who was the camp surgeon for the CCC and POW camps in Lawrenceburg.

Paula, who was about twenty years old, and her husband

owned a four-hundred-acre farm. Her husband could speak some German and was able to communicate with some of the POWs. She remembers that one of the Germans had been an editor at a magazine, and another one had painted houses for a living in Germany. She said that many of the men were highly educated and were not trained for the hard physical labor they did while in the POW camp.

She also remembers that one of the older POWs (about thirty years old) did not want to fight in the war nor did the majority of the other older men want to fight . . . it was mostly the younger men who wanted to fight.

Each day the men brought a sack lunch with them. The sack held an apple and two slices of bread with a little bit of potted meat between them. The Crowders were not supposed to feed the POWs, but she and her mother would cook for them anyway. Her mother said, "If I had a boy over there, I would appreciate it if someone would feed him." She said those boys were hungry.

The men hoed out the strawberries, worked in the hay, and did some clearing. One of her fondest memories is when the men were doing some clearing, her mother said, "Paula, I want you go down there and show that boy how to use that blade. He's going to cut his leg off!" Paula said she went down and showed him how to use the tool. She said, "They did not know how to use a sling blade to cut down the weeds. We were afraid they were going to hurt themselves."

One of the young POWs by the name of Rudolf was about the same size as Paula's husband, and they would send him clothes after the war. They kept in touch for several years until the Crowders moved to Franklin and lost touch with the young soldier.

Neal Frisbie

A native of Lawrence County—Frisbie was fourteen years old when the POWs were at camp. He drove a 1929 Ford Model "A" Roadster; and, no, he did not have a license. Every time the law would catch him they'd say, "Boy, you get home; your Mama is going to whip your butt." Frisbie would just laugh.

Frisbie started talking with Sergeant T. R. Blackburn (a guard at the POW camp) at the swimming pool one time when the sergeant was with his girlfriend (a local girl). Frisbie and Blackburn became good friends. The sergeant asked if he could borrow Frisbie's car to go courting with his girl. Frisbie would say that he did not have any gas. Blackburn would tell him that he would put gas in the car if Frisbie would let him borrow the car. So Frisbie let the sergeant use his car for courting.

The sergeant did not marry a local girl, and Frisbie does not remember the name of the girl he courted. Frisbie said, "I was just a kid, and I wasn't interested in the girl. I was just interested in getting gas for my old Ford." Gas was rationed back then for the war effort; and his family only had an A sticker, which was good for four gallons of gas a week. When the sergeant used the car, he put three to five gallons of gas in the car, using camp gas. They didn't use a lot of gas courting, so Frisbie had plenty of gas in his old car.

There was a place at the camp called a servicing pit, where they serviced the camp officers' vehicles. It had a ramp on which they pulled the vehicles, and they changed the oil and greased the vehicle. Neal did not have his car serviced there. (The pit is still there at the time of this publication.)

Frisbie used to squirrel hunt close to the camp. One time when he was hunting there, the Germans thought he was shooting at them. He was down in the deep hollow below the dam.

Frisbie wasn't sure why the law was called unless some of the officers thought he might be too close. They may have thought he might hit someone. Max Erwin, who was on the city police force, came down where Frisbie was hunting. Erwin laughed and said, "Them Germans up there are afraid you're gonna shoot 'em. You better get home, Boy." Frisbie went home, but he was back hunting a couple days later. However, no one called the law on him that time.

Wallace Palmore

Son-in-law of Robert Noack, guard at POW camp—Robert Noack, a clerk at the POW camp, was also an amateur photographer. Because of his love for photography, he had worked in a photo shop before he went into the service. He had taken pictures all his life.

Noack did not talk very much about the POW camp or his time there. The only thing he really talked about was how one day he and one of his buddies were in town at one of the stores. Noack saw Dorothy Prokesh, a local girl, walk by on the sidewalk. He told his buddy, "I'm gonna marry that girl." His buddy said, "You don't even know her." Noack said, "Watch." (Palmore said he did not know how they got together, but they married shortly after that.)

Noack was from New Jersey and was of German descent. One of his closest friends was Edward Wernet, who also worked at the POW camp. Edward Wernet was a witness at the Noacks' wedding. The Noacks married in Florence (Lauderdale County), Alabama. The Noacks and the Wernets swapped Christmas cards for years. They called Wernet "Pops" and Mrs. Noack had his address in her address book.

Palmore heard that the POWs were allowed to work on

farms without guards. He commented, "From what I am told, the boys were happy here and really did not want to leave."

Dan Mills

Native of Lawrence County—Mills was about nine or ten years old when the POWs were at the camp on Pine Bluff. Mills said, "We would ride our bikes over to the creek. It was really interesting to see the POWs in the creek. The guards would prop their guns up beside the creek to get in the creek, too. My buddies and I would jump in right along with them. I was very familiar with the POWs."

Mills stated that some of the men spoke a little English, but most of them did not. The thing that impressed Mills was how well-built the men were. Mills said, "They worked the stuffing out of those boys. They were very muscular from all the hard labor they did. Most of them were blonde and very good-looking men. Yet, they did not want to escape."

He remembers going to the Crowder farm (Dr. V. H. Crowder, Sr.), which was out Waynesboro Highway (across from the Lawrenceburg Veterinary Clinic). The POWs would be cutting wood on Dr. Crowder's farm. "Dr. Crowder's boy, Virgil, Jr., and I used to go out there with Dr. Crowder. We would talk to the boys who spoke English. They were cutting some kind of wood that was used for dye, as I understand it. That was a long time ago. I don't remember any personal things about them [POWs]," Mills reminisced. He continued, "They didn't talk a lot. Some of the men were friendly; others were just like Germans should have been. Of course, we didn't speak their language, and they didn't speak ours; so there wasn't a lot of communication. Some of them were not so nice, but we didn't have any episodes or confrontations or anything like that with the boys."

Mills finished by saying, "I don't think they had any SS members or anything of that kind. Most of those, I remember, were captured in North Africa by the British. They were old German army guys, but they were not Nazis or any of that stuff. They weren't so contentious."

Juanita Keys

Mount Pleasant native and historian—Keys worked at the unemployment office in Maury County in Columbia during the 1940s. She remembers that the World War II Veterans received one hundred dollars a month until they could find a job. If they made more than the one hundred dollars, they were off the program. They put the veterans in office positions whenever possible.

Keys also remembers that German POWs worked at the Rockdale Plant near Mount Pleasant. The men looked about eighteen or nineteen years old and appeared to be very nice. The unemployment office had to fill out forms on a monthly basis, including forms on the POWs. She only went to the Rockdale Plant one time but said that she remembered the occasion very well.

Milton Clyde Yancey

Interview with his son, Bill Yancey; photo courtesy of Bill Yancey—Milton Clyde Yancey was born in 1921. He was originally from Spring Hill, Tennessee. He left Spring Hill and moved to Oregon where, at the age of sixteen or seventeen, he joined the CCC there and worked in the lumber industry. Mr. Yancey was basically a lumberjack back in those days.

They cut trees with a hack or a saw, toppled them, and moved them out. They lived in CCC camps, where their food and all their essential needs were furnished. Mr. Yancey said the CCC was a true learning experience for his dad. He said he learned a lot of skills, including those of a pipeliner, heavy equipment operator, and master wood-carver. The CCC moved around a lot, working timberland and re-planting as the older trees were harvested. When they finished cutting in one area, they moved to another area.

The CCC camps were run similar to military camps, so as to keep order and maintain a disciplined group. They were groomed for the military. When World War II broke out, Mr. Yancey went into the army/air force and served in Germany. He was a crewman on a B-24 and was shot down twice.

Following his military service term, Mr. Yancey and his family lived in numerous locations. One daughter continues to live in Oregon. She still has a magazine article and several pictures of her dad and other enrollees in his CCC camp. His son, Bill, resides in Marshall County, Tennessee, not far from Spring Hill where his dad lived some seventy-five years earlier.

Milton Yancey created wood-carvings of trucks, dozers, and other equipment used for phosphate mining. Those items are on display at the Mount Pleasant Museum in Mount Pleasant in Maury County.

Ray Morris

Author's personal interview with only CCC survivor found— Ray Morris joined the CCC, Company 490, in Brownsville, Tennessee, when he was nineteen years old. He was paid thirty dollars a month: twenty-eight dollars went home to the family and two dollars was kept for spending. (Author's note: Most research shows that enrollees sent twenty-five dollars home and kept five dollars. This may have been a choice of the enrollee pending the family needs.) He sent his younger siblings to school

with the money he sent home. Morris was a boxer and would make a few extra bucks on the side on weekends. Sometimes he made as much as three dollars for a boxing match. He said it was a good life.

Morris said: "It was a great day when Roosevelt started this program. He really put the young guys to work by creating so many jobs." Morris always appreciated the work that he was allowed to do. His company planted a lot of pine trees. They also built roads. He considered it a good life and is glad that he had the opportunity to serve during that time.

He and a good buddy joined at the same time. They were given a choice to go to Oregon or go to West Tennessee. His friend held up his hand to go back to Tennessee, but Morris chose to go to Oregon by himself. It was a good way to see the country. A lot of men joined the CCC in order to see other parts of the country.

Morris went to Oregon, staying in several places including Burns and Eugene. He also went to the state of Washington. He said that he was "everywhere" while in the CCC. He was in the hospital for thirty days in Washington. He had been working in the desert and had developed arthritis. He was sent to the main hospital in Vancouver for observation. A specialist was brought in from Chicago to find out what was wrong with

him. The specialist determined that his tonsils were the problem. The doctor removed his tonsils; he recovered without
any complications and was able to go back to the camp.

Morris served two different hitches for a total of twenty-
four months. He was the seventh child of ten (the youngest
boy). There were five girls and five boys. His parents were
divorced. Most of his older brothers and sisters were married,
so it fell to him to help provide for his mother and younger
siblings. He grew up in West Tennessee in Madison County.
His oldest brother had served in the CCC, and that is how he
knew about the program. He knew it was a good way to help
his family.

His brother was a barber, and Ray was a boxer. The camp
had a boxing ring that was drawn up around an old store office.
Ropes were put up to make a ring for the boxing matches.
On Sundays everyone went to the boxing ring. At the boxing
matches they would have one knock-out with "no-holds-
barred"—no rules. Morris said he always won. They would
pass a cigar box to take up a collection for that round. Guys
would put in a nickel, or a dime, or whatever they had. There
wasn't much money back in those days, but he averaged about
three dollars every Sunday. The three dollars that he made boxing
helped his two dollars that he was paid for his work in the CCC.

When he first arrived in Company 490 and the truck pulled
up to the camp, the men at camp would start yelling "Fresh
meat, fresh meat!" Morris said, " When you got off the truck,
you either got whipped or you whipped somebody." Morris
was a pretty good boxer, so he usually whipped somebody.
He had a good start because he was talented as a boxer.

The CCC was a great program. It was a morale boost for
the country. The men did a lot of good work building trails,

fire stations, planting pine trees, and clearing land. They dug ditches, built flumes, and helped farmers. They would cut out a wide area and sod it to prevent erosion. They planted millions of trees.

When Morris received his first paycheck, two dollars, he got into a crap game and lost all of the two dollars. That early lesson taught him that he was not a gambler, and he never played craps again.

Morris remembers that when he was in Oregon they had such a big snowstorm, they had to dig a tunnel from the barracks to get outside.

Shown in photograph, FIRST ROW: Burke Golden, Hershal B. Matheny, Tyler Iverson, Harbert Q. Richardson, Willie B. Williams, James Y. Proctor, Alvin A. Smith, Melborn Walker, Raymond Kelley, Mose Gatlin.
SECOND ROW: Robert Black, Milton Nolen, Gilbert Crow, Johnnie J. Rhodes, W. C. Barnett, S. D. Barnett, Roy Hicks, Morris Ozment, Milburn R. Morris.
THIRD ROW: Charles Holt, Thomas J. Ray, Olender Owens, Oscar Vowell, Thomas Herndon, Robert C. Wright, James Reeves, George F. Rose, Edward F. Applewhite, George Roberts, Malcolm Compton.

COMPANY 490

Tenn. SCS-11

BROWNSVILLE, TENNESSEE

Morris is pictured on the far right in the second row.
Photo courtesy of Ray Morris

On a normal day, they were signed over to the forestry service first thing in the morning and turned back over to the army in the evening. The CCC offered several trades: barbers, auto mechanics, carpenters, woodworkers, and cooks. During Ray's second hitch in the CCC, he was promoted to second cook. He was also a warehouse attendant where men came in for tools that they needed for different jobs.

After leaving the CCC, Morris tried three times to volunteer for the army during World War II; but he was turned down each time because he had fallen arches.

Morris and Margaret, his wife, lived in Lawrenceburg for a couple of years during the 1950s. While there, Dr. Virgil Crowder, Sr., was their physician. (Dr. Crowder had been the camp surgeon for the CCC camp and the POW camp in Lawrenceburg.) Morris and his wife, Margaret, now live in Franklin, Tennessee. Morris is now in his early nineties; but his wit, wisdom, and mobility would lead you to think of him as a much younger man.

Morris still laughs today over an incident that happened soon after he arrived in Oregon. He had gotten up early one morning and was on his way to the mess tent for breakfast when he saw the "prettiest little cat" he had ever seen. The cat was black with a wide stripe down its back and up its tail. He watched the cat for a little while before he went to the mess tent. When he got in the mess tent, he began telling some of the group about the cat and how he thought it was so pretty. One of the men said, "What did that cat look like again?" Morris repeated his description of the cat, and the men burst out laughing. Morris was confused about the men's response, and he asked why they were laughing. They said, "Have you never seen a polecat?" They could not believe that a boy from the country in Tennessee had never seen a skunk before. After thinking about it, Morris thought that was pretty amazing too.

Alvin Clarence Atwell

Interview, information, and photo courtesy of his son, Greg Atwell—Alvin C. Atwell was born February 18, 1916, in Jersey, Arkansas. At an early age Atwell joined the CCC in Arkansas and, like many young men of the day, received grooming for the

up-and-coming war. In November of 1940, Atwell joined the army in Missouri with the 68th Armored Infantry Battalion, 14th Armored Division.

Atwell received a Bronze Star for heroic service that occurred on December 18 to December 21, 1944, near Ober Otterbach, Germany, where he encouraged and guided his platoon (while under fire) to hold a hazardous position of potential value to the enemy. His determined courage and unhesitating actions helped to maintain a high state of morale for his platoon.

Atwell received the First Oak Leaf Cluster to the Bronze Star for his heroic achievement at Rittershoffen, France, on January 18, 1945. An enemy mortar shell scored a direct hit on a half-track loaded with ammunition. Without regard for his own safety, Sergeant Atwell—amidst the flying shrapnel of the exploding ammunition—successfully extinguished the fire, thereby saving valuable and critically needed equipment and ammunition.

Atwell received a Silver Star for his gallantry in action in Germany and France from January 17, 1945, to May 5, 1945, many times acting as platoon leader and exposing himself to enemy fire, leading his men in the attacks. His inspirational leadership and uncanny use of position afforded by the terrain were great contributions to the effectiveness of his platoon.

Following his twenty-two-year military career (first sergeant) and retirement on January 1, 1963, Mr. Atwell listed his permanent address as Auburn Heights, Michigan. He served in the Army Reserve until November of 1970.

Sergeant Atwell's son, Greg, now resides in Maury County, Tennessee. Greg also enjoys the great outdoors similar to his dad's CCC tenure, where Greg has served for the past twenty years or so as platoon leader for his church's "Royal Rangers" group (a scout-oriented group of teenage boys).

Dennis Eddie Whittenberg

Resident of Hohenwald, Tennessee, on recollections of his father—Dennis recalls that his father, Dennis E. Whittenberg, was supervisor of transportation (trucks, dozers, and other equipment) for the POW operation in Lewis County near the Napier community. (Note: The actual operation centered more toward the old Laurel Hill CCC campsite that was owned by James H. Stribling of Lawrenceburg. Stribling also owned the Pine Bluff property, overlooking David Crockett State Park, which was the site of the actual POW camp.*)

The superintendent of the Lewis County work projects was Raymond Skillern of Rockdale, which is just south of Mount

---

*A last-minute find by the author revealed that James H. Stribling purchased the Napier Iron Works in 1936. Some of the woodcutting could have occurred in this area of the Railroad Bed Pike and the Natchez Trace junction.

Pleasant, Tennessee. (Note: Skillern was also plant manager of the Tennessee Products Corporation furnace located on Rockdale Hill. Some of the wood cut at the Napier POW project was utilized for the Rockdale furnace and other furnace operations in the area.)

Dennis recalls that his father had a green pickup truck that he drove from place to place during the course of his workday. He remembers that his father on many occasions brought four or five POWs into Hohenwald and let them roam the streets for an hour or so. He would tell the POWs to be back at the truck at a set time. The men would buy candy bars and other snack foods that were unavailable at the camp, then meet back at the truck to go back to the job site. Dennis commented that no one thought anything about the POWs roaming the streets and that there was never any problem from the men.

Dennis Eddie Whittenberg remembered that while serving in the military, he was stationed in Germany; and he recalled meeting one of the local Germans, Joe, who told Whittenberg that he was a former POW in America. During their conversation, Joe mentioned that he had served his encampment in Lawrenceburg, Tennessee.

A Lewis County Article

An article in the December 13, 2012 issue of the *Lewis County Herald* spoke of several in the Lewis County area who were familiar with the German POWs who worked in the Napier community at a work site there. (The fact of an actual POW camp in the Napier area, or former Laurel Hill CCC campsite, was not substantiated by this writer but may have existed. Through our research, there was much POW activity in and around this area of Lewis County and into that corner of nearby

Lawrence County.) The article did mention two sisters, Wilma Jones and Josephine Warf, who had met and stayed in contact with one of the POWs. They recalled someone named Willi (possibly Willi Müller as recorded on a list of known POWs from the Pine Bluff, Lawrenceburg, POW camp) who worked at the Napier site. Willi had sent Wilma a wedding picture of him and his bride from Germany. This *Lewis County Herald* article by Graham Kirby gave some fascinating details of other POW and World War II statistics.

Author's final note: This chapter holds special meaning to me; I met so many wonderful people while working on this book. Your stories have inspired me. So many of you (or your parents) went through some very tough times: the CCC camp, being held as a prisoner of war and then coming home to be a guard at a prisoner-of-war camp, growing up at the Children's Home, and enduring the Depression. Not one of you ever complained about the hardships you encountered. You considered it to be a "part of life." Thank you all for being so kind and generous with your time and stories. May you all be long remembered for your bravery and sacrifices.

CONCLUSION

By Tim Pettus

MANY YEARS AGO I became interested in the Jim Stribling story. Being a forty-year banker myself, I guess it was the great run of the First National Bank that he founded, the big house on Pulaski Street, the vast holdings of this man, and his charities—the Christian Home, Salem Church, and numerous others. Over the years, I have collected stories regarding his business dealings, his religious endeavors, and a little of his personal side. This information was handed down to me by the late Jim Stribling Brock Leonard, Stribling McLean, and Martha Jewell Boston. I am so thankful that much of what I've learned can now, through this book, be preserved for future generations to enjoy and remember. How could this one man achieve so much, touch so many, and become a financial and political power broker in Middle Tennessee, and then yet, be so misunderstood? In the end he just wanted to help people, especially orphans and farmers.

Many folks disliked him in the ordinary course of business. He, in fact, did have to foreclose on properties. It was a business. However, what few know is that at his death, he had $250,000 in note receivables in his lockbox marked "forgiven." He certainly would not have wanted this attention as he shunned the limelight. He avoided the "show-off" factor of wealth, even living in an old farmhouse much of his adult life. He would have probably not permitted this book, had he been living.

Even though a majority of this book is about the local CCC and POW camps, neither would have existed without Mr. Stribling. Come to think of it, so much of Lawrence County would not be evident today without Jim Stribling.

Our family is so appreciative that the Gandys would produce this book, mostly, through their love of history in Middle Tennessee.

And, finally, a big thanks to Curtis Peters, whose now many years of research and display of CCC and POW camp memorabilia, has ensured through the [Old Jail] museum that this story will live on for many years to come.

ABOUT THE AUTHOR

KATHLEEN GRAHAM-GANDY, a native of Mount Pleasant, grew up in the northern part of Giles County. Although her family moved from Mount Pleasant when she was an infant, they continued to visit Mount Pleasant often to visit relatives. Her husband, Charles, was also born in the Mount Pleasant area on Mt. Joy Road. His family moved to Lewis County when he was an infant.

Graham-Gandy has a natural tendency towards history, as she is always listening for new stories about her hometown and the surrounding area. She and Charles have been working for many years putting together the genealogy of their families. They hope to publish this collection for each family in the near future.

Graham-Gandy retired from banking in 1999. She spent several years as a newspaper correspondent with a local newspaper, *The Mt. Pleasant Review*. It was this experience that led to friendships with locals that brought about her first historical book, *Mount Pleasant's 100 South Main Street*. These same connections have led to this publication as well. "If a man wants friends, he must show himself friendly" works for a woman too. Relationships are the core ingredient of both publications. And the friendships gained through this book's interviews are an eternal treasure that she could never repay—even with an autographed copy of this publication.

Graham-Gandy's books are easy reading and full of pictorial supplements to keep the history visible as it is read. Her next project centers on a journal kept while she and Charles built a power line to a cabin on the Gandy family's homesite. In this book, Kathy stretches from history to humor. The working title of this next adventure is: *How to Build a Power Line with a Blonde Groundman.* This will be a self-deprecating account of true-to-life history in the making.

Kathy and Charles have a blended family that includes four sons and ten grandchildren. Graham-Gandy is involved in church, civic, and community activities. She and Charles are active with the Gideons International where both have served at the state level in Kentucky and have spoken at different functions. Charles continues to speak for the Gideons at local churches throughout the Maury County area. Along with her sons and grandchildren, she is very proud of her youth group at First Assembly of God in Columbia, Tennessee. They have developed relationships that she will cherish for a lifetime.

INDEX

One Man's Vision... One County's Reward

How the Life of James H. Stribling Affected His Fellow Man

ORDER FORM

You may order additional copies of *One Man's Vision . . . One County's Reward* directly from the publisher. The easiest way is to visit our Web site at www.shockinnerprizes.com and purchase a copy through PayPal. If you do not have Internet access, you may make a copy of this page on any copy machine and fill out the information below, or you may send your request neatly printed on a clean sheet of note paper. Be sure to include your check or money order for the total amount and mail to:

Shock Inner Prizes, Inc.
Attn: Book Publishing Division
8369 Old Highway 43
Mount Pleasant, Tennessee 38474

For questions call: 1-800-771-0442 or E-mail: sales@shockinnerprizes.com

You must include your street address for shipping information (no P.O. Box addresses accepted) and your phone number.

Acceptable forms of payment are money order, cashier's check, or personal check. Payment by money order or cashier's check will ship within 5 working days. Payment made by personal check will be shipped within 5 working days from the time your check clears our bank. *Tennessee residents must add 9.75% sales tax.*

Shipping and handling charges apply as follows:

for 1–2 copies, add $5.00 S&H
for 3–5 copies, add $9.00 S&H
for 6 or more copies, add $1.50 S&H per book

Please send me _____ copies of *One Man's Vision . . . One County's Reward* at $19.95 each, plus tax (if applicable) and shipping and handling charges.

NAME (please print): _____

STREET ADDRESS: _____

APT. NO.: _____ PHONE: _____

CITY: _____ STATE: _____ ZIP: _____

I have enclosed (check one):

❏ a personal check ❏ a cashier's check ❏ a money order for $ _____

Please allow 2 to 3 weeks for delivery.